# Pregnancy

## All your questions answered

# Pregnancy

## All your questions answered

**Bounty**
Books

*Pregnancy – All Your Questions Answered* has been produced in association with *Practical Parenting* (an IPC Media Limited publication) Practical Parenting ® is a registered trademark of IPC Media

First published in Great Britain in 2007 by Hamlyn, a division of Octopus Publishing Group Ltd

This edition published in 2014 by Bounty Books, a division of Octopus Publishing Group Ltd Endeavour House, 189 Shaftesbury Avenue, London WC2H 8JY www.octopusbooks.co.uk

ISBN: 978-0-753727-89-8

A CIP catalogue record for this book is available from the British Library

Printed and bound in China

Notes
This book is not intended as a substitute for personal medical advice. The reader should consult a physician in all matters relating to health and particularly in respect of any symptoms which may require diagnosis or medical attention. While the advice and information are believed to be accurate and true at the time of going to press, neither the author nor the publisher can accept any legal responsibility or liability for errors or omissions that may be made.

Some of the material in this book has appeared in *Healthy Pregnancy* (2003), *Pregnancy & Birth* (Gill Thorn, 1995) and *Your Pregnancy Week by Week* (2006), also published by Hamlyn.

# contents

# introduction

You are probably thinking about having a baby, or have recently discovered that you are expecting one. If so, congratulations! You are about to embark on a very special journey, after which your life will never be the same again. As pregnancy is a journey that is unique for every mum-to-be, this guide aims to be as comprehensive as possible, covering the whole range of different experiences, questions and concerns.

The months of pregnancy leading up to the birth of a baby are a thrilling time. Mothers love sharing the milestone moments with family and friends, showing pictures from ultrasound scans and thinking about their baby's arrival. Many women discover a new side to their partner, who suddenly becomes proud and protective of the growing bump, and wants to learn all about the baby's development (particularly its size in relation to various fruits and vegetables!).

No matter how smoothly your pregnancy progresses, however, yours would certainly be unusual if you did not feel the odd anxiety. There may be a burning issue – such as home versus hospital birth – that you want to consider further, or you may be suffering from a minor complaint that you want to be reassured about.

For answers to all your questions about pregnancy, you need to look no further than this book from the experts at *Practical Parenting* magazine. *Pregnancy – All Your Questions Answered* is a fully comprehensive guide in an accessible question-and-answer format. From conception to delivery, the book includes detailed advice on all aspects of pregnancy, giving a week-by-week account of the way your body is changing and your baby is developing. It explains how to ensure you are as healthy as possible during your pregnancy, and explores all the different options for antenatal care, labour and birth.

Not all pregnancies and births are straightforward, so there is also information on complications, such as diabetes and pre-eclampsia, as well as multiple births, difficult births, caesarean section, assisted delivery and overdue babies. You can reassure yourself by reading about the

**Above:** Having read about the baby's development, your partner will feel prepared for the new arrival.

common complaints that arise as pregnancy progresses, and learn how to deal with them.

In addition to over 200 questions often asked by pregnant women, there are a number of special features on topics such as relaxation techniques, your partner's role and water birth. There are also many quotes and true stories, which underline the variety of women's experiences. As a midwife, I have found that having access to the right information and support enables women to feel relaxed, confident and in control of their pregnancies. I hope that this book will give you the knowledge to help make your own experience a very positive one.

*Anne Richley*

**Anne Richley** is a community midwife and the mother of two children. She regularly provides expert advice in *Practical Parenting* magazine.

1

# getting started

# Choosing to have a baby

Deciding to have a baby is one of the most momentous decisions you are likely to make in your life, and the idea that you are going to become a parent can take some getting used to. Planning ahead can help you to start your pregnancy in good health and a positive frame of mind. By adopting a healthy lifestyle you can enhance your chances of conceiving, reduce the likelihood of problems during pregnancy and spare yourself a certain amount of worry. You are also more likely to feel that you are in control of your body and your pregnancy.

## What's dad thinking?

**Many men take great delight in young children. They are keen on the idea of becoming a father, and they are enthusiastic and eager to share the preparations. Others are pleased, but reserved about it. Your partner may have moments of doubt: he may worry about being a good father, about taking on the financial responsibility for you and the baby and about your safety during pregnancy and birth. He may also be concerned about changes in your social life, your sex life and your relationship with each other.**

## Common concerns

It is normal to have anxieties when you are thinking about having a baby. You may fear losing your freedom, passing up a career, becoming dependent on your partner or simply facing up to the responsibilities of parenthood. You may also worry about the physical demands of pregnancy, about its effects on your body, about illnesses that might affect your baby or about the possibility of having a child with a disability.

Other concerns might centre around being a good mother and coping with day-to-day childcare. You may also wonder how much your partner will really help you. Working through all sorts of doubts can be a large part of preparing yourself mentally for pregnancy and you will find that many of them disappear once you are actually pregnant.

Not everyone can plan their pregnancy well in advance, and many women have a perfectly healthy pregnancy with no special preparations at all. However, if you and your partner have the luxury of time to get in the peak of health and fitness before you conceive, you will improve your chances of conception and also have a greater chance of a healthy pregnancy and a healthy baby. It is worth finding out about the positive changes that you can make in anticipation of pregnancy (see Changing your lifestyle, pages 12–13), and it can also be helpful to discover just how your reproductive system functions (for more information see Reproduction, pages 14–15).

# Choosing to have a baby **Common questions**

**Q** Is there a perfect age for pregnancy?

**A** Physically, the best time to have a baby is in your early 20s. However, many of the risk factors associated with giving birth when you are older could affect any woman, whatever her age; being overweight or having suffered infertility problems just happen to be more common in older women. The risk of chromosomal abnormalities increases with age but most problems, including heart defects, spina bifida, cleft palate and talipes, are no more common in older mothers.

**Q** How far in advance should I start preparing for pregnancy?

**A** You should start preparing at least three months ahead of trying for a baby, but ideally aim for six months or more. This will give you sufficient time to build up good nutritional reserves and eliminate all traces of the ill-effects of alcohol and smoking from your system. Encourage your partner to prepare with you, because the quality of his sperm depends on his diet and lifestyle.

**Q** What should I do about contraception?

**A** If you are taking the pill or using an intra-uterine device (IUCD) you might want to use another form of contraception for about three months before attempting to get pregnant. This will allow your body to return to normal, as both forms of contraception can alter the balance of nutrients such as zinc, copper and certain vitamins. Allowing your periods time to settle down to a regular pattern also makes dating your pregnancy much more accurate.

**Q** Does it matter if I am fit when I conceive?

**A** The special needs of pregnancy often become obvious to women too late, when they realize how much harder everything is if they are unfit! If you increase your suppleness, strength and stamina before becoming pregnant you will be able to carry a baby more easily, reduce the risk of backache and other discomforts, and find you get less tired (see Exercise and pregnancy, pages 102–109).

**Below:** Talking through your hopes and fears is an important part of preparing for pregnancy.

# Changing your lifestyle

If you and your partner have the chance to improve your health before you become pregnant, take it! Healthy parents tend to have healthy babies and fit mothers tend to experience fewer problems during pregnancy and birth.

## Where to start

If you have any specific health worries, or if you suffer from any conditions that you think might affect your pregnancy, discuss these with your doctor before stopping contraception. Mention any long-term medication you are on, as well as any herbal supplements or homeopathic remedies that you use, as some of these can affect your ability to conceive or harm the fetus (see pages 110–111). At the same time, you can arrange to have your immunity to rubella (German measles) checked.

Before conceiving, focus on your general fitness, weight and diet. Take steps to make improvements in each area if necessary (see Health and wellbeing, pages 84–121). If you drink alcohol regularly, take recreational drugs or smoke you should seriously consider stopping altogether.

## Folic acid supplements

If possible, you should take folic acid supplements (400 mcg daily) for at least three months before and after conception. Folic acid is known to reduce the risk of babies having spina bifida, as well as other neural tube defects and cleft palate.

**Above:** Regular exercise gets your body fit for pregnancy – don't forget to stay hydrated.

## Five ways to **prepare for pregnancy**

1 Find ways of reducing stress in your life. Try to shed unnecessary work commitments and reorganize your social life.
2 Go to your GP for a check-up so that you start pregnancy with a clean bill of health, or see if your midwife provides preconceptual advice and information.
3 Redress the balance between work and play, activity and relaxation, your own needs and those of others in your life.
4 Take more exercise and improve your diet.
5 Change habits you know are bad for you such as smoking and excessive drinking of alcohol.

# Lifestyle **Common questions**

**Q** I take regular medication for an ongoing condition. Can I continue to do so while trying for a baby?
**A** Before stopping contraception, talk to your doctor if you have any condition that needs regular medication (including asthma if you use an inhaler). Your medication may have no known problems, or there may be an alternative treatment approach that can be tried. If your condition requires treatment with drugs that could pose hazards, talking it through with an expert will help you to decide what to do.

**Q** Is it safe to take over-the-counter medicines during pregnancy?
**A** All drugs alter your body chemistry, so treat them with great caution around the time of conception and during pregnancy. Check with your doctor, pharmacist or a qualified alternative practitioner before taking any medication that is not essential to your health. This warning includes over-the-counter (OTC) remedies for minor ailments such as colds and 'flu, aromatherapy oils, herbal or homeopathic remedies, and vitamin or slimming pills.

**Q** How does alcohol affect pregnancy?
**A** If you drink heavily during pregnancy, you double your risk of miscarriage and increase the chances of having a baby with a major abnormality. You should consume no more than a maximum of one to two units, once or twice a week. Over eight units a week is thought to cause fetal alcohol syndrome. It is best for you and your baby if you cut out alcohol completely.

**Q** What effects can smoking have on a baby during pregnancy?
**A** Smoking during pregnancy is associated with more miscarriages, vaginal bleeding, premature births and low birth-weight babies. If you are over 35, there is also a significant increase in the risk of your baby having a minor malformation and five times the risk of low birth weight (a major cause of infant illness) compared with a younger smoker. The good news if you have smoked for many years is that stopping before you conceive gives your baby the same chance of good health as a non-smoker's baby.

*'I worried about everything when I was expecting Jack, but you cannot put things on hold just because you're pregnant. I want us all to enjoy ourselves as a family and that means using common sense. Lots of risks are very small and I don't want Jack and Chloe to get the idea that pregnancy stops you doing things that are fun.'*
*Sue, mother of Jack and Chloe, and nine weeks pregnant*

# REPRODUCTION

## The basics: getting to know your body

**Before you start trying to conceive it is a good idea to familiarize yourself with the workings of your reproductive system, and with that of your partner.**

### Female reproductive system

Before you get pregnant, the uterus (womb) is roughly the size and shape of a pear and weighs about 60 g (2½ oz). The two ovaries lie on either side, between finger-like projections called fimbriae at the end of the Fallopian tubes, through which fertilized eggs travel to the uterus.

- **Ovaries** All the eggs you will ever produce are stored in your ovaries before birth. When you begin menstruating one egg is released approximately every 28 days until you reach the menopause. The release of the egg is called ovulation, and usually each ovary

produces an egg on alternate months. The ovaries also produce the hormone oestrogen, which thickens the lining of the womb ready to receive the fertilized egg.

- **Eggs** Each month about 20 eggs (ova) begin to ripen inside the ovary follicles in your ovaries. One egg (ovum) will ripen first and will be released from the follicle.

- **Fallopian tubes** You have two Fallopian tubes, one running from each ovary to the uterus. When an egg is released from an ovary, it is drawn into the Fallopian tube. Slight contractions of the Fallopian tube help to move the egg towards the uterus. The journey from ovary to uterus takes a couple

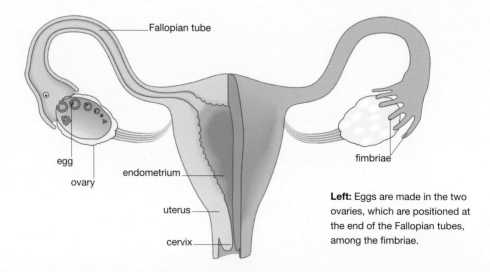

Fallopian tube

egg

ovary

endometrium

uterus

cervix

fimbriae

**Left:** Eggs are made in the two ovaries, which are positioned at the end of the Fallopian tubes, among the fimbriae.

of days, during which time the egg may be fertilized by a sperm.

- **Uterus** The egg then moves into the uterus, which is like a bag with a thick muscular wall. If the egg is fertilized, it attaches to the endometrium, the spongy lining of the uterus. The endometrium has been prepared ready to receive the fertilized egg; if the egg is not fertilized, the lining is shed – this is your period.
- **Cervix** The neck of the uterus at the top of the vagina, through which the baby passes at birth, is the cervix. It is normally closed, leaving a tiny opening through which blood seeps during a period.

# Male reproductive system

The male system maximizes the chances of impregnation. A man does not have a store of sperm when he is born. Sperm production begins at puberty and continues until very late in life, although it starts to slow down in late middle age. It takes about 70–80 days to produce a mature sperm, ready for ejaculation. Of the hundreds of million sperm in any one ejaculation, only a couple of thousand survive the journey into the uterus and on to the Fallopian tube.

## Ejaculation

In each ejaculation, between 2 and 6 ml (½–1½ tsp) of semen are released, each millilitre of which contains between 35 million and 200 million sperm. Not all of these are normal, healthy sperm – about a quarter of them cannot swim and have no chance of making it to the egg.

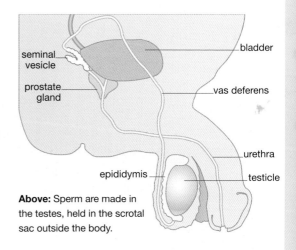

**Above:** Sperm are made in the testes, held in the scrotal sac outside the body.

- **Scrotal sac** This bag of skin contains and protects the testes. It holds them outside the body where temperatures are slightly cooler, maximizing sperm production.
- **Testes** Sperm are made in the testes, or testicles, and are constantly replenished.
- **Sperm** Each sperm is about 0.05 mm long and consists of a head containing genetic information, a middle section that provides the energy for the sperm to propel itself, and a tail, which moves from side to side as the sperm swims.
- **Epididymis** The sperm mature in this part of the testis.
- **Vas deferens** When the sperm are mature, they pass along the vas deferens (sperm ducts) from the epididymis to the seminal vesicles.
- **Seminal vesicles** Sperm are stored here until ejaculation. They mix with fluid made in the seminal vesicle, and fluids from the prostate gland, to form semen, which is projected along the urethra.
- **Urethra** During ejaculation, contractions at the base of the penis force semen along this tube, which runs from the bladder to the tip of the penis.

# Trying to conceive

**Above:** Trying for a baby provokes a variety of feelings, from joy to apprehension.

Once you feel that you and your partner are fit, and ready for pregnancy, it is time to start trying to conceive. The decision to abandon contraception may produce a mixture of emotions: excitement, happiness, anxiety or apprehension. Try not to become too worried about counting days and scheduling intercourse – studies show that you are more likely to conceive if you are relaxed and happy!

## Stopping contraception

Barrier methods of contraception, such as condoms or a diaphragm, allow you to conceive as soon as you stop using them. However, if you have been taking the contraceptive pill or using an intra-uterine device (IUCD, or coil), you should aim to have at least one 'normal' period before you start trying to conceive.

Some women experience a burst of fertility as soon as they stop taking the pill, while others find that their menstrual cycle takes a few months to settle down completely. If you want to wait until you are totally fit and healthy before attempting to conceive, you could stop taking the pill or have your coil removed and then use a barrier method until the time you want to get pregnant.

# Conceiving **Common questions**

**Q** How long should I expect to be trying for a baby before I conceive?

**A** Unfortunately, it is impossible to predict how long it will take you to conceive. All couples are different, and all sorts of things, such as age, general health and the type of contraception you have been using, affect conception. Generally, you should allow at least three months for trying to conceive and anything up to a year is normal. If you want to maximize your health and fitness beforehand, you should allow an additional six months.

**Q** My sister-in-law used an ovulation kit. What is this and how does it work?

**A** An ovulation-predictor kit is a simple device for detecting the increase in luteinizing hormone (LH), which indicates you are about to ovulate. Most pharmacies sell these kits. They are 99 per cent accurate and very easy to use: you simply urinate onto a test-stick each day around the middle of your menstrual cycle.

**Q** A friend suggested keeping a temperature chart? How can this help?

**A** Just after ovulation, your body temperature increases very slightly and stays at this level until after your period. By taking your temperature at the same time every morning and plotting the readings on a chart, you can pinpoint when ovulation occurs (just before the temperature rise). You will need to take readings for a few months in order to work out an average pattern for your cycle.

**Q** Would it be harmful to my baby if I became pregnant by accident while on the pill?

**A** It is very unlikely your baby will be harmed, as the amount of hormone in the contraceptive pill is relatively small. If you stopped taking the pill as soon as you discovered you were pregnant, the synthetic hormones would soon clear from your body and your own pregnancy hormones would dominate.

## Ovulation

It's amazing how many women have no idea when in the month they are most likely to conceive. One simple way of working out your time of ovulation is to keep a calendar. Note the day when your period starts and how many days it lasts. If you have a straightforward 28-day cycle, you probably ovulate on day 14. Otherwise, working out your ovulation date is a little more complicated, because ovulation generally occurs 14 days before the start of your next period, and this can be difficult to predict if your cycle is irregular.

Another option is to monitor your cervical mucus. The mucus that your cervix produces to help sperm swim up to the uterus is often discharged from your vagina. By noting any changes in its texture, you can spot when you are ovulating. When you are fertile, the mucus looks like egg white and is stretchy.

# Natural sex selection

There are various natural methods that you can use to try to influence the sex of your baby. You can choose one or try a combination of them. Bear in mind that, even if you get the result you want, you will never know whether the method worked or if it was just chance!

## Timing intercourse

One of the most popular methods of trying to influence the sex of your child is timing when you have intercourse. This method is based on what is known as the 'Shettles theory' that male sperm swim faster than female sperm but die sooner. For a boy, abstain from sex for 2–3 days before you ovulate, then have intercourse as close to ovulation as possible, so the speedier male sperm will reach the egg first. For a girl, have sex 2–3 days before ovulation, so that the male sperm will have died by the time the egg is released, and the longer living female sperm will have a greater chance of reaching the egg.

## Creating the right environment

Male sperm are said to prefer an alkaline environment, while female sperm are more resistant to an acidic one. Some women have therefore tried to make their vagina more acid or more alkaline by flushing it about half an hour before intercourse with a solution of bicarbonate of soda (alkaline) for a boy and with diluted lemon juice or vinegar (acid) for a girl. However, doctors do not recommend this practice, as douching the vagina can cause bacterial vaginosis and infection.

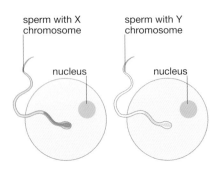

**Above:** Sex is determined by whether the fertilizing sperm has an X or Y chromosome 23. The egg on the left will become a girl; the egg on the right, a boy.

'We first heard of the Shettles theory before we had any children, and we managed to achieve the genders we wanted for all five of ours! Although it is supposed to be harder to conceive a girl, we had two daughters and three sons. To conceive our sons we made love on the day I ovulated, and when we were trying for the girls we had sex on the third and second days before I ovulated.'
Sarah, mother of Jake, Harry, Ryan, Melissa and Emily

**Above:** A diet rich in leafy green vegetables is said to increase the likelihood of conceiving a girl.

## Diet

Some women swear by dietary methods. They believe that you are more likely to produce a boy if you eat foods that are rich in sodium and potassium, which might include meat, dried and salted fish, rice, pasta, potatoes and beans, and certain fruits and vegetables such as bananas, apricots and celery. If you are trying to have a girl, on the other hand, you should eat foods that are rich in magnesium as well as calcium, for example, dairy products, eggs, nuts, soya beans, leafy green vegetables and fresh fruit juice.

## Genes and inheritance

The genetic information that will determine your baby's characteristics comes from you and your partner. When the sperm and egg fuse, the 23 chromosomes contained by each join up to form 23 pairs of chromosomes. Each chromosome contains thousands of genes that determine everything from eye and hair colour to intelligence, personality and physical health. Because half of the genes come from you and half from your partner, your baby will have a unique combination of genetic material. As a result, she could inherit your eye colour and your partner's nose shape, your short legs and your partner's mathematical ability. Although the environment in which your child grows up and the experiences she has will contribute to the person she becomes, her genetic make-up is determined at the moment of conception.

## Sex selection **Common questions**

**Q** What determines the sex of a baby?
**A** Each egg or sperm contains 23 chromosomes, one of which is a sex chromosome. Eggs always contain the X version of chromosome 23, while sperm contain either the X or the Y version. If the sperm that fertilizes the egg contains a Y chromosome, the baby will be a boy; if it contains an X chromosome, the baby will be a girl. Left to nature, a good balance of the sexes develops: about 103 boys are born for every 100 girls.

**Q** Is there a down side to trying to influence the sex of my baby?
**A** If you are keen enough to take measures to influence the sex of your baby, you may be very disappointed if they fail. This could lead to problems bonding with your baby and may even cause post-natal depression. If this is a possibility, it might be better to adopt a more laid-back approach, letting nature take its course and resolving to accept whatever sex of baby you have.

# Fertilization

When your partner's sperm meets your egg and the two fuse together at the moment of fertilization, a miraculous event occurs: the beginning of a brand-new life. From this point onwards, the fertilized egg assumes a life of its own, growing and developing at an amazing rate until, some nine months later, a fully formed, unique, complex human being emerges into the world.

## The journey of the egg

Once the egg has been released from one of your ovaries (ovulation), it is drawn into the Fallopian tube. Slight contractions of the tube assist in moving the egg in the direction of the uterus, helped by tiny hairs, called cilia, which wave and shift the egg along. The egg can survive in the Fallopian tube for about 24 hours and, if it is not fertilized, it will be reabsorbed by your body.

As the egg is released, your body prepares for the possibility that it may be fertilized: the lining of your uterus, the endometrium, becomes thick and spongy, ready for a fertilized egg to implant. If fertilization does not take place, the endometrium comes away and you will start to bleed as another menstrual cycle begins.

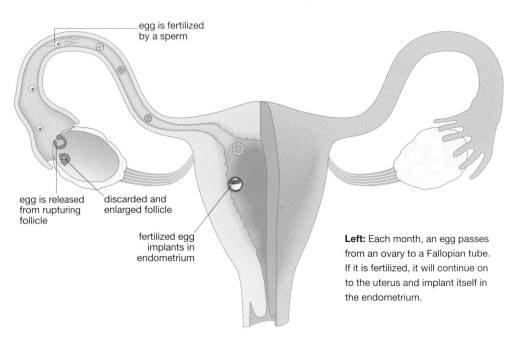

egg is fertilized by a sperm

egg is released from rupturing follicle

discarded and enlarged follicle

fertilized egg implants in endometrium

**Left:** Each month, an egg passes from an ovary to a Fallopian tube. If it is fertilized, it will continue on to the uterus and implant itself in the endometrium.

# The journey of the sperm

After ejaculation, the sperm swim very quickly from the vagina into the cervix (the neck of the uterus), through the uterus and into the Fallopian tube towards the waiting egg. To help the process, the egg releases chemicals that tell the sperm where it is, attracting them towards it.

The sperm race to penetrate the egg, but only one sperm out of the millions released at ejaculation will succeed in fertilizing the egg. As soon as the egg has been penetrated, it releases chemicals that 'seal' it, so that no other sperm can break through. Once the sperm has broken through the surface of the egg, its tail breaks off.

# After fertilization

When the egg and the sperm have fused, they become a new type of cell, called a zygote. The sperm and egg each contained 23 chromosomes, so the newly formed zygote contains 46 chromosomes. The zygote then travels slowly along the Fallopian tube, dividing into identical cells as it goes – first two, then four, then eight, and so on. By about day 4 it is a solid ball of cells and is called a morula. When it reaches the uterus it is a hollow ball of 50–100 cells and is called a blastocyst. It takes around six days for the blastocyst to reach the uterus and implant. Once implanted, it then continues to grow and develop until the blastocyst becomes an embryo.

# Fertilization **Common questions**

**Q How often should I be having sex to increase my chances of conception?**
**A** The key to getting pregnant is to have sex at least once every 48 hours during your fertile period. This ensures that there are plenty of sperm available whenever there is an egg ready to be fertilized. It may also help to stay in bed a while after having sex. Although sperm are designed to swim towards your cervix, you can help them on their way by lying down – or even sticking your legs in the air!

**Q Can an egg fertilize, but fail to implant?**
**A** Yes, in some cases an egg that has been successfully fertilized by a sperm fails to implant in the uterus. This is usually because of an abnormality in the fertilized egg that means it cannot survive. If this happens, you usually will not even know that the egg was fertilized. You may just have a slightly later period than usual.

**Q I am delighted to have just found out that I am pregnant, but I am not sure when to tell people. Is it best to wait until after 12 weeks?**
**A** When to tell people you are pregnant is a personal choice. Many women wait until after 12 weeks, when there is less risk of miscarriage. But others want to share their news at once. It is understandable that some women feel cautious, particularly if they have had a previous miscarriage. But if the pregnancy were to end and it had been a secret, this too could be very hard for a couple. Trust your instincts and if you want to share your news, do.

# Expecting twins

The discovery that you are expecting twins can be a shock, and it is natural to worry about how you will cope with two babies. There is something different about expecting twins: other mothers-to-be often want to ask you what it is like, and you will also receive extra care from medical professionals, adding to the feeling that there is something special happening.

## Finding out

If you have had no reason to suspect that you might be expecting twins, you may not have a routine ultrasound scan until you are 12 weeks pregnant or more, by which time the two babies will be clearly distinguishable in the scan image. If you have been given fertility treatment, you will probably have an early ultrasound scan at around six weeks into your pregnancy, and even at this stage of your pregnancy you may be able to detect two tiny heartbeats on the monitor screen.

## What kind of twin?

Identical twins occur when one egg splits into two after fertilization. As the twins develop from two halves of the same fertilized egg, they contain identical genetic information, so they will be the same sex, look very alike and may even have similar personalities. Around one in three sets of twins are identical, and two-thirds of these will share a placenta while in the uterus.

Fraternal (non-identical) twins occur when a woman produces two separate eggs that are then fertilized by two different sperm. These babies will not be any more or less alike than any other pair of siblings, and each will be contained within its own amniotic sac and have its own placenta, although the latter may fuse during the pregnancy.

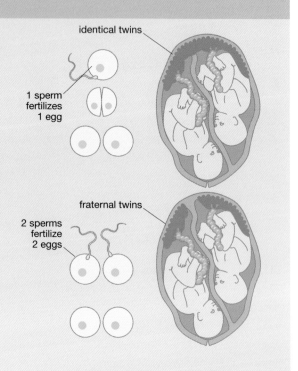

identical twins

1 sperm fertilizes 1 egg

fraternal twins

2 sperms fertilize 2 eggs

# Twins **Common questions**

**Above:** A family history of twins increases your chance of conceiving fraternal twins yourself.

**Q What are the chances of having twins?**
**A** You are more likely to conceive fraternal twins (see box) if there is a family tendency to do so, especially on the maternal side. Your age is also a factor in this: women over 30 years old produce more follicle-stimulating hormones than earlier in life so they are more likely to release more than one egg at a time when they ovulate.

**Q Is it true that fertility treatment increases your chances of having twins?**
**A** Yes, if you have undergone fertility treatment, you will have a greater chance of conceiving more than one baby. Fertility drugs make you more likely to release more than one egg at a time, while in the case of IVF more than one embryo is often implanted (see pages 28–29), so you may end up having twins or triplets. On average, 25 per cent of women using either fertility drugs or IVF conceive twins.

**Q What are conjoined twins?**
**A** If a single egg fails to split properly after fertilization, conjoined twins (sometimes known as Siamese twins) will develop. Conjoined twins occur only very rarely – about once per

200,000 live births. There are various types, depending on where the twins are joined. It may be possible to separate conjoined twins after birth, but the condition carries serious health risks, especially if the twins are sharing vital organs or blood supply.

**Q My mother has a twin brother. Does this family history make it more likely that I will have twins myself?**
**A** Identical twins do not tend to run in families but fraternal (non-identical) twins do, especially through the maternal side. So, because your mother has a twin brother, the chances of you conceiving fraternal twins are higher than average. This would also be the case if you are a fraternal twin, have twin siblings or have already produced one set of twins yourself.

## Triplets

Triplets are now more common as a result of fertility treatments. In some countries, women under 40 have only two embryos implanted with each IVF cycle, so the most they conceive is twins (although one egg may split, producing triplets). There are three types of triplet:

- **Three identical triplets** occur if one egg splits into three after fertilization.
- **Two identical and one non-identical triplets** occur if two eggs are released and only one splits in two.
- **Three non-identical triplets** occur if three separate eggs are fertilized.

# Fertility problems

If you are struggling to conceive, it can seem as if the whole world is pregnant except you. The reality is that about one in seven women has difficulty conceiving, and even women in fertile couples having regular unprotected sex have only a 20 per cent chance of getting pregnant each month.

## Common causes of female infertility

- **Problems with ovulation** A fine balance of different hormones is needed for the various stages of ovulation to occur. If any of these hormones is absent or not present in the right levels, ovulation may not happen. The ovaries may also be damaged, perhaps as a side-effect of radiotherapy or as a result of surgery or an infection.

- **Polycystic ovary syndrome (PCOS)** Usually the eggs in the ovaries develop inside follicles until one is mature enough to be released. With PCOS, the follicles become cysts, so that the eggs are unable to mature.

- **Endometriosis** This condition occurs when the cells that normally make up the endometrium (see page 15) grow elsewhere inside the woman's body. The cells then bleed when she has her period, causing internal organs to become glued together with blood and endometrial

**Below left:** Some of the internal organs where deposits of endometriosis are commonly found.

**Below right:** Fibroids of various sizes can form within and outside the uterus.

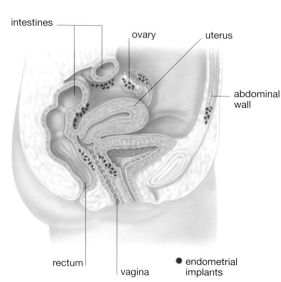

intestines — ovary — uterus — abdominal wall — rectum — vagina — ● endometrial implants

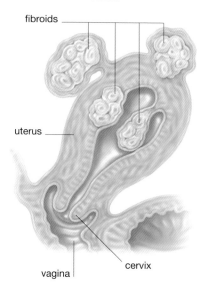

fibroids — uterus — cervix — vagina

tissue. This condition can affect fertility if the ovaries, Fallopian tubes or uterus become damaged.

- **Damaged Fallopian tubes** Damage to the Fallopian tubes or blockage by scar tissue can be caused by a previous ectopic pregnancy, by an infection such as chlamydia or by endometriosis.
- **Fibroids** These benign tumours can grow inside and outside the uterus and do not usually affect fertility. Sometimes, however, they can press against the Fallopian tubes or interfere with the implanting of a fertilized egg. They can be removed surgically, if deemed necessary.

## Common causes of male infertility

- **Low sperm count** This can range from none to a lower than average number; the normal range is 35–200 million sperm per millilitre of semen.
- **Abnormal sperm** The sperm may not be properly formed.
- **Poor sperm mobility** The sperm are neither fast nor agile enough.
- **Failure to ejaculate** Some men suffer from retrograde ejaculation, where the semen goes backwards into the bladder during sex rather than into the vagina.
- **Blocked vas deferens** The vas deferens or sperm ducts (see page 15) may become blocked because of a defect or an infection.
- **Testicular failure** Undescended testicles, injury to the testicles, chemotherapy, mumps after puberty or injury can all be a cause of lowered sperm production.

## Fertility **Common questions**

**Q How long should I keep trying to conceive before going to someone for help?**
**A** If you have been trying for a baby without success for 12 months, it is worth talking to your doctor about your concerns. In some cases, it is worth seeking advice after only six months, for example if you are over 35 and do not have regular periods; if you or your partner have had a sexually transmitted disease (STD), a pelvic or abdominal injury or surgery; or if there is a tendency to fertility problems in your family.

**Q What can we expect my doctor to do?**
**A** Your doctor will take a medical history and ask questions about your menstrual cycle, how long you have been trying to conceive and your lifestyle. He or she may give you an internal examination, check your hormone levels to see whether you are ovulating and will carry out a smear test if it is due. Your blood will be checked for STDs, as some, such as chlamydia, can affect fertility. Your partner's penis and testes will be examined, and he will be asked to provide a semen sample to be sent to a laboratory for testing. Your doctor will probably also refer you to a fertility specialist for further investigation.

**Q What does a fertility specialist do?**
**A** A fertility specialist will carry out further investigations. These may include an ultrasound scan to look closely at your ovaries and a biopsy – removing a tiny part of the endometrium – to check whether it is becoming thick and spongy enough after ovulation. Other tests check the correct functioning of the Fallopian tubes.

# Overcoming fertility problems

For many couples, the stress and anxiety involved in trying for a baby are often to blame for difficulties in conceiving. It is easy to get very hung-up on counting fertile days, filling in charts and having sex to order, but becoming obsessive about these things can often have the opposite effect to the one you are looking for.

**Below:** If you or your partner has a fertility problem, your specialist will recommend suitable treatments.

## What to do

If conception is taking a few months, try to remain relaxed about it. Remember that sex should be fun and a means of showing your love for each other, not just a way to make a baby. You may find that if you stop counting, plotting and measuring and just try to have lots of sex without thinking too hard about the consequences, you will get lucky without too much trouble.

If you have been trying to conceive a baby for a long time without any success, and you have seen your doctor in order to investigate your or your partner's potential

**True story**

**Infertility reversal**

'I first started trying for a baby 12 years ago. When month after month ended in tears, I went to my doctor. Tests showed I didn't ovulate, had no female hormones and was suffering from polycystic ovarian syndrome (PCOS). It was noted as "unexplained infertility". My marriage dissolved soon after. But three years on, I met David, who became my partner.

'Even though I knew I was infertile, we began to talk about having a child together. We decided that I should go back to the doctor, to see if there was any hope of treatment. I was amazed when he looked at my notes and said the original tests might just have shown that I wasn't ovulating that day. I wasn't amused.

'I came off the pill and was given some medication to help me encourage ovulation. I was due to start this with my next period, but it was already six days late. In my experience, the best way to bring on a period is to do a pregnancy test! So I did the test and waited. When I saw that the result was positive, my heart felt too big for my chest. I cried, laughed, cried again. When David came home, we cried some more.

'A week later we came back to earth when I started to bleed. It wasn't serious, but after that we were in hospital nearly every week with various problems. A 3D scan really helped me through – I saw my baby move and knew she was real.

'Our long-awaited girl was born by caesarean. The surgeon held her up and said, "Look what you've done!" After all we'd been through, we had to call her Faith.'

**Jo, mother of Faith**

fertility problems, the next step is to start treatment. There are four basic methods of dealing with fertility issues: drug treatment; sperm and egg donation; surgery; and assisted conception such as in vitro fertilization (IVF) or intracytoplasmic sperm injection (ICSI). (For more information on these treatments, see Assisted conception, pages 28–29, and Sperm and egg donation, pages 30–31.)

## Drug treatments

Drug treatments are designed to stimulate your ovulation. They are often the first port of call for women with fertility problems, as they are relatively simple to use, safe and have a track record of being used successfully for many years.

Ovulation is controlled by a fine balance of hormones, including one called follicle-stimulating hormone (or FSH). Levels of FSH can be raised by taking a drug called clomifene (formerly spelt clomiphene). This stimulates the ovaries and leads to a higher rate of ovulation. You will be monitored while taking the five-day course of clomifene pills, so that your doctor can determine whether any mature eggs are being produced. It may be a couple of months after taking the drugs before you start to ovulate regularly.

# ASSISTED CONCEPTION

## Choosing to have IVF

**During in vitro fertilization (IVF), the egg is fertilized by the sperm outside the body, in a laboratory. The fertilized egg is then implanted in the uterus. Intracytoplasmic sperm injection (ICSI) is a specialized type of IVF, in which a single sperm is injected directly into an egg.**

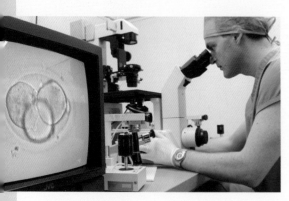

**Above:** In the laboratory, eggs and sperm are prepared for an attempt at assisted conception.

Once you have been accepted onto a course of IVF treatment, the first step is for doctors to give you drugs that suppress the activity of your ovaries, a process that involves 'sniffing' a hormone spray for approximately 21 days. This is followed by a course of injections that will stimulate your ovaries to produce eggs. The procedure ensures that you produce a number of eggs at the same time. Your blood will be tested regularly and you will be given ultrasound scans so the doctors can monitor the eggs' development. Timing is crucial because the eggs need to be collected a matter of hours before they

are released. When the follicles are almost ready, you will be given an injection of human chorionic gonadotrophin (HCG), a hormone that will trigger ovulation.

## What happens next?

When the eggs are ready, you will be given sedation or a general anaesthetic and the doctor will remove several eggs using a tiny hollow needle inserted into your ovary through your vagina wall, or sometimes passed through the abdomen, guided by an ultrasound scan. You should be able to go home afterwards to rest.

In the laboratory, your eggs will be placed together with your partner's sperm. After a few days, eggs that have been fertilized will have divided many times and become embryos. Up to three embryos will then be placed into your uterus through your cervix, using a catheter.

In some countries, only two embryos will be used if you are under 40, to reduce the risk of conceiving triplets. If you are over 40, you can have three embryos implanted if you wish, as it is less likely that all of them will implant. If more than three embryos are produced, extras can be frozen and used for another IVF cycle.

As with a normal conception, you can do a pregnancy test after about two weeks. If you are pregnant, you will be scanned and your antenatal care planned. If not, you may want to consider more treatment, or take a break to think about what to do next.

## Pros and cons

IVF means that a couple can conceive a baby using their own eggs and sperm. On the down side, it involves a lot of medical intervention, which can be painful and distressing, so several cycles can take their toll emotionally. Also, the drugs that boost ovulation can have unpleasant side-effects. IVF can also be expensive if you have to pay for it yourself.

## Chances of success

Success depends on the nature of your fertility problems and your age. The success rate across the United Kingdom is around 28 per cent for under 35s, after which it starts to fall away. In the United States, the average success rate is 28–35 per cent.

## The effects of IVF

Various stages have different side-effects:
- Taking drugs to suppress your ovaries may produce symptoms that are similar to those of the menopause: hot flushes, sweating, insomnia, dizziness, headaches and vaginal dryness.
- Taking HCG to stimulate ovulation may produce symptoms similar to pre-menstrual tension (PMT): anxiety, tearfulness or stress, bloating, sore ovaries or general aching and tiredness.

### Five tips for couples **undergoing IVF**

1 **Decide early on who you are going to tell. It might help to have a friend or family member to whom you can talk.**
2 **Consider donating eggs or sperm. Some clinics give priority to couples who are prepared to do this for other couples with fertility problems.**
3 **Learn to give yourself injections. You will save time and effort going to your doctor's surgery for the long course of hormones.**
4 **Know when to stop. It can be more difficult to give up than to begin, but IVF is a hard slog, and it can be empowering to decide that it is no longer for you.**
5 **Keep communicating with each other. If either of you feels in need of a break or is unable to cope with any more, do not be afraid to say.**

- The egg collection procedure may leave you feeling tired from the effects of the anaesthetic, and your ovaries and abdomen will ache.
- Embryo transfer may leave you drowsy and emotional. You are likely to have sore breasts and a painful abdomen.

## Intracytoplasmic sperm injection (ICSI)

This technique was developed to help men who have a low sperm count. It achieves fertilization through the direct injection of a single sperm into the egg's cytoplasm (fluid centre), enabling the sperm to bypass the egg's protective outer layer. Eggs and sperm are collected as in IVF.

# Sperm and egg donation

Assisted-conception treatments such as in vitro fertilization (IVF) rely on a couple's sperm and egg being fertilized outside the body. However, some couples do not conceive a baby for the simple reason that the woman is not producing any eggs or the man is not producing any sperm.

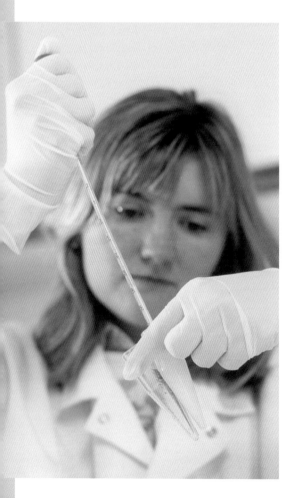

## Sperm donation

If you are not ovulating or your partner is not producing sperm, then your only chance of having a baby together may be to accept sperm or eggs from a donor. Sperm donation is a good option if the woman is fully fertile but the man is experiencing fertility problems and any treatments used to boost his sperm count have failed.

The sperm will be frozen after donation and then defrosted immediately before the procedure. The clinic will work out when you are ovulating and your doctor will sometimes recommend that you take fertility drugs, such as clomifene, to make absolutely sure that you will have released an egg when the sperm are introduced. The defrosted sperm are usually inserted directly into your uterus.

## Egg donation

If a woman is not ovulating and drug therapies, such as clomifene, have not helped, but the man is still producing healthy sperm, then egg donation could be the right option for you. The quality of the eggs that a woman produces declines as she ages, so egg donation is particularly valuable for women who choose to become mothers in later life. This procedure can also help if your eggs have been destroyed by cancer treatments.

The egg-donation procedure involves both you and your egg donor taking drugs to synchronize your cycles, to ensure that she is

**Left:** Donated sperm is gathered, frozen for storage and then defrosted directly before insemination.

# Fertility problems **Common questions**

**Q** What is embryo donation?

**A** Some couples who have extra embryos, created by IVF, donate them to other infertile couples. Receiving an embryo in this way is an option if there is a risk of you and your partner passing on a genetic disorder of which you are both carriers. The procedure involves the same basic technique as IVF.

**Q** What is IUI?

**A** IUI or intrauterine insemination is the term for what was once known as artificial insemination. In this process, sperm are artificially placed in the uterus, often by means of a catheter. The procedure is frequently used when a woman's cervical mucus is hostile to sperm, when couples cannot naturally have intercourse due to disability or injury, and in cases of male

infertility. In IUI, the egg and sperm are produced naturally, but are given help in reaching the uterus.

**Q** I am beginning to accept that I may never have children, but how do I break the news to my family?

**A** Anyone in a long-term relationship may have received comments from friends and relatives about 'the patter of tiny feet', the ticking of biological clocks or the wisdom of buying a large car. Such remarks can hurt if you are struggling to conceive, and it can be hard to know how to cope. One strategy is to plan your response in advance, deciding either to make light of it or to be completely honest and upfront about your situation.

producing eggs at the time when your uterus is ready for an egg to implant. Once her eggs have been removed, they will be combined with your partner's sperm just as in normal IVF (see Assisted conception, pages 28–29).

## Surgery

Fertility problems in women are often caused by damage to the Fallopian tubes (see page 25). If this is the case, there are two main surgical procedures that can be performed to repair the damage.

- **Fimbrioplasty** is a procedure used to open up a blocked Fallopian tube. The opening of a Fallopian tube is made up of finger-like sections, called fimbriae (see page 14).

These can sometimes fuse together, sealing off the entrance and stopping eggs from passing through. The operation peels back the fimbriae, opening up the tube so that the egg can travel through.

- **Tuboplasty** is an operation performed to open up Fallopian tubes that have become blocked or narrowed. A balloon catheter is inserted down the Fallopian tube, and the balloon at the end is inflated in order to unblock the tube.

# Common anxieties

During pregnancy, your body is being bombarded with a variety of hormones that can affect your mood, triggering a rollercoaster of emotions. You may feel tearful, without knowing quite why. You may be deliriously happy one minute only to be gripped by a seemingly irrational fear seconds later. Don't worry, you're not the only one. Most expectant mothers – and partners – go through many anxious moments.

## Why worry?

Becoming a parent involves adjusting to some huge changes in both your role and lifestyle, which can be difficult. If this is your first baby, you might worry that your partner will see you differently after the birth: not as a lover but in your new role as a mother. You may also have some regrets about the loss of freedom that having a child entails. If you already have an older child or children, you may worry about how they will adjust to the arrival of a new baby brother or sister.

You will probably be expecting changes in your financial circumstances or in your housing arrangements. If your pregnancy was not planned, you may be very concerned about being unable to support a baby financially or about your house being too small.

Of course, it is important to think through all the practicalities of returning to work and enlisting your family to help out with child care. However, some people would always feel that they don't have enough money, enough bedrooms or a big enough car to commit to having a baby, and yet, with hindsight, do not regret an unplanned pregnancy.

**Left:** Joyful anticipation and concerns about the future are both a natural part of pregnancy.

# Common anxieties **Common questions**

**Q** My pregnancy was not planned and I was drinking and smoking when I conceived. Will this have harmed my baby?
**A** Many women feel guilty about having drunk alcohol in the weeks before they knew they were pregnant or worry that they have eaten the 'wrong' types of food. Do your best to adopt a healthy lifestyle as soon as you find out that you are pregnant. By stopping smoking, giving up alcohol and eating a healthy diet you will give your baby the best start possible. Screening tests, including ultrasound scans, can help reassure you about the general health of your baby (see pages 190–193).

**Q** I miscarried last summer and now that I am pregnant again, I am worried the same thing will happen. What can I do?
**A** Women with a history of difficult pregnancy, perhaps a stillbirth or miscarriage, can be particularly fearful about 'something going wrong'. If this is the case, it is important to talk about your worries. Speaking to others who have had a similar experience may provide you with the emotional support that you need. You might also ask your midwife or doctor to see you more often, and you will be given extra ultrasound scans if that is considered necessary (however, the excessive use of ultrasound should be avoided).

**Q** Since becoming pregnant, I feel my husband has lost interest in me and no longer finds me attractive. Is this normal?
**A** As their shape changes during pregnancy, some women begin to worry that they are no longer attractive to their partner. You may think you look fat or get a shock when you catch sight of your growing bump in the reflection of a shop doorway or a mirror. Talk to your partner about it – you may find he is worried that you will reject his advances, as many women go off sex during pregnancy.

**Q** I love being pregnant, but I am worried that I will not be able to get through giving birth. What can I do?
**A** Many fears about the birth stem from a lack of accurate information. It is a good idea for both of you to find out as much as you can about labour by attending antenatal classes. Here you will be encouraged to talk about your feelings and to discuss not only your fears but also your hopes.

*'Throughout the pregnancy I was convinced that something would go wrong and I just kept waiting for the bubble to burst. It was such a relief talking to other women in antenatal classes and finding out that I was not the only one who felt that way.'*
*Michelle, mother of Louise*

# your changing body

# Your body
## at 1–8 weeks

For many women the first sign that they are pregnant is a missed period. However, women who have an irregular menstrual cycle may only decide to do a pregnancy test when they experience other symptoms, including tiredness, tender breasts and a need to pass urine more frequently.

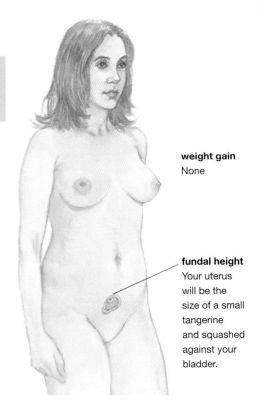

**weight gain**
None

**fundal height**
Your uterus will be the size of a small tangerine and squashed against your bladder.

## How are you?

You may have very mixed emotions when you discover that you are pregnant. Even if you have planned to have a baby, the reality of being pregnant may be overwhelming. While many women want to shout the news to everyone immediately, others prefer to wait until after they are 12 weeks pregnant, when there is less risk of a miscarriage.

You will probably have started to feel very tired (which will not be helped by the frequent need to pass urine during the night) and you may well be suffering from nausea or vomiting. Other early symptoms of pregnancy include pelvic congestion (an achy and bloated feeling in your pubic area), tender breasts and a

metallic taste in the mouth. Although your body may feel different, it will not look very different to normal, so others will not be able to tell that you are pregnant.

## Your due date

Your midwife will use a chart similar to the one shown (right) to give you an estimated date of delivery (EDD). This date will be used to check your baby's growth and development. Your EDD will be 40 weeks from the first day of your last menstrual period (LMP), not from the day you think you conceived. This is more accurate because not all women ovulate at the same stage of their cycle. However, because the date is based on an average 28-day cycle, only 5 per cent of women actually give birth on their EDD. To work out your EDD, look up the day and month of the first day of your last period, then read the date on the line below.

### 1–8 weeks: things to do

- **Start taking folic acid supplements (400 mcg daily) if you have not done so already.**
- **Make an appointment to see a midwife at around eight weeks of pregnancy.**

# 1–8 weeks **Common questions**

**Q** I am seven weeks pregnant and I am being sick every day. What can I do?
**A** In the majority of cases the sickness is normal and will not harm your baby, who will still get what he needs from you – however little you eat – as long as your diet is balanced. Try to eat little and often throughout the day. Ginger or peppermint is also thought to help nausea, and some women swear by travel bands. These bands apply pressure to the acupuncture points in the wrist that control sickness. Try sucking ice cubes if you cannot face drinking anything and see your doctor if you find yourself becoming dehydrated.

**Q** My pregnancy was unexpected. I know we can have a great family life, but my partner is not sure. How do I convince him?
**A** Worries about the future can outweigh optimism when it comes to fatherhood. If your partner's reactions are lukewarm, try to find out why. He may have unhappy memories of his own childhood, be afraid of the changes a baby will bring or not feel ready for such responsibility. Some men feel that they have no interest in babies, although they like older children. Others may simply not be drawn to children at all. Discussing his views openly could help him to overcome his anxieties.

## Your estimated date of delivery (see Your due date, left, for how to use this table)

| | | | | | | | | | | | | | | | | | | | | | | | | | | | | | | | |
|---|---|---|---|---|---|---|---|---|---|---|---|---|---|---|---|---|---|---|---|---|---|---|---|---|---|---|---|---|---|---|---|
| January | 1 | 2 | 3 | 4 | 5 | 6 | 7 | 8 | 9 | 10 | 11 | 12 | 13 | 14 | 15 | 16 | 17 | 18 | 19 | 20 | 21 | 22 | 23 | 24 | 25 | 26 | 27 | 28 | 29 | 30 | 31 |
| Oct/Nov | 8 | 9 | 10 | 11 | 12 | 13 | 14 | 15 | 16 | 17 | 18 | 19 | 20 | 21 | 22 | 23 | 24 | 25 | 26 | 27 | 28 | 29 | 30 | 31 | 1 | 2 | 3 | 4 | 5 | 6 | 7 |
| February | 1 | 2 | 3 | 4 | 5 | 6 | 7 | 8 | 9 | 10 | 11 | 12 | 13 | 14 | 15 | 16 | 17 | 18 | 19 | 20 | 21 | 22 | 23 | 24 | 25 | 26 | 27 | 28 | | | |
| Nov/Dec | 8 | 9 | 10 | 11 | 12 | 13 | 14 | 15 | 16 | 17 | 18 | 19 | 20 | 21 | 22 | 23 | 24 | 25 | 26 | 27 | 28 | 29 | 30 | 1 | 2 | 3 | 4 | 5 | | | |
| March | 1 | 2 | 3 | 4 | 5 | 6 | 7 | 8 | 9 | 10 | 11 | 12 | 13 | 14 | 15 | 16 | 17 | 18 | 19 | 20 | 21 | 22 | 23 | 24 | 25 | 26 | 27 | 28 | 29 | 30 | 31 |
| Dec/Jan | 6 | 7 | 8 | 9 | 10 | 11 | 12 | 13 | 14 | 15 | 16 | 17 | 18 | 19 | 20 | 21 | 22 | 23 | 24 | 25 | 26 | 27 | 28 | 29 | 30 | 31 | 1 | 2 | 3 | 4 | 5 |
| April | 1 | 2 | 3 | 4 | 5 | 6 | 7 | 8 | 9 | 10 | 11 | 12 | 13 | 14 | 15 | 16 | 17 | 18 | 19 | 20 | 21 | 22 | 23 | 24 | 25 | 26 | 27 | 28 | 29 | 30 | |
| Jan/Feb | 6 | 7 | 8 | 9 | 10 | 11 | 12 | 13 | 14 | 15 | 16 | 17 | 18 | 19 | 20 | 21 | 22 | 23 | 24 | 25 | 26 | 27 | 28 | 29 | 30 | 31 | 1 | 2 | 3 | 4 | |
| May | 1 | 2 | 3 | 4 | 5 | 6 | 7 | 8 | 9 | 10 | 11 | 12 | 13 | 14 | 15 | 16 | 17 | 18 | 19 | 20 | 21 | 22 | 23 | 24 | 25 | 26 | 27 | 28 | 29 | 30 | 31 |
| Feb/Mar | 5 | 6 | 7 | 8 | 9 | 10 | 11 | 12 | 13 | 14 | 15 | 16 | 17 | 18 | 19 | 20 | 21 | 22 | 23 | 24 | 25 | 26 | 27 | 28 | 1 | 2 | 3 | 4 | 5 | 6 | 7 |
| June | 1 | 2 | 3 | 4 | 5 | 6 | 7 | 8 | 9 | 10 | 11 | 12 | 13 | 14 | 15 | 16 | 17 | 18 | 19 | 20 | 21 | 22 | 23 | 24 | 25 | 26 | 27 | 28 | 29 | 30 | |
| Mar/Apr | 8 | 9 | 10 | 11 | 12 | 13 | 14 | 15 | 16 | 17 | 18 | 19 | 20 | 21 | 22 | 23 | 24 | 25 | 26 | 27 | 28 | 29 | 30 | 31 | 1 | 2 | 3 | 4 | 5 | 6 | |
| July | 1 | 2 | 3 | 4 | 5 | 6 | 7 | 8 | 9 | 10 | 11 | 12 | 13 | 14 | 15 | 16 | 17 | 18 | 19 | 20 | 21 | 22 | 23 | 24 | 25 | 26 | 27 | 28 | 29 | 30 | 31 |
| Apr/May | 7 | 8 | 9 | 10 | 11 | 12 | 13 | 14 | 15 | 16 | 17 | 18 | 19 | 20 | 21 | 22 | 23 | 24 | 25 | 26 | 27 | 28 | 29 | 30 | 1 | 2 | 3 | 4 | 5 | 6 | 7 |
| August | 1 | 2 | 3 | 4 | 5 | 6 | 7 | 8 | 9 | 10 | 11 | 12 | 13 | 14 | 15 | 16 | 17 | 18 | 19 | 20 | 21 | 22 | 23 | 24 | 25 | 26 | 27 | 28 | 29 | 30 | 31 |
| May/Jun | 8 | 9 | 10 | 11 | 12 | 13 | 14 | 15 | 16 | 17 | 18 | 19 | 20 | 21 | 22 | 23 | 24 | 25 | 26 | 27 | 28 | 29 | 30 | 31 | 1 | 2 | 3 | 4 | 5 | 6 | 7 |
| September | 1 | 2 | 3 | 4 | 5 | 6 | 7 | 8 | 9 | 10 | 11 | 12 | 13 | 14 | 15 | 16 | 17 | 18 | 19 | 20 | 21 | 22 | 23 | 24 | 25 | 26 | 27 | 28 | 29 | 30 | |
| Jun/Jul | 8 | 9 | 10 | 11 | 12 | 13 | 14 | 15 | 16 | 17 | 18 | 19 | 20 | 21 | 22 | 23 | 24 | 25 | 26 | 27 | 28 | 29 | 30 | 1 | 2 | 3 | 4 | 5 | 6 | 7 | |
| October | 1 | 2 | 3 | 4 | 5 | 6 | 7 | 8 | 9 | 10 | 11 | 12 | 13 | 14 | 15 | 16 | 17 | 18 | 19 | 20 | 21 | 22 | 23 | 24 | 25 | 26 | 27 | 28 | 29 | 30 | 31 |
| Jul/Aug | 8 | 9 | 10 | 11 | 12 | 13 | 14 | 15 | 16 | 17 | 18 | 19 | 20 | 21 | 22 | 23 | 24 | 25 | 26 | 27 | 28 | 29 | 30 | 31 | 1 | 2 | 3 | 4 | 5 | 6 | 7 |
| November | 1 | 2 | 3 | 4 | 5 | 6 | 7 | 8 | 9 | 10 | 11 | 12 | 13 | 14 | 15 | 16 | 17 | 18 | 19 | 20 | 21 | 22 | 23 | 24 | 25 | 26 | 27 | 28 | 29 | 30 | |
| Aug/Sep | 8 | 9 | 10 | 11 | 12 | 13 | 14 | 15 | 16 | 17 | 18 | 19 | 20 | 21 | 22 | 23 | 24 | 25 | 26 | 27 | 28 | 29 | 30 | 31 | 1 | 2 | 3 | 4 | 5 | 6 | |
| December | 1 | 2 | 3 | 4 | 5 | 6 | 7 | 8 | 9 | 10 | 11 | 12 | 13 | 14 | 15 | 16 | 17 | 18 | 19 | 20 | 21 | 22 | 23 | 24 | 25 | 26 | 27 | 28 | 29 | 30 | 31 |
| Sep/Oct | 7 | 8 | 9 | 10 | 11 | 12 | 13 | 14 | 15 | 16 | 17 | 18 | 19 | 20 | 21 | 22 | 23 | 24 | 25 | 26 | 27 | 28 | 29 | 30 | 1 | 2 | 3 | 4 | 5 | 6 | 7 |

# Your body
# at 9–12 weeks

By now, you have probably got used to the idea that you are pregnant. At this stage you will have your first antenatal appointment with your midwife or doctor, and you will have been offered an ultrasound scan.

## 9–12 weeks: things to do

- Continue to take folic acid supplements and eat iron-rich foods, for example, red meat, dried apricots, raisins, pulses, green leafy vegetables and dark oily fish (maximum two portions of oily fish per week).
- Make an appointment to see your midwife or doctor if you have not done so already. They will advise you to take blood tests and may offer you a dating scan.

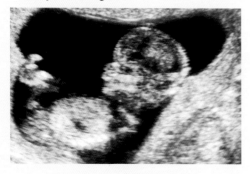

- If you decide to have chorionic villus sampling (CVS), a prenatal screening test to detect genetic defects (see pages 194–197), it would be done around now.
- Ask your midwife or doctor for the appropriate certificate to claim free prescriptions and dental care.

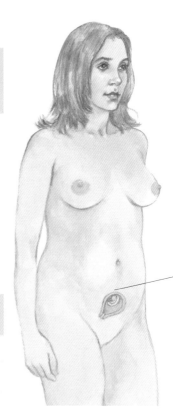

**weight gain**
Up to 1 kg (2 lb), but sickness may cause weight loss.

**fundal height**
The top of your uterus should be just above your pubic bone.

## How are you?

9–12 weeks is an exciting period emotionally for parents-to-be, because it is towards the end of this time that most couples start to tell friends and family their news. The tiredness and nausea often experienced at the beginning of pregnancy should lessen now, although for a small minority of women these symptoms will continue. You may also feel very hungry. Your breasts will now be bigger and you may find that your veins become more prominent.

From nine weeks of pregnancy, you might notice that your waist seems to be getting thicker and that your clothes feel tighter, but this has nothing to do with the size of your baby. The sensation is more likely to be the result of general congestion: your circulation will have become more sluggish and you may also be suffering from constipation and wind.

# 9–12 weeks **Common questions**

**Q** I have noticed a significant increase in vaginal discharge. Is this normal?

**A** As long as the discharge is white, non-itchy and has no smell, there is nothing to worry about. An increase is normal during pregnancy and usually results from hormonal activity. If it seems itchy, is discoloured or has a strong smell, see your midwife or doctor, who can take a swab to rule out the possibility that you have an infection.

**Q** I seem to have terrible constipation and wind. Why is this, and is there anything I can do?

**A** The hormone progesterone relaxes the bowel, slowing it down and causing constipation and wind. To relieve this, try exercise, particularly yoga – the gentle exercises encourage the bowel to become less sluggish. When you eat, chew the food slowly and give it time to digest. Drinking peppermint tea is also said to help relieve trapped wind. If constipation continues to be a problem, talk to your midwife, who will probably recommend a mild laxative.

**Q** I barely get through a night without waking, sometimes with an urgent need to go to the toilet. Why is this?

**A** Your metabolic rate increases by 20 per cent during pregnancy, which means that your body is working harder and, although you might feel tired, it is hard to 'switch off' as your mind is still working overtime. In the early weeks, it is very common to wake during the night to go to the toilet, as the uterus is squashed against the bladder, but as the uterus expands it rises further above the bladder, relieving the pressure on it.

**Q** My gums have started bleeding when I brush my teeth. Does this mean I have gum disease?

**A** Not necessarily. Pregnancy hormones soften the gums and there is a tendency for them to bleed. Looking after your teeth in pregnancy is very important – softer gums means that you are at greater risk of infection, so you should pay greater attention to brushing and flossing.

*'It didn't feel like I was really pregnant until I actually saw my baby on the scan and saw it move. At last I felt I could tell my family, friends and people at work that I was going to have a baby, although I think that some of them had already guessed!'*

*Kate, 19 weeks pregnant*

# Your body
## at 13–16 weeks

As you enter the second three months of pregnancy, you will probably start to 'bloom'. Many women feel at their most feminine during this stage of pregnancy, because their breasts become larger, their abdomen rounds and the condition of their skin and hair improves. By the second trimester you will have accepted and become more confident in your pregnancy, and you may well have shared the news with others.

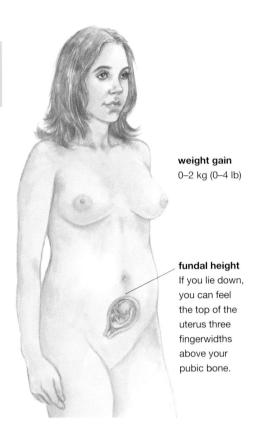

**weight gain**
0–2 kg (0–4 lb)

**fundal height**
If you lie down, you can feel the top of the uterus three fingerwidths above your pubic bone.

## 13–16 weeks: things to do

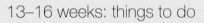

- Increase your intake of calcium by eating plenty of dairy foods, tinned fish (a maximum of two portions of oily fish per week), white bread, spinach, baked beans, kidney beans, almonds and oranges.
- Make sure that you have had all the blood tests that you need by the end of this period. It is important to establish your blood group during pregnancy in case of any bleeding.
- If you are Rhesus negative (see pages 140–141) and have any bleeding after 12 weeks of pregnancy, you will be advised to have an injection of Anti-D. You may also be advised to have the injection if you are Rhesus negative and no bleeding occurs.

## How are you?

During 13–16 weeks of pregnancy, your tiredness and nausea should improve and your energy levels should pick up. You will also become aware of your changing shape and find that your usual clothes are too tight. Changes in skin condition are commonly experienced at this stage.

Your uterus has now risen out of your pubic cavity and is the size of a grapefruit. If you have had a baby before, your bump is likely to be more obvious, because your muscles have been stretched and are not as toned. Your veins expand during pregnancy and therefore become more prominent: you might notice them as blue lines not only on your breasts, but also on your legs and abdomen.

# 13–16 weeks **Common questions**

**Q** Since I got pregnant, I have found it hard to focus mentally and suffer regularly from memory loss. What is going on?
**A** Many pregnant women suffer from short-term memory loss, and the effect may even persist a few weeks after the birth – probably because they are so distracted and absorbed by their pregnancy and the lack of sleep that follows. The best action to take is to relax and resist becoming frustrated. Make lists and try to adjust to being less efficient than usual.

**Q** I suffer terribly from heartburn, mostly at night-time. Is there anything I can do?
**A** Heartburn is common in pregnancy and is felt as an unpleasant burning sensation when stomach acids leak into your oesophagus. This is because the valve that normally stops this from happening relaxes during pregnancy. You can alleviate the problem by standing and sitting tall, as slouching squashes the stomach, making the problem worse. At night, sleep with more pillows to prop you up. Try adjusting your diet so that you do not eat late at night, and avoid spicy or fried foods. Some women find that drinking peppermint tea after a meal helps prevent heartburn.

**Q** Why do pregnant women get acne?
**A** During pregnancy it is normal for your skin to change, and it can happen at different stages of pregnancy. The skin tends to retain more moisture in these months because of the increased volume of blood in the body, and for many women it is a time when they experience skin and hair problems not seen since adolescence. Good skin care does not only involve cleansing, toning and moisturizing, but also maintaining a balanced diet, drinking plenty of water and taking regular exercise. Eating foods rich in vitamin C can generally improve the condition of the skin.

**Q** Why should I go to antenatal classes?
**A** It is a good way of meeting other pregnant women and building a support network for after the birth. Most classes encourage partners to come along, which helps them feel involved. You will be given information on everything to do with childbirth, for example, pain relief, positions in labour, signs of labour, types of birth, feeding and baby care. You will get the opportunity to tour the maternity unit – which is worthwhile even if planning a home birth. You can see how to get there, where to park and the ward you will go to, as well as the options that are available. You will be able to ask questions in an informal setting.

*'I felt more feminine than ever before when I was pregnant. It gave me an excuse to experiment with clothes and change my hairstyle, and I loved having a decent cleavage!'*
*Cilla, mother of Callum*

# Your body
# at 17–20 weeks

At 17–20 weeks, you will look pregnant, with a noticeable bump and a vanishing waistline. Many women feel happier once they finally look like they are pregnant, but others find it difficult to adjust to their changing body image. Once your baby starts to move you will feel reassured that everything is going well, and you will begin to develop more confidence in your own pregnancy.

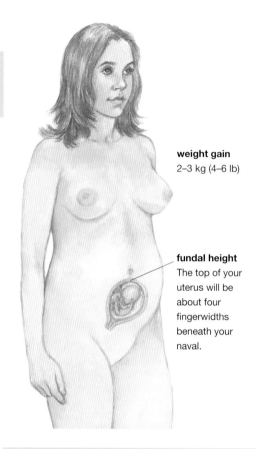

**weight gain**
2–3 kg (4–6 lb)

**fundal height**
The top of your uterus will be about four fingerwidths beneath your naval.

## How are you?

Many women bloom at this stage of pregnancy: their nausea decreases, their energy levels increase and they begin to look noticeably pregnant. Learning about the different options for birth, going to antenatal classes and talking with other women who have children all make pregnancy more enjoyable, and you can have lots of fun looking for maternity clothes to show off your bump.

By 17–20 weeks, you might well have experienced the excitement of feeling your baby move and you may have heard her heart beat. You will probably be feeling very protective of your unborn child.

You may notice some changes in the pigmentation of your skin, such as a dark line on your stomach or a discoloration on your face. These usually fade after the baby is born.

## 17–20 weeks: things to do

- Include plenty of iron-rich foods to avoid getting anaemia and be sure that you are getting enough vitamin C to help your body absorb the iron.
- Think about enrolling in an antenatal class. Although it is probably too early to begin them, you might need to go on a waiting list to avoid disappointment.
- Pay attention to your posture. During pregnancy, your ligaments stretch and your joints separate slightly, making you more prone to back problems. Bend and lift properly, with knees bent and the load held close to the body.

# 17–20 weeks **Common questions**

**Q** Why am I still feeling nauseous?

**A** About 70 per cent of pregnant women suffer from nausea and vomiting but this usually gets better around the 14th week. For some, however, sickness continues throughout pregnancy, or disappears and reappears later. Keep your blood sugar level constant. Have a light snack before bed so your body has some energy through the night. Carry snacks with you, such as dried fruit or rice cakes.

**Q** I am itching all over – is this normal?

**A** About 17 per cent of expectant mums suffer from itching, called pruritus gravidarum, in pregnancy. This can keep you awake at night and you may find that whenever you become warm, your skin, especially your abdomen, starts to itch. Calamine lotion is very soothing, as is a cool bath. Moisturize your skin by gently massaging it with baby oil. If the itching is due to stretching, this can also help to nourish it.

**Q** Why is my sense of smell stronger?

**A** Pregnant women often develop an increased sensitivity to smell. This may be because hormones cause congestion and swelling in the tissues lining the nose, altering signals reaching the nerves responsible for the sense of smell.

**Q** I am 17 weeks pregnant and my breasts have grown by two cup sizes. Will they stop?

**A** Your breasts grow a lot in the first trimester and throughout pregnancy, but will slow down. Your ribcage will also expand, so get a maternity bra that initially fits on the tightest fastener. Make sure your breasts are always properly supported. If you plan to breastfeed, wait until around 36 weeks before buying a nursing bra.

*'I didn't realize that being pregnant involves more than just an ever-growing bump. I've put on weight all over my body and feel fat and cumbersome. Luckily, my partner has been wonderful: he's continually reassuring me that my bump is perfect and that I look beautiful.'*
*Debbie, 20 weeks pregnant*

**Right:** Swimming is great for relaxation, as the water supports your body while you exercise.

# Your body
## at 21–24 weeks

This can be an exhilarating stage of pregnancy. You will have a rounded bump, which is growing week by week. Your baby's movements will be reassuring; you may even feel him jumping in response to a loud noise. By this time, you will have also been given a detailed ultrasound scan, enabling you to see your baby's image and the incredible development of the tiny life inside you.

## How are you?

Many women get very excited about their pregnancy at this stage but, equally, they can be gripped by fear in the middle of the night about potential problems with the baby or the birth. Tell your midwife or doctor if you have any worries – they can help to reassure you and put things into perspective. You may want to find out more about labour and think about what sort of birth you would like. However, it is also normal for women to want to avoid these concerns and just concentrate on enjoying their pregnancy.

Your body will now look very different and you may no longer be able to wear your normal clothes. Moving into your maternity clothes will probably emphasize your changing shape.

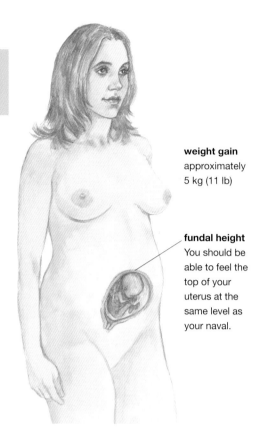

**weight gain**
approximately 5 kg (11 lb)

**fundal height**
You should be able to feel the top of your uterus at the same level as your naval.

## 21–24 weeks: things to do

- Continue to eat iron-rich foods, and also eat foods rich in vitamin D, for example, oily fish, eggs, milk, fortified margarine and breakfast cereals. This vitamin is essential for the development of your baby's bones and teeth.
- Make time to rest and set aside time each day to think about your baby because it is important to be prepared emotionally and practically, as well as physically.
- Start to think about when you would like to give up work and how practical it will be to continue working until close to your due date.

# 21–24 weeks **Common questions**

**Q** I have been having vivid dreams, some erotic and others horrific and to do with pregnancy and the baby. Is this normal?
**A** Yes, it is. We do not know why this happens, but the cause is most likely to be a change in hormones as well as the disturbed sleep that you experience in pregnancy. Women sometimes feel at their most feminine and sexual when pregnant, which could account for the erotic dreams. Try to relax before bed with a warm bath and a milky drink. If you have been keeping any worries to yourself, talk to your midwife. Discussing your emotions may help to relax your mind.

**Q** Since getting pregnant, I keep waking in the night with cramp in my legs. Can anything prevent this?
**A** Cramp is a common complaint and some think a lack of calcium could be to blame. It might help to add calcium to your diet by eating yogurt, dried figs or broccoli. Gentle, regular exercise or a massage can help by improving your circulation. Ask your partner to give you a leg massage before bed, using a carrier oil with three drops of citrus or lavender oil added. (Use citrus oil only after 12 weeks of pregnancy and lavender oil after 28 weeks.)

**Q** I am six months pregnant and I have piles. What can I do about them?
**A** Piles, also known as haemorrhoids, are swollen blood vessels inside and outside the anus. They are one of the most common complaints of pregnancy, causing itching, bleeding and pain. They are due to hormones making the veins more elastic, and can be exacerbated by the weight of the baby and constipation. Your doctor can prescribe a cream to reduce the swelling. Piles tend to disappear after the birth, but can be removed surgically if they persist.

**Q** I feel as if I am puffing up like a balloon. Should I be worried?
**A** Swelling (oedema), particularly of legs and feet, affects around half of all pregnant women. It occurs because of the increased volume of blood, sluggish circulation and retention of excess fluid. Sit with your feet up and rest them on a pillow when in bed. Wear support tights, drink plenty of water and take regular exercise. If swelling is accompanied by a rise in blood pressure or protein in your urine (checked at antenatal appointments), it could be a sign of pre-eclampsia. However, oedema is usually completely normal.

*'I do not mind people asking me when the baby's due, but I cannot believe the way in which people I do not know comment on my size. I would not dream of passing comment on the size of their non-pregnant stomach – maybe I should!'*
*Jessica, 24 weeks pregnant*

# Your body
## at 25–28 weeks

You will probably be relieved to have made it to the last three months, taking comfort from the fact that, if your baby were to be born at 28 weeks, he would have a very good chance of survival. Nevertheless, the realization that the birth is not far away can bring a whole new set of anxieties about your health, your baby's health and the impending labour.

## How are you?

If your baby is active or pressing on your bladder, you may find yourself having to get up during the night in order to visit the toilet. This can leave you feeling very tired. By this stage of pregnancy, your baby is curled up inside you, and, although he no longer has much room to move about freely, he will still kick, roll and wriggle. If he is in a head-down position, you may notice more jabbing at the top of your bump or kicking in the ribs.

By 25–28 weeks, your breasts are getting ready for your baby's first feed. You may notice that they start leaking a few drops of colostrum (the first milk, which is rich in antibodies) as your body prepares for breastfeeding.

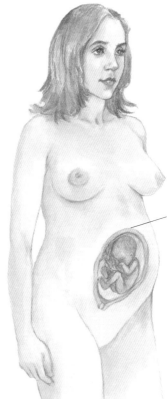

**weight gain**
approximately
8 kg (18 lb)

**fundal height**
The top of your bump is four fingerwidths above your naval and three or four fingerwidths below the top of your ribcage.

## 25–28 weeks: things to do

- Drink sufficient amounts of water and eat plenty of fibre-rich foods, such as wholegrain cereals, fruit and vegetables, to avoid becoming constipated.
- Eat foods containing essential fatty acids, which are found in seeds (including sunflower and linseed) and oily fish (such as sardines) – all important 'brain foods'.
- Attend all your antenatal checks, which will be more frequent at this stage of pregnancy.
- Your blood should be retested for antibodies and anaemia, which is common at this stage of pregnancy

# 25–28 weeks **Common questions**

**Q** I am only 25 weeks pregnant but my breasts are leaking already. Is this normal?
**A** Yes, it is. From around the 16th week of pregnancy, women start to produce colostrum, the 'foremilk' that is rich in antibodies, in preparation for the birth. Some women find that their breasts leak and they need to wear breast pads. It can happen during sex, which can feel embarrassing, but is normal.

**Q** I am 26 weeks pregnant and have got this far without stretch marks. Could I still get them?
**A** More than 50 per cent of women develop stretch marks during pregnancy and they often appear towards the end. Anyone who has had rapid weight gain or loss is more vulnerable, but it seems the biggest influence on whether or not you will get them is your skin type. The collagen and elastin content of skin is partly down to genetics, so if your mum and/or sister have them, it increases your chances of developing them.

*'I love aqua-natal classes, as we all go out afterwards and talk about our pregnancies. It is great being able to indulge in pregnancy and baby talk, with people who have the same hopes and fears as I do.'*

*Maggie, 27 weeks pregnant*

**Q** I have terrible backache. Do you think this is sciatica?
**A** Sciatica in pregnancy is caused by the weight of the uterus pressing on the sciatic nerve and it is also the result of the pregnancy hormone relaxin, which softens and stretches your ligaments. As your baby grows, your stomach muscles may become weaker and this puts more strain on your lower back. When the baby's head moves down into your pelvis, the sciatic nerve may become pinched. Symptoms usually affect one side of the body and range from pins and needles to a severe, shooting pain that runs down one leg. Improving your posture could go some way to alleviating the problem, but you should also seek advice from your midwife, who may refer you to a physiotherapist.

**Q** I am 28 weeks pregnant and nervous about having sex. Can it trigger labour?
**A** The vast majority of women are able to continue having sex without any problems at all. Women with a low-lying placenta, bleeding, or a history of premature labour or recurrent miscarriage may be advised to avoid intercourse. Sex can help trigger labour at the end of your pregnancy, but only if your body is ready for this. Semen contains prostaglandin, the hormone that is used to induce labour. Also, when aroused your body releases oxytocin, which stimulates the uterus and can start contractions.

# Your body
## at 29–32 weeks

The period of 'blooming' may now seem a long way in the past. By this stage of pregnancy, you are starting to really feel the weight of your baby and to experience discomfort as your stomach gets squashed by your expanding uterus. Other organs are pushed aside as well, and you may start to feel breathless whenever you move about.

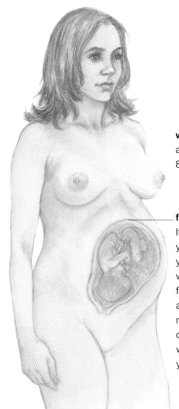

**weight gain**
approximately
8 kg (18 lb)

**fundal height**
If you place your hand on your abdomen, with your little finger just above your naval, the top of your uterus will be close to your thumb.

## How are you?

This period of your pregnancy can be one of mixed emotions as the birth becomes more imminent. At times you may be very excited and impatient to meet your baby, while at others you may be fearful of the prospect of labour and becoming a mother. Originally, you may have intended to work until late into your pregnancy, but you may now discover that being heavily pregnant is causing you to feel tired and breathless.

At 29–32 weeks, your centre of gravity changes and you may find yourself developing the familiar pregnancy 'waddle'. Be aware of your posture, however, because it is easy to slouch when your shape changes and this can cause you to develop back problems. You may also start to retain fluid (oedema), so that your fingers and feet become swollen – particularly at the end of the day. It is a good idea to take off any rings while you still can.

## 29–32 weeks: things to do

- Drink lots of cranberry juice, to reduce the risk of getting a urinary tract infection (see page 158).
- Eat brown rice, strawberries, eggs, spinach, onions and green beans, which are all good sources of manganese – essential for the healthy development of your baby's bones and joints.
- You should have started to attend antenatal classes by now.
- If you are not familiar with the maternity unit, arrange a visit and ask a member of staff to show you around.

# 29–32 weeks **Common questions**

**Q** I do not seem to be suffering from haemorrhoids, but have noticed that my vagina feels slightly swollen. Is this the same thing?

**A** Yes, you are probably developing varicose veins in your vulva. You may also feel a general heaviness around your vagina and your pelvic floor may ache – both common symptoms. Wear a chunky sanitary towel for support, avoid standing for long periods and remember to do your pelvic floor exercises regularly (see pages 108–109). It is likely that the swelling will go away after the birth.

**Q** I am convinced that my bump is much smaller than everyone else's in my antenatal class and now I am worried that my baby is not growing properly. What can I do?

**A** Tell your midwife about your worries. She can reassure you and explain what she is doing at your antenatal check. One of these checks includes feeling the top of the uterus to make sure that it is growing at the right rate and noting the size of your bump. If there is any cause for concern, your midwife will closely monitor you and can refer you to the hospital for growth scans. Obviously some babies are bigger or smaller than average and women's bumps always vary in size depending on how many babies the woman has had before, the amount of fluid around the baby, the height of the woman and her baby's position. Bear in mind that it is also very difficult to judge the size of a fully clothed bump.

*'I love going for my antenatal checks. When I hear my baby's heartbeat, I could happily stay in the room and carry on listening, until I go into labour!'*
*Kristina, 31 weeks pregnant*

## Sleep

At around 30 weeks of pregnancy, women often find it hard to get comfortable in bed and have a good night's sleep, thanks to the size of their bump, the frequent urge to empty their bladder, their baby's movements and a mind that becomes active in the middle of the night. There are various things that you can try:

- Lie on your left side with one pillow underneath to support your bump and another between your knees.
- Some gentle exercise taken during the day can help you to sleep better at night, so try going for an evening walk or having a swim after work.
- Avoid any stimulants, such as tea, coffee and fizzy drinks, and have a drink of warm milk instead.
- Enjoy a soak in a warm, but not hot, bath before bed.
- Do not allow yourself to get overtired, as this can make it even harder for you to fall asleep.
- Try to keep yourself cool at night, particularly if you have been suffering from frequent night sweats.

# Your body
## at 33–36 weeks

As your due date approaches, you are probably becoming very excited, although your pregnancy is now starting to take its toll on you physically. You may not be feeling as energetic as you have been in previous weeks and, if you have not done so already, you will be preparing to stop work. For many women, this time is characterized by a return to the discomforts of early pregnancy.

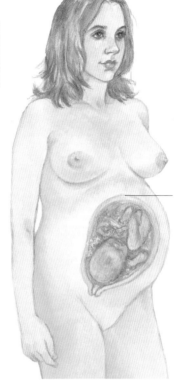

**weight gain**
approximately 10 kg (22 lb)

**fundal height**
If you lie down, the top of your uterus will be approximately a fingerwidth below the bottom of your ribs.

## 33–36 weeks: things to do

- Make sure you eat a varied diet rich in fresh fruit and vegetables. This will not only give you energy but also help to build up your baby's immune system.
- Vitamin K is essential for blood clotting and is particularly important as you approach the birth. Good sources include green leafy vegetables, cantaloupe melon, fortified cereals and wholemeal bread.
- From 34 weeks, start drinking one cup of raspberry leaf tea twice a day in order to tone your uterus and prepare it for labour.
- Get yourself measured for a nursing bra, ideally at 36 weeks.
- Continue to take regular gentle exercise to give you stamina to cope during labour.

## How are you?

As your baby is now resting, probably head down, in your uterus, rather than 'floating' inside you, you will feel pressure on your bladder – which means frequent trips to the toilet, day and night. Your stomach is getting squashed higher up as your uterus grows, and this could entail a return to the indigestion and heartburn that you may have experienced in the early weeks.

You may be feeling tired, particularly if you are waking frequently during the night to pass urine, so try to rest during the day. You may feel discomfort under your ribcage as your baby pushes against it with a foot or his bottom. Your breasts will grow a little more and, if they have not done so already, may start to leak colostrum in preparation for breastfeeding.

# 33–36 weeks **Common questions**

**Q** Is there anything I can do to alleviate my backache?

**A** As you get bigger and heavier you are more likely to get backache, and many women start to experience backache towards the end of pregnancy, especially if they are prone to back problems. It is important to be aware of your posture, standing straight, with your bottom tucked in. When you bend to pick up objects, bend your knees, squat down with a straight back and then stand, keeping the object close to your body.

**Q** I sometimes notice my bump tightening. Does this mean I will go into labour early?

**A** What you are describing are Braxton Hicks tightenings. These mild, irregular tightenings have, in fact, been there throughout your pregnancy but you just haven't been able to feel them until now. Braxton Hicks tightenings get more frequent and intense towards the end of pregnancy, and some women notice them from about week 25. They are in fact practice tightenings, getting your uterus ready for labour. Unlike the contractions that happen in labour, they are not painful and are irregular.

**Q** I want to breastfeed but I am 35 weeks pregnant and I have not leaked any milk. Does this mean that I will have a problem with the feeding?

**A** Some women do not leak anything until after the birth, while other women leak colostrum from early on in their pregnancy. Neither has any effect on their ability to breastfeed. There will be many changes to your breasts during pregnancy: they will become more sensitive,

they will get bigger, and the area around the nipple (areola) will darken. After your baby is born, put him to the breast frequently to encourage your milk to come in, which will happen on about the third day after the birth. Until then he feeds on a thick creamy substance called colostrum that helps to protect him from infections.

'My mum told me that I would have a shorter labour if I drank raspberry leaf tea from 34 weeks of pregnancy. Prepared to try anything, I drank it religiously towards the end of my first pregnancy. When I remonstrated with my mother following a 36-hour labour, she told me that it might have been 72 hours if I hadn't had any!'

*Anne, mother of Ruby and George*

# Your body
## at 37–40 weeks

When you reach 37–40 weeks
of pregnancy, you have the
reassurance of knowing that your
baby could be born at any time
and would not be considered
premature. Normal gestation is,
in fact, anything between 37 and
42 weeks, and not just the precise
'textbook' 40-weeks pregnancy.
There will be days when you are
extremely excited and impatient to
meet your baby and others when
you feel panic-stricken at not being
fully prepared.

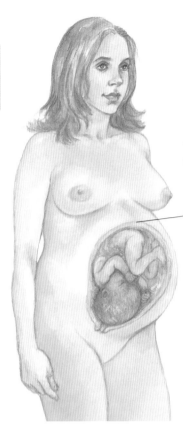

**weight gain**
approximately
13.5 kg (30 lb)

**fundal height**
At full term
your uterus
will be as high
as it gets –
just under the
breastbone.

## How are you?

Women often find that their 'nesting instinct'
kicks in around now and they start to prepare
for their baby's birth. You might get a last burst
of energy and find that you are cleaning out
cupboards, washing baby clothes, wanting to
decorate the baby's room and feeling tearful if
everything is not just right.

You will probably be getting up at night,
possibly several times a night, in order to
empty your bladder or lying in bed awake,
desperately tired, with an active baby inside
you. Many women feel that their baby may as
well be born now, as they are getting no more
rest and sleep than if she had already arrived.
At this stage of your pregnancy, you may feel
so large that you have difficulty moving about
or even eating a meal.

## 37–40 weeks: things to do

- Eat plenty of iron-rich foods to stock up your
  iron reserves. Even if you are not anaemic,
  you will inevitably lose a certain amount of
  blood during the birth. Dried fruit such as
  raisins and apricots contain iron in an easily
  digestible form.
- Attend your antenatal checks.
- Complete your birth plan and discuss it with
  your midwife (see page 186).
- Make sure that your labour ward bag is ready
  (see page 203).
- Continue to fill your diary with places to go
  and people to visit. If you go past your due
  date, which you may well do, time will drag if
  you have nothing planned.

# 37–40 weeks **Common questions**

**Q** I am 37 weeks pregnant and have Group B Strep infection. Is my baby at risk?

**A** Group B streptococcus is a common vaginal bacterium carried by about one-third of women, often without symptoms but sometimes associated with a vaginal infection (typically with itchiness and excessive discoloured, smelly discharge). It is usually harmless in healthy adults but can sometimes cause a serious infection when passed to babies during labour or birth. If you are considered to be at risk or are showing symptoms, a swab can be taken to check for infection. If you know you carry the infection you will be offered intravenous antibiotics during labour to help protect your baby.

**Q** I find it very hard to get a full night's sleep and am worried that I will not have enough energy when I finally go into labour. What can I do?

**A** Many women find that, towards the end of their pregnancy, their baby is active when they are ready to sleep, and this can keep them awake. Also, as your baby gets bigger, her head puts pressure on the bladder, causing you to wake several times a night to go to the toilet. There is nothing worse than lying in bed unable to get to sleep. It is far better to switch on the light and read a book or magazine, or get yourself a warm drink and wait until you feel sleepy, then try again. Try to make up for lost sleep during the day by taking a nap when you feel tired.

*'To be honest, I am fed up. I cannot sleep properly or eat a decent meal or walk more than a few metres before sitting down to rest. I know it is well-intentioned, but I have found it hard to adjust to being "public property". Sometimes people I hardly know come up and pat my bump and it is not hard to resent it. Pregnancy is not my favourite time of life. I cannot wait for the baby to arrive.'*

Siobhan, 39 weeks pregnant

**Above:** Try to rest as much as necessary during the day to make up for sleep lost at night.

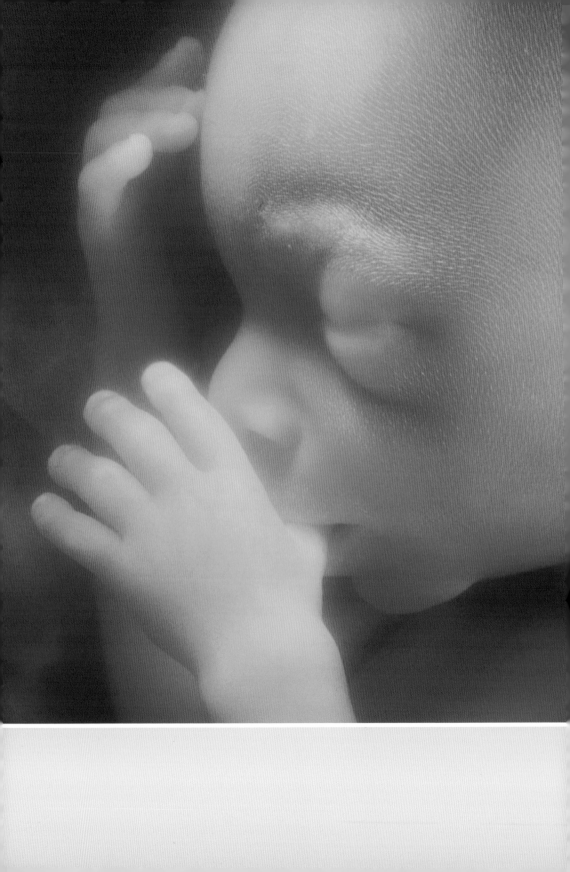

3

# your growing baby

# A LIFE-SUPPORT SYSTEM

## How your body cares for your baby

**Normally, the development of the fetus from a tiny group of cells to a fully grown baby occurs inside the uterus with the help of the placenta, the umbilical cord and the amniotic fluid.**

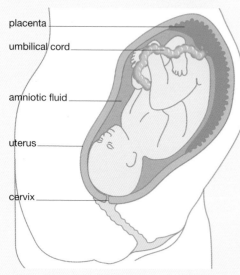

placenta

umbilical cord

amniotic fluid

uterus

cervix

**Above:** The placenta, umbilical cord and amniotic fluid provide your baby with the necessities of life.

## The placenta

The placenta is a disc-shaped structure attached to the wall of the uterus and connected to the baby via the umbilical cord. It is a network of arteries and veins from your baby that interfaces with your circulation. At term, it weighs approximately one-sixth as much as the baby.

Blood vessels from your baby (the umbilical arteries) lead into the placenta, where they divide into fine blood vessels (capillaries) that enter finger-like projections of the placenta (the placental villi). These villi increase the surface area of the placenta and are bathed in your blood, which is transported to the uterus by branches of your uterine arteries (the spiral arteries). This means that your blood and your baby's blood can come very close to each other without actually mixing.

## Three facts about the **placenta**

1 The placenta enables oxygen and nutrients to cross from your blood into your baby's blood, and also allows carbon dioxide and waste products to go from your baby's blood into your blood for disposal.

2 The placenta also manufactures a number of hormones, including human chorionic gonadotrophin (HCG), which is important for sustaining the pregnancy during the first few weeks, human placental lactogen (HPL), which is important for fetal growth, oestriol (a type of oestrogen) and progesterone, which maintains the lining of the uterus.

3 The placenta also protects your baby against rejection by your antibodies and helps to block the passage of many potentially harmful substances, for example drugs and other chemicals.

The placenta is usually well out of the cervix's way, but occasionally it implants in the lower uterus, a condition known as placenta praevia (see page 130). This may be noted at the 20-week scan, but in nine out of ten cases, it will have moved out of the way before you are due to give birth.

## The umbilical cord

The cord is usually about 50 cm (20 in) long, 1–2 cm (½–¾ in) wide and contains two arteries and one vein, which spiral around each other. Inside the cord is a jelly-like substance called Wharton's jelly, which cushions the blood vessels. Occasionally a knot forms in the cord. In most cases this does not cause any problems because blood is still able to pass through it.

## The amniotic fluid

Your growing baby is surrounded by fluid, which protects both baby and uterus. For most of the pregnancy, this amniotic fluid comes from your baby's urine. The quantity increases from 150–200 ml (5–7 fl oz) at 16 weeks to 1000 ml (1¾ pt) at 36 weeks.

Amniotic fluid is constantly being recirculated: your baby swallows it as she

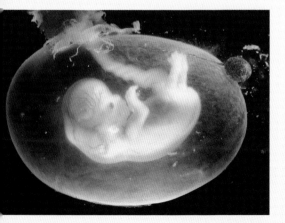

## When your waters break

**When your waters break, before or during labour, it is amniotic fluid that is expelled. This is usually clear and straw-coloured, but can be greenish in colour, indicating that your baby has opened her bowels in the womb, producing meconium (a mixture of waste secretions, cells and pigments). This is often a sign of fetal maturity, but may also indicate fetal distress.**

practises breathing and then passes it out again as urine. Any process that interferes with your baby swallowing or passing urine can produce either too much amniotic fluid (polyhydramnios) or too little (oligohydramnios). The quantity of amniotic fluid can be measured by ultrasound and a normal amount is one indication that your baby is thriving.
• It allows your baby to move around freely
• It protects her from knocks
• It keeps her at a constant temperature
• It helps her lungs to develop normally.

## Nuchal cord

In a small number of pregnancies, the cord winds around the baby's neck (referred to as a nuchal cord). This rarely causes any complications. However, as the baby descends during labour, the cord may tighten, particularly if it is wrapped more than once around the neck. This may lower the baby's heart rate, resulting in signs of fetal distress. Once the baby's head is out, the midwife can usually gently loop the cord over it. Because it is the baby's lifeline, it is not usually advisable to cut it at this stage.

**Left:** The growing baby is suspended in an amniotic sac, attached to the placenta by an umbilical cord.

# The first four weeks

At the beginning of each menstrual cycle, hormones stimulate your ovaries to release an egg, which begins its journey down the Fallopian tube. It is in the Fallopian tube that fertilization usually takes place. Within hours of fertilization, the fertilized egg (known as the zygote) divides into two, then four, then eight and so on.

## Early growth

Approximately four days after fertilization, the zygote has become a solid cluster of cells called a morula. About a week after fertilization, the ball of cells – now hollow in the centre and called a blastocyst – reaches the uterus. The blastocyst will attach itself to the wall of your uterus and begin to embed deep into its lining. This process is called implantation.

The cluster of cells very quickly produces an outer layer, which will develop into the placenta and amniotic sac, and an inner layer, which will develop into the embryo. The outer layer has root-like structures that bury into the lining of the uterus. These become the route by which nutrients and oxygen are transported from your circulation to what will soon be the developing placenta and embryo.

In week 4, the embryo starts to grow lengthwise, so that the initially round cluster of cells assumes a leaner shape. The outer cells extend tiny finger-like projections (villi), which link up with your circulation. Within each of the embryo's body cells are 46 chromosomes in 23 pairs, with one of each pair being inherited from each parent (see page 19). As cell division takes places, so long as the chromosomes have been copied correctly, each new cell will have the same number of chromosomes and contain the same genetic information.

Your body is producing high levels of human chorionic gonadotrophin (HCG), especially in the morning. This happens after successful conception, that is, once a fertilized egg is implanted in the lining of the uterus. High levels of HCG, which makes pregnancy tests read positive, are necessary to sustain pregnancy. A plug of mucus develops at the entrance of the uterus to protect the embryo from infection.

## The division of cells

At four weeks the cells are dividing and multiplying rapidly, and three layers of cells have now formed:

1 **The outer layer (ectoderm)** will develop into your baby's brain, nervous system, skin, hair, nails and teeth.
2 **The middle layer (mesoderm)** will become his heart and blood vessels, bones, muscles and reproductive organs.
3 **The inner layer (endoderm)** will eventually develop into his lungs, liver, bladder and digestive system.

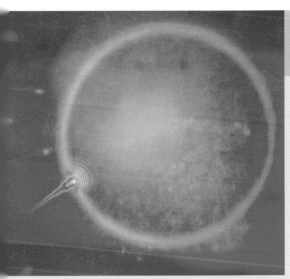

**Above:** The moment when a sperm penetrates an egg during fertilization – and the start of a new life.

*'When I became pregnant my life changed overnight. I did not resent the changes, but I felt ill, emotional and mixed up and had no idea how to help myself or where to go for advice. I could not relate to my baby as it all seemed too remote. I thought there must be something wrong with me. I didn't realize that other women also felt emotionally drained or found life very difficult in the early weeks.'*

Francesca, mother of Toby

## The first four weeks
# Common questions

**Q** I have just found out that I am pregnant, but I have been taking paracetamol because of a bad back. Could I have harmed my baby?

**A** Paracetamol is one of a handful of drugs that are widely regarded as being safe to take throughout pregnancy (on the advice of your doctor), so stop worrying. As long as you have been taking the correct dose, it will not have harmed your baby. The reason it is thought to be safe is that it had already been used widely for a long period of time without any adverse effects on mums-to-be before the question of its safety in pregnancy was ever raised.

**Q** Does it really matter what I eat and drink so early in pregnancy?

**A** By 12 weeks of pregnancy the embryo will be almost fully developed, which means that the majority of development happens at the start of your pregnancy. Sometimes, things go wrong for no apparent reason, but you can take steps to improve the chances of a successful pregnancy. Avoiding certain foods (see pages 98–101) and taking folic acid (see page 12) will give the tiny embryo extra protection. You should also avoid drugs, smoking and alcohol, all of which can affect your baby's development. It is also best to avoid close contact with certain chemicals and and toxic substances around this time. If you have a problem with dependency or addiction, confide in your midwife who can help to refer you for additional support.

# Your baby at eight weeks

Medically speaking, by eight weeks, the embryo is officially called a fetus (meaning 'young' or 'little one'), although you have probably referred to it as 'your baby' from the very beginning. She is living in warm amniotic fluid, which keeps her at a constant temperature and cushions her from any knocks or pressure.

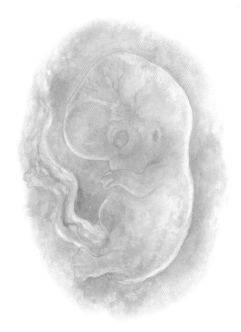

**Above:** By week 7 your baby has a regular heartbeat and limbs that are recognizable as arms and legs.

## Amniotic fluid

Amniotic fluid is the straw-coloured, watery substance that surrounds your baby, protecting her and enabling her to move freely. It also keeps the temperature in the uterus constant and has an important role in the development of the lungs and kidneys.

- At 37.5°C (99.5°F), the temperature of the fluid is higher than that of your body.
- Until 14 weeks, amniotic fluid is absorbed by your baby's skin. Once her kidneys start to function and she develops a sucking reflex, she swallows the fluid and excretes it back into the amniotic sac. However, all her nutrients come from the placenta via the umbilical cord.
- Amniotic fluid contains a range of different substances, including glucose, fructose, salt, proteins, amino acids, citric acid, urea, lactic acids and fatty acids, and is a good conductor of sound.

## Development milestones

- **At five weeks** The embryo has a head end and a tail end and all the building blocks for the vital organs are in place. There is a curved back, like the letter C, with a stripe down it, which marks the beginning of the central nervous system. The head can already be distinguished from the body and the developing heart can be seen as a bulge, no bigger than a poppy seed.
- **At six weeks** The most advanced system at this stage is the central nervous system, with the brain developing at one end. The liver begins to develop before the rest of the digestive system. The embryonic heart is already beating. Limb buds have appeared and, at the base of the head, there are folds that will eventually develop into facial features.
- **At seven weeks** The heart has four clearly defined chambers and a regular beat. The lungs are developing, the muscles and

bones are forming, and the limbs are beginning to take shape. The head and brain are growing rapidly, and a neck is developing to separate the relatively large head of the baby from her body. Nasal and oral cavities are now developing and there is a dark tinge where the eyes are forming.

- **At eight weeks** Bones start to harden and lengthen at this stage, forming distinguishable joints. The baby is now recognizably human. Her body is losing its curved appearance and the limbs are more in proportion. Blood vessels are visible beneath transparent skin. The eyes are wide apart, on the sides of the head. The outer parts of the ears are developing. Fingers and toes are distinguishable, despite the webbing between them.

*'My pregnancy came as quite a shock, as we weren't planning to try for a baby until after our wedding. I guessed I was pregnant because my boobs were sore, but when the blue line on the test kit appeared, I felt a mixture of excitement and shock. However much I had imagined I might be pregnant, it was completely different when I realized I was.'*

*Donna, eight weeks pregnant*

# 5–8 weeks
# Common questions

**Q How does the embryo sustain life during these early weeks?**
**A** At this early stage the embryo already takes oxygen via the developing placenta, to which it is attached by a stalk, and there is a basic circulation in place, from you to your baby, and tiny blood vessels are now forming.

**Q How soon is it possible to see the baby on a scan?**
**A** In certain cases where it is necessary to confirm a pregnancy very early on, an ultrasound scan may be given, although it is usually not possible to see the embryo as such at less than eight weeks. You may be offered a trans-vaginal ultrasound scan, in which a probe is placed into the vagina. This may just be able to show the 'flickering' of your baby's heart at six weeks.

**Q Does the embryo move about at this stage, and will I be able to feel it?**
**A** Initially, the embryo starts to make tiny 'twitching' movements at around seven weeks. These may be detected by sensitive ultrasound equipment. By eight weeks, messages pass along the nerves to the baby's muscles, enabling her to make spontaneous movements, such as gentle kicking, but you will not be able to feel these until approximately 18 weeks of pregnancy.

# Your baby at 12 weeks

By 12 weeks, your baby has grown to about the size of a lemon. This stage of pregnancy, which marks the end of the first three months, often feels like a milestone for many women because the risk of miscarriage is reduced after week 12. This is often the time that couples decide to announce the pregnancy. Although just three months have passed, the major development of your baby is complete and the emphasis is now on growth.

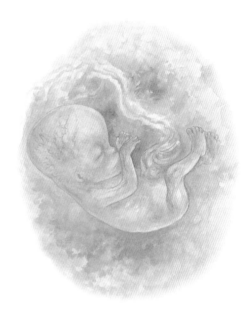

**Above:** At 12 weeks, nails start to appear on your baby's fingers and toes and genitals begin to form.

*'I was unsure of my dates so the midwife arranged an ultrasound scan. The sonographer pointed out a tiny shape, like a seahorse, with a flickering heartbeat. Although I'd had a positive pregnancy test, it only felt real when I could see the baby with my own eyes!'*

*Liz, nine weeks pregnant*

## Development milestones

- **At nine weeks** Your baby's heart is almost fully developed at nine weeks, and it is beating at approximately 170 beats per minute. A band of muscle, which will later become the diaphragm, separates the cavity of the chest and the abdomen. The growth of the hands and feet is particularly rapid: the fingers have separated and the feet have lengthened. The upper lip is formed and the ears are becoming more recognizable.

- **At 10 weeks** The structure of the brain is now complete and cells are continuing to multiply. The palate of the mouth is forming and tooth sockets have formed. The umbilical cord is now fully formed and blood is beginning to circulate through it. The stomach and intestines are developed

# 9–12 weeks **Common questions**

**Q** I am due for my first scan. What is the scan for and is there anything I should do to prepare?

**A** This first scan is referred to as a 'dating scan' and will usually be done at weeks 10–12. Drink plenty of water or juice beforehand because, when your bladder is full, it helps the sonographer to get a clearer picture of your baby. It will be at this point that the number of babies you are carrying will be confirmed – although, if you are pregnant with twins, you might already have a suspicion because early pregnancy symptoms tend to be much worse. The sonographer will take measurements of your baby, from which he or she will work out when your baby is due.

**Q** How can the sonographer determine my estimated delivery date (EDD) from the dating scan?

**A** The sonographer measures the baby from crown to rump – that is, from the top of the head to the end of the bottom, as if the baby were sitting down – and it is this measurement that can be used to determine how many weeks pregnant you are. These scans are most accurate when they are done at around week 10 because there is more variation in fetus size later in pregnancy.

and the muscles of the digestive tract are functional. The face is taking shape and now looks distinctly human. The finger and toes are no longer webbed.

- **At 11 weeks** The ovaries and testes have developed inside the body, but the baby's sex is still not obvious from the outside because the genitals have not yet developed. Limbs remain short and undeveloped because they have not yet had much use.

- **At 12 weeks** The baby has unmistakable facial features including chin and nose, although the eyelids remain fused shut over the eyes. The baby's circulation is fully functioning and the kidneys are working. Bones are becoming harder. The muscles of the intestines are moving. Genitals are starting to form.

## Three facts about the dating scan

1 There is no evidence that ultrasound scanning is harmful either to you or your baby, although excessive and unnecessary use should be avoided. Scans can be inconclusive, however. It is possible that the presence of twins will be missed, for example, if one baby is behind the other.

2 Although the main purpose of the first scan is to measure the baby to work out your EDD, some major abnormalities can be picked up on a scan taken at around 12 weeks.

3 Measurements made on later scans will be compared with the first scan to make sure the baby is growing properly.

# THE FIRST TRIMESTER

## How your baby has grown

**In the 12 weeks since the sperm fertilized the egg, triggering cell division, amazing changes have taken place within your uterus.**

### Your baby's development

At 12 weeks of pregnancy, your baby weighs about 14 g (½ oz) and is approximately 6.5 cm (2½ in) in length. During the last three months, your baby's body has developed in many different ways.

**Skin and hair:** Skin is translucent. Fingers and toes are no longer webbed and the nails are beginning to develop.

**Muscles:** Developing muscles have become linked with the nervous system. The diaphragm has formed.

**Bones:** All bones are in place. Bones continue to harden.

**Organs:** All major internal organs are formed, but still maturing.

**Circulatory system:** This is fully functioning. The heart is pumping blood.

**Digestive system:** This is now fully formed and functional.

**Below:** At 12 weeks, your baby's fingers are no longer webbed and facial features are distinct.

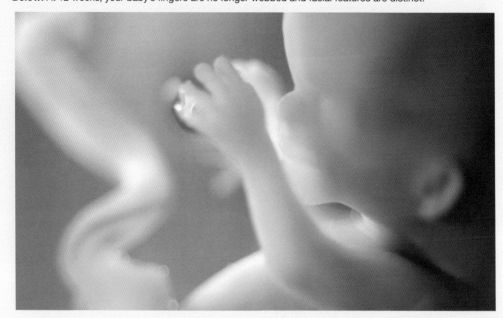

**Endocrine system:** This is starting to manufacture growth hormone and produce alphafetoprotein (AFP, see page 192).

**Nervous system:** The brain is now complete but still developing. Messages pass between the spinal cord and muscles.

**Renal system:** Kidneys are functioning.

**Respiratory system:** Your baby is practising breathing movements.

**Ears:** The ears have moved from the neck to the side of the head. The outer ears continue to develop but the middle and inner ears are fully formed.

**Eyes:** Although still wide apart, the eyes have moved from the sides of the head to the front. Eyelids are fused shut.

## How smoking can affect your baby

- Smoking affects the growth of your baby by diminishing the supply of oxygen.
- It increases the risk of miscarriage, premature birth and cot death.
- It also increases the risk of stillbirth or of death within the first week of life.
- Babies of smokers generally have a lower birth weight.
- They are also more likely to suffer from breathing difficulties.
- Babies of smokers are more likely to smoke as adults.

# True story

**A tough decision to make**

'We were on holiday when I discovered I was pregnant. I thought I might be, as I wasn't enjoying the taste of alcohol, my breasts were fuller and felt sore and tender, and my appetite had increased. But I was in denial. Eventually, Simon said we should do a pregnancy test, and when the blue line showed up, I burst into tears. I was worried and confused and really didn't know what to do with myself.

'Luckily, I had lots of support from Simon's mum, but for a few days I felt lost. It took us about a week to come to a decision about what to do. We went off for a meal and talked it through. By the time we'd finished, we came to the conclusion that this baby was meant to be.

'We started to look at the situation philosophically and decided that it had happened and we should go with it. Having made a decision, I looked up just as a shooting star swooped down from the sky. It seemed like a good omen.

'Coming to terms with expecting a baby has taken a lot of adjustment. But when we went for a dating scan at 12 weeks, it was a real turning point. I felt tearful and did cry, but this time it was with joy. We could see our baby on the screen, and it was a really emotional moment.

'Since finding out about the pregnancy, I've made some major changes. I'm definitely not such a party animal and I have given up smoking. At the beginning, I was still having the odd puff on a cigarette, but now I am not even tempted. The incentive of my baby has made giving up much easier than I thought it would be.'

*Tamsin, 12 weeks pregnant*

## Your baby at 16 weeks

By 16 weeks, your baby is fully formed and is continuing to grow rapidly. Although you will not have been aware of it, he started moving when you were seven or eight weeks pregnant. However, 16 weeks is the earliest stage at which you can feel your baby move. He is already making a lot of movements, but they will be very subtle. At first, you may not be sure whether he is moving at all.

**Above:** At 16 weeks your baby looks completely human and can make different facial expressions.

### Quickening

These first movements that you can feel are referred to as 'quickening'. If this is your first baby, you will probably not notice anything until around 18–22 weeks of pregnancy. Your baby has plenty of room and is constantly exercising by moving and changing position. If a bright light is shone onto your abdomen at 16 weeks of pregnancy, your baby may even raise an arm to shield his eyes.

Bear in mind that babies should not begin to move significantly less as you get closer to your delivery date. If you feel that the baby's movements are reducing, contact your midwife or the maternity unit so that you and your baby can be checked over.

### Development milestones

- **At 13 weeks** The organs are now formed and will mature over the following weeks. The hands and feet are fully developed, and the arms and legs are growing longer. The joints and bones are continuing to harden. The baby is sprouting fine hair (lanugo) over his body.

- **At 14 weeks** The thyroid gland is starting to produce hormones. The external genitals are developing further and, in most cases, can now be identified on an ultrasound scan. The baby's face is well developed at this stage, and very faint eyebrows are beginning to appear.

- **At 15 weeks** The baby's body is generally in proportion now, and his legs are longer than his arms. As well as the soft coating of hair over the body, fluffy hair is growing on the baby's head. The skin is still very thin and translucent.

- **At 16 weeks** The face of your baby now looks human in appearance and can produce different expressions. The baby is able to hold his head up straighter and

# 13–16 weeks **Common questions**

**Q** Can my baby hear me if I talk to him?

**A** Yes, you can talk to your baby because the amniotic fluid that surrounds him will conduct sound. As well as your voice, he will be able to hear your heart beating and your stomach rumbling. Research shows that a newborn baby is very attuned to his mother's voice, presumably because he has got used to hearing it (even though it is muffled) from within the uterus.

**Q** Why does the size of babies vary so much?

**A** There are many things that determine a baby's size, some of which you have influence over and some of which you do not. Your baby inherits genes from two biological parents so, if both parents are small, he will probably be small as well. Your baby is more likely to be smaller if you smoke because he is receiving less oxygen and nutrients than he should. If you eat a healthy balanced diet your baby is less likely to have a low birth weight. Medical conditions, such as diabetes or high blood pressure, can also affect a baby's size.

**Q** My friend has given me a handheld Doppler monitor she used every day to listen to her baby's heart. Is this safe?

**A** A Doppler is an ultrasound device, used by your midwife, to listen to your baby's heartbeat. The heartbeat will be amplified so that you can hear it too. It will sound very fast and will be about 150 beats per minute at this stage. It works by bouncing sound waves off red blood cells, which shows how fast they are moving, and how fast the blood is flowing. There is no conclusive evidence that it is unsafe, but it could be argued that we still know relatively little about it and more research is needed. Current ultrasound guidelines include not giving a women or her baby any unnecessary exposure, so it should not be used as a toy.

yawn, and he may even suck his thumb. Nails are appearing on the fingers and toes, and the skeleton has developed to such an extent that it would be visible on an X-ray. The baby is practising breathing movements, which encourages the development of the lungs.

*'She became absorbed in her own body and obsessed with her pregnancy. I felt pushed out. After the scan it seemed far more real to me than it had previously.'*
*Michael, partner of Cheryl, 14 weeks pregnant*

## Your baby at 20 weeks

Your baby's growth starts to slow down from 20 weeks and she is approximately half the length of a full-term baby. No new structures will be formed now: she has everything she needs, although she is not mature enough to survive if born at this stage. She is about the size of a mango and, if she is to arrive on her due date, she is halfway there.

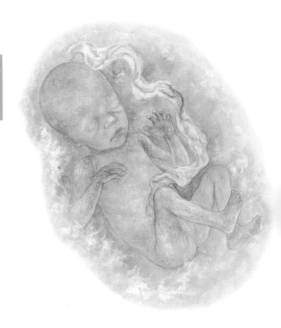

**Above:** Your baby has lots of room and will change position frequently; she can even somersault.

## Development milestones

- **At 17 weeks** The baby begins to lay down brown fat, which plays an important part in generating heat after the birth. The placenta is also growing quickly. The chest is making breathing movements, although oxygen is still being supplied via the umbilical cord.
- **A 18 weeks** The last organ to develop is the lungs, which takes several weeks. At this stage, tiny air sacs are beginning to form. The muscles are strengthening. The kidneys are working. The body and head are more in proportion now and the facial features are very clear.
- **At 19 weeks** The placenta is fully formed. Millions of cells are growing in the brain and nerves begin to connect the brain to the muscles. Permanent tooth buds are appearing behind the buds of the milk teeth. The skin is waxy and covered in vernix (see right).

- **At 20 weeks** Development focuses on the lungs and digestive and immune systems. The kidneys pass about 7–17 ml (2–5 tsp) of urine every 24 hours. Areas of the brain are developing specific to taste, smell, hearing, sight and touch. The heartbeat is stronger and can be heard using a stethoscope. The legs are almost in proportion with the rest of the baby's body.

### Vernix

This greasy white coating is produced by oil glands in your baby's skin. It keeps her skin supple and protects it from immersion in the amniotic fluid. It is very thick around the eyebrows and is anchored in place by the lanugo. It lubricates and protects the skin during birth. In some hospitals it is cleaned off straight away after birth; it rubs off naturally after a couple of days if this is not done.

# 17–20 weeks **Common questions**

**Q** I'm 17 weeks pregnant and feel really low and miserable, and the slightest thing has me in tears. Will it affect my baby?

**A** Mood swings and tearfulness are common in pregnancy because of the increased hormones in your body and because of sheer tiredness. Normal mood swings are unlikely to harm your baby. However, 10–15 per cent of women do get antenatal depression (in varying degrees). Talk to your midwife about how you are feeling as soon as possible. It is important to address this and to explore the cause, as there is an increased risk of developing post-natal depression, which, it is thought, can potentially affect the emotional development of your baby.

**Q** I am 18 weeks pregnant and have started to feel my baby move, but sometimes it seems nothing happens for days. Should I be worried?

**A** No. You may certainly be aware of some movement, but your baby is still relatively small so there may be days when you do not feel very much. Your baby is much more aware of the outside world than she was earlier in your pregnancy. If she hears a sudden loud noise outside your body, she may move around vigorously in reaction to it and this may be when you are most aware of her movements.

**Q** My 20-week scan report said my placenta was anterior. In my last pregnancy, it was posterior. Is this important?

**A** No. The sonographer will always comment on the position of your placenta. In most pregnancies the placenta is situated on the back wall of the uterus (posterior) but in some it is on the front wall (anterior). Either position is fine. The only time the position of the placenta becomes an issue is if it is low in the uterus and covers the cervix. This condition is called placenta praevia (see page 130), and you would need a caesarean if it remained there.

> '*Andrew and I found the 20-week anomaly scan a real thrill. Even though this is our second baby, it was still a momentous occasion. And there's always the worry that a problem shows up – but everything looks fine. We left the hospital relaxed and relieved. It feels as though the pregnancy is flying by.*'
>
> *Zoe, 22 weeks pregnant*

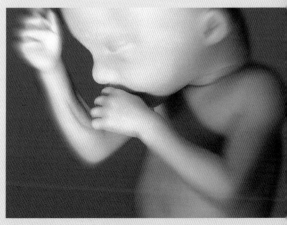

**Above:** Scans have shown 20-week babies sucking their thumbs and grasping the umbilical cord.

# Your baby at 24 weeks

Although medical and legal opinions vary from country to country, in most parts of the world your baby is considered to be 'viable' and therefore capable of a separate existence, at around 24 weeks of pregnancy. If he were to be born prematurely at this time, he might be able to survive in a special-care baby unit (SCBU) with the help of medical expertise and a ventilator to assist with his breathing.

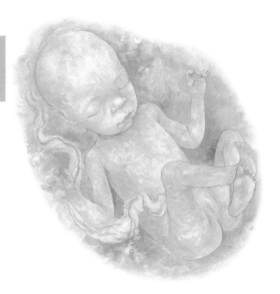

**Above:** By 24 weeks, your baby may have recognizable family features.

## Development milestones

- **At 21 weeks** The growth of the brain is very rapid and it is around this time that memory is thought to develop. The tongue is now fully developed. The baby already has a high number of red blood cells and white blood cells are now produced.
- **At 22 weeks** The baby is now aware of himself and how different parts of the body are related to others. His skin looks too big for his body because there is still very little fat present.
- **At 23 weeks** The bones, muscles and organs are steadily growing and the lungs continue to develop. The eyes are still closed, but their colour is already starting to develop.
- **At 24 weeks** The lungs continue to develop daily, forming more air sacs. The baby is getting plenty of practice at breathing, by taking small amounts of fluid in and out of the lungs, which causes his chest to move up and down. The centres of the bones are getting harder. Brainwaves demonstrate that, at this stage, your baby is almost as active as a newborn and increases in his pulse rate show that he reacts to sounds, such as loud noises.

'My baby has definitely developed a pattern of waking and sleeping. She seems most active at night, when I am lying in bed, and sleeps during the day when I am moving around. My midwife tells me that the motion of my movements rocks the baby to sleep and I love the idea of that.'
Sandra, 22 weeks pregnant

# 21–24 weeks **Common questions**

**Q** My baby is very active. I am worried that he could damage me. Is this possible?

**A** A baby's kicks can be uncomfortable but he won't harm you, because the uterus in which he is confined is made out of thick muscle. Also, he is surrounded by amniotic fluid, which acts as a 'shock absorber', cushioning his movements. It is good for babies to be active.

**Q** My partner loved coming to the anomaly scan at 20 weeks, and said that he felt really connected to the baby for the first time. How can I keep him feeling this way?

**A** Encourage your partner to feel the baby with you. If he lays his head on your abdomen, he may be aware of your baby's heartbeat as well as feeling some small ripples of movement. This will be a very special moment for him as it could be his first real opportunity to bond. If the baby has older siblings, let them enjoy this moment too, as it can help them feel that the new baby is already part of their family.

**Q** I am 22 weeks pregnant and am worried about getting chickenpox from my friends' children. Is there anything I can do to avoid it? Can it damage my unborn baby?

**A** Most adults are immune to chickenpox, but if you can't remember having it as a child you can have your blood tested for antibodies. Developing chickenpox during pregnancy is rare, but could affect a baby's development if the virus was contracted before 20 weeks or after 36 weeks of pregnancy. If you develop chickenpox, your baby could contract the virus (varicella infection of the newborn). If you have

**Above:** Hearing and feeling the baby through your abdomen allows your partner to bond with his child.

contracted chickenpox during pregnancy, you can have an injection of immunoglobulin. This contains chickenpox antibodies, which will lessen the effect on your baby.

**Q** Why does my baby get fits of hiccoughs?

**A** These are probably a result of your baby moving his chest in practice 'breathing'. These movements are thought to help babies to expand their lungs in preparation for their first real breath after they are born. You will feel the hiccoughs as a series of rhythmical movements which can last for up to 30 minutes. Don't worry about them. Hiccoughs are certainly not doing him any harm – and many women find the sensation amusing.

# Your baby at 28 weeks

You may feel that you are more in touch with your baby by 28 weeks, as you begin to recognize her wakeful times and the sounds that she likes. You may even feel that she responds to your moods. There is evidence to show that the mother's hormones (such as the stress hormone, cortisol) do actually cross the placenta, so your baby may be relaxed or agitated according to how you feel.

## Development milestones

- **At 25 weeks** The lungs are now filling with tiny air sacs (alveoli), each one wrapped in a network of blood vessels. There is no air inside them at the moment – just fluid from the amniotic sac, which passes in and out as your baby practises breathing.

*'Now I've got a proper bump I've been starting to feel real movements. I've completely bypassed the faint fluttery first movements and gone straight to the feisty kicking stage.'*
Clair, 25 weeks pregnant

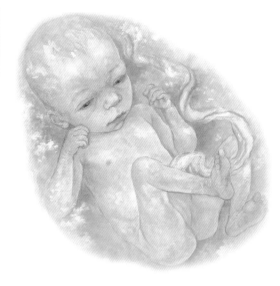

**Above:** Your baby may be head down at this stage, but if not there is plenty of time for her to turn.

- **At 26 weeks** The nervous system is maturing and the brain is increasing in size. The baby can experience pain. The eyes are almost fully formed and may be partly open. A thin layer of fat now starts to accumulate under the skin.
- **At 27 weeks** Bones, muscles and organs continue to grow. The eyelids are open and the baby looks much the same as she will at full term, only smaller and thinner.
- **At 28 weeks** Most of the smaller airways and alveoli in your baby's lungs have developed by this stage. The amount of fat on her body is increasing, making it easier for your midwife or doctor to identify the position that she is in when they feel your abdomen. In baby boys, the testicles may have descended into the scrotum by now, although in some cases this will not happen until after birth.

## 25–28 weeks **Common questions**

**Q** I'm 26 weeks pregnant and I'm having real problems sleeping and feel so exhausted the whole time. Can I ask my doctor for some sleeping pills or would they harm my baby?

**A** Like all medicines, sleeping tablets are best avoided during pregnancy. Try to get to sleep naturally if you can. The best means of doing this is to make sure that you are relaxed and comfortable. Try to get some light exercise during the day. Avoid eating heavy meals late in the evening or you will not have time to digest them, but if you are peckish, have a light snack or a glass of warm milk. Make sure that the bedroom is at a comfortable temperature: being too hot or too cold will make sleeping difficult. Although it sounds easy, try not to worry about being unable to sleep, this will just make it more difficult. Distract yourself by getting up to watch the television for a while, or read a book or magazine. When you feel sleepy, try again. Why not ask your midwife about yoga or relaxation classes? You may learn techniques that you can use when you find it difficult to get to sleep.

**Q** Is it true that babies respond to music in the womb?

**A** Yes, and it can be beneficial. Try singing the same songs or nursery rhymes to your baby on a regular basis from six months. Singing combines a right-brain process (music) with a left-brain activity (language) and will encourage connections between the two halves of your baby's brain to grow. From seven months, play classical music to your baby. This may help to speed the development of the right-brain spatial skills and is said to increase the likelihood that your child will excel in sports!

**Q** I know I have some way to go still, but at 28 weeks pregnant I am beginning to panic about fitting a baby into my busy lifestyle. What can you recommend?

**A** This is a great time to start preparing yourself mentally for the adjustments you are inevitably going to have to make once your baby arrives, by including your baby in your everyday routine. Try to make time every day when you can think about your baby. Imagine how she looks now, and what position she is in and what she will be like when she arrives. Talk to her as you stroke your bump.

**Below:** If you wake up at night, try reading until you feel sleepy again.

# THE SECOND TRIMESTER

## How your baby has grown

**At this stage of pregnancy, your baby is fully formed, growing rapidly and responsive to a range of stimuli, including touch, sound and light.**

### Your baby's development

At 28 weeks your baby weighs approximately 1.1 kg (2½ lb) and is about 25 cm (10 in) in length. Throughout the second trimester, your baby's body has continued changing rapidly.

**Below:** By the end of the second trimester, your baby can listen to and recognize your voice.

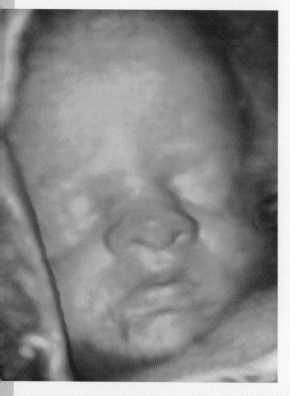

**Skin and hair:** Skin appears paler, as fat is laid down, and is no longer translucent. Hair continues to grow on the head and eyelashes and eyebrows are clearly defined. Lanugo starts to disappear.

**Muscles:** The baby's muscles are now well developed and have gained strength from vigorous movement. Your baby can make a fist and punch against the uterine wall.

**Circulatory system:** The heart is beating approximately 150–160 times per minute – about twice as fast as an adult heart.

**Digestive system:** Meconium (the baby's first bowel movement) is collecting in the colon. The baby drinks and excretes amniotic fluid.

**Nervous system:** Brain cells are multiplying rapidly and folds and grooves are appearing on the brain's surface. More links are being made between the brain and the rest of the nervous system. Your baby can respond to pain, touch, sound, taste and light, and also has a memory.

**Respiratory system:** The tiny air sacs (alveoli) and airways are developing.

**Ears:** Your baby can recognize your voice and may respond to loud noises and music.

**Eyes:** The eyes have now opened. Your baby can look around and follow the light of a torch shone across your abdomen.

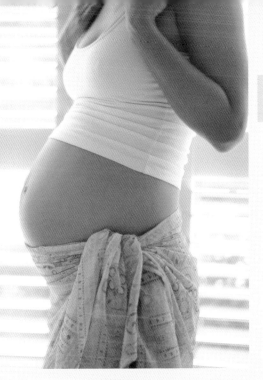

## Gender according to shape

Among all of the myths that are associated with pregnancy one of the most common is that the shape of your bump – to the front or all round – is dictated by the sex of the baby that you are expecting. The reality is that the shape of your bump depends on the way the baby is lying in your uterus coupled with a number of factors related more to you than to your baby, including how much weight you have put on during your pregnancy, your height, if your muscles have been stretched during previous pregnancies and the shape of your pelvis.

# True
## story

### Big bump anxieties

'I had my first antenatal class this week. We are only booked in for three in total, and the other two won't be until 32 weeks and 33 weeks. This was a daytime session just for mums-to-be, and we were shown some antenatal exercises and stretches to relieve aches and pains and to prepare us for labour.

'The teacher started off by asking us to talk to the person on our right-hand side, and tell them about any problems we'd experienced. I felt a bit awkward because I didn't really feel I had any problems to talk about. Most of the other women had had lots of niggles, so I guess I had just been really lucky so far.

'I have become a bit anxious since going to class, however. I am worried that my bump isn't big enough for my dates. I was comparing myself to the other expectant mums and everyone else looked much bigger. A few women even commented on how small I looked, and initially it did make me feel smug. But now I am feeling a little worried that perhaps I am not growing enough. It might be because I'm tall, so my bump just doesn't show so much.

'In the end I mentioned it to my midwife at my check-up this week, and she carefully double-checked the size of my bump by measuring from the top of it to the bottom with her tape. She reassured me that I was absolutely fine and had nothing to be concerned about, so I feel a bit better about it now.'

*Justine, 28 weeks pregnant*

# Your baby at 32 weeks

At 32 weeks your baby looks like a smaller version of a full-term baby, but she is still very delicate. She remains active, but is now not as quick to turn. As she grows, she no longer 'floats' in the amniotic fluid but instead rests in the uterus, most often in the head-down position. If your midwife confirms that your baby has not yet turned head down, you can try encouraging her to do so by adopting an all-fours position (see page 205). Do not worry, though. There is still plenty of time for her to move into her final position, ready for the birth.

## Development milestones

- **At 29 weeks** The baby's head now looks in proportion to the size of the arms and legs. The eyes are capable of focusing and blinking. A layer of fat has been building up beneath the skin, and the lungs are continuing to develop.
- **At 30 weeks** The baby is becoming plumper and the skin is looking more smooth, although it is still covered in greasy white vernix.
- **At 31 weeks** The cells lining the air sacs of the lungs secrete a substance called surfactant, a lubricant that prevents the tissues of the lungs from sticking together.

**Above:** Your baby no longer has much room and will be drawing up her knees into the fetal position.

This is essential for enabling the baby to breathe outside the uterus.

- **At 32 weeks** The hearing – the baby's main link with the outside world – is becoming more finely attuned. The lining in the air sacs continues to secrete the lubricant surfactant. A few creases are developing where she is laying down fat, at the top of her thighs and on her arms. The hair on her head continues to grow and there may still be a light covering of soft lanugo across the back of her shoulders and along the tops of her arms, although most of it will have been shed by now.

# 29–32 weeks **Common questions**

**Q** I am 31 weeks pregnant and worried about having a premature baby. If I go into early labour is there anything that can be done to stop it?

**A** This will depend on whether or not your cervix has started to dilate. A drug can be administered via a drip to relax the uterus and stop the contractions but, if your cervix is opening, then labour will probably continue. Women who show signs of premature labour are often advised to have two steroid injections which will help with the development of the baby's lungs.

**Q** I'm 32 weeks pregnant and have put on 10 kg (22 lb). I feel huge! Am I gaining too much weight?

**A** Mums-to-be vary hugely in the amount of weight they put on during pregnancy – the average is 9–14 kg (20–30 lb) – and gain at different rates (see pages 88–91). The most important thing is to eat a healthy, balanced diet that is rich in vitamins and minerals.

**Q** My friend's baby was diagnosed as 'small for dates' at a recent check-up. What does this mean?

**A** 'Small for dates' babies (also known as fetal growth restriction, small for gestational age or intra-uterine growth restriction) are simply those that are suspected to be smaller than expected for their gestation, and are often diagnosed around this time. It is not something to be unduly worried about. If your baby is thought to be small, you may be offered some ultrasound scans to monitor the growth more closely and will need more frequent antenatal checks. You may also be offered a scan that looks at the blood flow through the placenta to the baby, to check that it is working efficiently.

*'I am enjoying antenatal classes. I like being with other mums-to-be, especially when they ask lots of questions. It makes me realize that I am not the only one worrying about what may seem like trivial things. I know that none of us really knows what to expect from labour, but at least the classes are showing us how to cope with the various situations that might arise.'*

*Isabel, 31 weeks pregnant*

# Your baby at 36 weeks

Your baby's development is almost complete by 36 weeks, although he would still be considered premature or preterm if he were to be born at this time. Your life is probably revolving around waiting for your labour to start and making sure that all your arrangements for the birth and for the first few weeks afterwards are in place.

**Above:** At 36 weeks, your baby's cheeks have filled out and become chubby.

## Development milestones

- **At 33 weeks** The focus now is on growth. The immune system is still developing, and the final weeks are crucial for the final stages in the development of the lungs.
- **At 34 weeks** The baby continues to lay down fat. The lungs are almost mature. Most of the soft, downy lanugo has disappeared from the body, and the hair on the head is becoming thicker.
- **At 35 weeks** The rate of growth slows and all major organs are fully mature, apart from the lungs.
- **At 36 weeks** The lungs continue to develop and, every day, more fat cells are being laid down in a layer under his skin. Muscles are now strong, after weeks of movement. The baby's cheeks are plump and the fingernails reach his fingertips. There is a good covering of hair on the baby's head, and well-formed eyebrows and eyelashes.

## Communicating with your baby

By this stage of pregnancy you are probably communicating with your baby on a regular basis, even if you are not always aware of it. Many women inadvertently stroke their abdomen or talk to their baby. Your baby is increasingly aware of the sounds, movements and emotions that you communicate to him. Get your partner to massage your bump with gentle, sweeping, rhythmic movements.

# 33–36 weeks **Common questions**

**Q** I am 34 weeks pregnant and my midwife says that my baby's head has engaged. I thought this happened at 36 weeks, so does this mean my baby will be born early?

**A** It suggests that your baby is lying in a favourable position and your pelvis is roomy. First babies engage on average at 36 weeks, but subsequent babies may not do so until you are in labour. Every baby has to engage sooner or later in order to be born normally, but this does not predict when you will go into labour. The timing depends on your pelvis size, how firm your abdominal muscles are, the amount of hormones flowing and your baby's position.

**Q** I am eight months pregnant and huge. Is my baby too big to be born normally?

**A** This is a common fear, but the majority of women's babies grow to the right size to fit through their pelvis. If the head engages into the pelvis, this is a good indication that the baby will fit. Try not to worry – the vaginal wall is made of muscle and stretches during the birth to accommodate your baby. In a labour where the head won't fit through the pelvis, there are plenty of warning signs, such as an increased heart rate in the baby, and the midwife will always be looking out for signs like this.

**Q** Can the baby tell how I am feeling?

**A** At this stage, your body responds to your different emotions by producing hormones, which are transmitted to your baby through the placenta. This is referred to as sympathetic communication. In this way, your baby is aware of whether you are frightened and upset, or happy and relaxed.

**Q** How far is my baby aware of what is going on around her?

**A** Your baby can now not only hear your voice and other sounds, but also respond to them. She also blinks and responds to light – her eyes are open when she is awake. In fact, your baby is capable of a whole range of reflexes. She reacts, remembers and is practising her breathing, swallowing and sucking movements, ready for after the birth. Her brain cells are increasing rapidly, and will continue to do so after the birth.

*'I always took my little boy to all my antenatal checks. My midwife used to ask him to guess where she would be able to hear the heartbeat and then he would help put the gel on my tummy. He was very accepting when Amy was born and I feel sure it is because he was so involved from the start.'*
*Ngaio, mother of Amy and Adam*

# Your baby at 40 weeks

Your baby is now ready to be born. At birth, major changes will occur in the baby's heart and lungs. Up until birth the exchange of oxygen and carbon dioxide has been through the placenta. As soon as she is born and takes her first breath, the blood in her lungs will become oxygenated and she will begin to breathe normally.

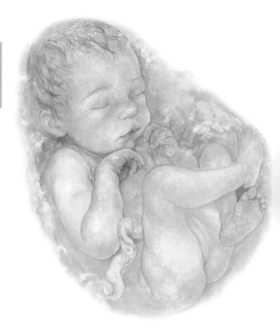

**Above:** At 40 weeks, your baby has completed her development in the uterus.

## Development milestones

- **At 37 weeks** All major development is complete at this stage of pregnancy. The baby continues to grow in size and strength and to lay down fat. The cells in the brain will continue to multiply and develop for the first few months of life after birth. In boys, the testicles usually descend into the scrotum.
- **At 38 weeks** Fat is still being laid down. The heart is beating at approximately 110–160 beats per minute. The baby has 300 bones, compared to an adult's 206. This is because some of them will fuse together later.
- **At 39 weeks** The immune system continues to develop, with some of your antibodies passing to the baby through the placenta. This offers the baby protection against disease and infection for the first few weeks of life.

- **At 40 weeks** The baby looks the same in the uterus as she will when she is finally born. Even inside the womb, the baby now practises making a sucking action and turning her head to one side – as if she is feeding!

## The fontanelle

The bones of your baby's skull remain soft so that they can ride over each other and mould to the shape of the birth canal. As a result, her head may be slightly pointed when she is born and she may have some swelling on either side of the head. This is only temporary. However, there will be a soft spot on the top of her head, called the fontanelle, for about 18 months, until the bones fuse together.

# 37–40 weeks **Common questions**

**Q** Will I be able to tell when my baby's head starts to descend into the pelvis?

**A** You might do: once her head is well down and engaged, you may notice that your bump has 'dropped' and looks lower. Your baby's movements will probably seem less vigorous, too, although you should still be feeling at least 10 movements a day. If this is not your first baby, this dropping often does not happen until labour, because your muscles do not have the tone they had first time round and so don't hold the baby in place so well.

**Q** I'm 37 weeks pregnant and last week my midwife told me that my baby is in the posterior position. What does this mean?

**A** This means that, at the moment, your baby is lying with her back towards your back, although she might turn during the first stage of labour so that she is lying with her back towards your front (anterior), which is the ideal position. There are things that you can start doing now to encourage her to turn into the anterior position (see page 205).

**Q** What happens if I go past my due date?

**A** Nothing initially. A normal pregnancy lasts anything between 37 and 42 weeks. You might be offered an induced labour once you have reached 41 weeks. After a certain period, the placenta, the source of your baby's nutrition, will not work as efficiently, though it's difficult to say exactly when this will happen. If you are keen to avoid induction, you should be offered ultrasound scans and monitoring of your baby's heartbeat to assess her wellbeing.

*'The waiting to go into labour was unbearable. My partner and I used to sit and talk about what our baby would look like and whose colour hair he would have. I felt such a longing to see and hold him.'*

*Dawn, mother of Jack*

# THE THIRD TRIMESTER

## How your baby has grown

**After spending nine months in the womb, your baby is now completely developed and ready to begin his journey into the world.**

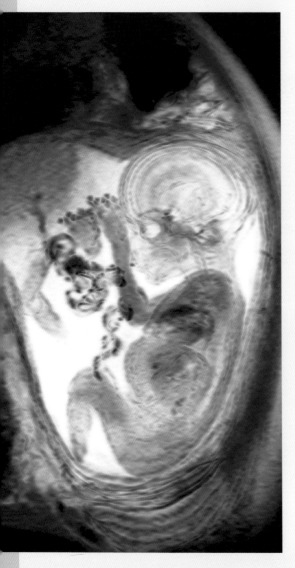

## Your baby's development

At 40 weeks of pregnancy, your baby weighs about 3.5 kg (7¾ lb) and measures approximately 36–37 cm (14–14½ in) from crown to rump or 47–51 cm (18½–20 in) from head to foot. The physical development that takes place within the uterus is now complete.

**Skin and hair:** The baby's skin is smooth, with folds of fat on the arms and top of legs. Some vernix may still be present. Most of the lanugo has been shed and your baby has a head of hair, as well as perfectly arched eyebrows and eyelashes.

**Muscles:** Muscles are strong from all the exercise inside the uterus. Your baby responds to sound and movement.

**Bones:** The soft bones of the skull will overlap slightly as the baby is squeezed through the birth canal.

**Organs:** All internal organs are now fully formed. The organs are surrounded by 20 per cent of your baby's fat.

**Circulatory system:** The heart is beating 110–160 times per minute.

**Digestive system:** Meconium has been collecting in your baby's intestine. He may pass

**Left:** At 40 weeks, your baby has fully formed internal organs and a mature respiratory system.

# True story

**Preparing for a breech birth**

'Trevor and I are thoroughly enjoying our antenatal classes. I think Trevor was a little bit apprehensive to start with, but he has got more out of them than he thought he would. It has been lovely to meet other parents and we have a great teacher who makes the experience very relaxed. The only problem is, after learning all about natural birth, I really want one. But according to my last scan, my baby is breech and the doctors are advising a caesarean.

'I've been given the option of an ECV, where they try to turn the baby externally, and one of the women in my antenatal class had it done yesterday. Although it didn't work, she reassured me by saying it's not uncomfortable or painful. I have also been advised to get on all fours as much as I can.

'Another tip sounds bizarre, but I am so desperate I've given it a go, though I don't know if it's worked yet. It's an acupuncture treatment called moxabustion, where an acupuncture point on your little toe is heated. I can't imagine how it works, but I'll try anything. The acupuncturist showed Trevor how to do the treatment, so he does it twice a day. The baby definitely moves afterwards, so I have not given up hope.

'My bump feels hard, tight and cumbersome now, but I'm still measuring small and my scans show fluid around the baby is on the low side. They are monitoring me closely now, and I know that, whatever happens, I am going to meet my baby soon.'

*Emma, 38 weeks pregnant*

some meconium during labour or soon after the birth.

**Nervous system:** This is now formed and sufficient for survival, although brain cells are continuing to multiply and will do so for some time after the birth. At this stage, your baby is capable of approximately 70 different reflex system behaviours.

**Respiratory system:** This is now fully mature.

**Ears:** Your baby can recognize familiar sounds, such as your voice and your partner's voice and music.

**Eyes:** A baby does not have to see very far in the uterus, but by birth your baby can focus between 20 and 30 cm (8–12 in), the distance between your breast and face.

4

# health and wellbeing

# Work and pregnancy

Choosing the right time to tell your employer that you are pregnant is always tricky. Although she may be delighted for you personally, she may be less happy professionally as she will have to arrange cover while you attend antenatal appointments or decide how to cope while you are away.

## Your rights and priorities

It is important to find out what benefits you are entitled to as a pregnant woman. Read your contract of employment, get in touch with a benefits agency – and, of course, ask your midwife for help, as she can provide you with lots of information. Once you have told your employers that you are pregnant, you can claim any entitlements in terms of time off for your antenatal appointments or risk assessments of your job. Bear in mind that you do not immediately have to tell them exactly when you are intending to give up or return to work.

## Know your body

Many women feel tired, sick or emotional during the first three months of pregnancy, when most of the physical changes are hidden. Reduce stress and carry on working more easily by making some simple adjustments to your lifestyle.

- Do not take on more work than you can realistically cope with.
- Avoid travelling at peak times.
- Eat regularly throughout the day to keep up your blood sugar level.
- Have a rest after eating lunch.
- Take care not to stand for hours on end without a break.
- Schedule your evening meal so that you can get to bed earlier.

**Above:** Plan your work day – you may find that you have more energy in the mornings or evenings.

# Work **Common questions**

**Q Could my job be putting me at risk?**
**A** Some types of work present more risks than others, and your employer must make the necessary checks to ensure your safety. You are entitled to change your working conditions or hours to avoid any risk that remains. If this is not practical, your employer must offer you a suitable alternative job. If they cannot, they have to suspend you on full pay. Problematic conditions range from working with dangerous chemicals, which could affect your unborn baby, to needing a seat if your job usually involves standing for some time. Long periods spent on your feet can cause problems such as varicose veins and low backache.

**Q I sometimes feel like I'm going to fall asleep at my desk. Any tips to keep awake?**
**A** It is mortifying to nod off at work, but very common. Get fresh air whenever you can, keep a cool facial misting in your bag, eat energizing snacks and avoid heavy meals or sugary foods. If all else fails, take yourself off somewhere quiet for a five-minute nap.

**Q How much time can I have off for antenatal appointments?**
**A** You are entitled to fully paid, reasonable time off to attend all your antenatal appointments. However, your employer can ask for proof of your appointments, and you may need a letter from your doctor or midwife stating that parentcraft and relaxation classes are part of antenatal care.

**Q When can I start my maternity leave?**
**A** The earliest you can begin your maternity leave is the start of the 11th week before your baby is due. Your employer has the right to start your maternity leave early if you are absent with a pregnancy-related illness during the last six weeks of your pregnancy.

*'I used to keep going through my lunch hour, as I knew if I sat down I wouldn't want to get up again! Eventually I realized there was no need to carry on as though I wasn't pregnant. Most people were sympathetic when I tried to leave on time.'*
*Abi, eight months pregnant*

**Below:** Keep some easy tasks for those times of the day when you feel most sleepy.

# Pregnancy weight gain
## What is normal?

If you are within the normal weight range when you conceive, and you gain steadily as your baby grows, you are likely to be healthier and to suffer fewer problems during pregnancy. Women gain weight at different rates, but you may only be weighed once during pregnancy to establish your Body Mass Index (see page 90).

## Guidelines for weight in pregnancy

On average, women put on no extra weight during the first three months of pregnancy, about 3 kg (7 lb) in weeks 13–20; another 5.5–6.5 kg (12–14 lb) in weeks 21–30, and a further 3 kg (7 lb) in weeks 31–36. In the last month your baby gains weight, but you lose a little because the volume of amniotic and other body fluids falls.

Your total weight gain during pregnancy consists of the baby, the placenta, extra blood and other fluids including amniotic fluid (the water surrounding the baby), the increased weight of your uterus and breasts, plus stores of fat. If you put on no extra fat, you can expect to return to within a kilo (a couple of pounds) of your pre-pregnancy weight 2–3 weeks after giving birth.

Your weight tends to regulate naturally if you eat healthily and according to your appetite. You should avoid getting so tired that you want to tuck into high-calorie snacks to give yourself extra energy.

Here are some guidelines for weight gain during pregnancy:

- If you gain nothing for a couple of weeks, or put on a significant amount and cannot think of a reason (such as a holiday during which you ate more than usual), check with your midwife that all is well.
- If you are in your teens, try to gain weight towards the upper end of the normal range

**Left:** If you eat a healthy, balanced diet, you will gain the right amount of weight during pregnancy.

# True story

**Coping with weight gain**

'I've reached the lumbering whale stage now, and I have to admit that, even though I know it's natural, the weight gain causes me to fret. Before I had my first child, Ruby, I was very overweight and I suppose I'm the same as anyone with weight issues – it's hard to stop obsessing about it.

'It's difficult to eat healthily because I feel hungry all the time. I didn't put on any weight until about 17 weeks, then I suddenly gained a lot of weight in my second trimester – exactly the same as with Ruby.

'Over the years I've got into the habit of weighing myself regularly, and if I didn't do it now I'd probably go mad wondering how much I weighed. I hate to see the scales go up rather than down – it's just that weight-watcher's mentality.

'However, I tell myself that I lost almost 40 kg (90 lb) before I had Ruby and another 20 kg (45 lb) afterwards, so I can do it again.'

*Clair, 30 weeks pregnant*

(say, 13.5–15.5 kg/30–34 lb). This can boost your baby's birth weight. Babies that have a low birth weight are more likely to suffer health problems.

- One effect of smoking or using street drugs is a low birth weight for your baby. Talk to your midwife (who can refer you for counselling) or seek other support if you cannot give these up, and try to gain weight towards the upper end of the normal range as described above.
- Don't be tempted to think that restricting your diet will help you to have a smaller baby and an easier birth! A baby that is poorly nourished often suffers restricted growth, which can lead to a more complicated labour.

## Eating disorders

The change of body image experienced as pregnancy advances can be very hard for some women to cope with and sometimes results in pregnant women suffering eating disorders, such as anorexia or bulimia. Don't become obsessed by weight gain during pregnancy; avoid weighing yourself if you are likely to find the pregnancy-related weight gain disheartening. Talk to your midwife if you become affected by any eating problems. She will give you support and refer you for counselling. Remember that losing weight rapidly can lead to you becoming under-nourished or dehydrated, and may prevent your baby from receiving the nutrition required for healthy development.

# Pregnancy weight gain
## Body Mass Index

The Body Mass Index (BMI) is a guide to the best weight range for good health when you are not pregnant, regardless of your age or body type. You usually start to gain weight after about 12 weeks of pregnancy, so your midwife will record your BMI at your booking visit, to help her to assess risk. If you are within the normal weight range for your height, you are less likely to suffer problems such as high blood pressure or diabetes during pregnancy. A BMI of 20–25 is ideal for optimum health.

## Calculating your BMI

You can use this simple method to calculate your BMI:

**1** Measure your height in metres and multiply this figure by itself.

**2** Measure your weight in kilograms.

**3** Divide the weight by the height squared. For example, the BMI for someone who weighs 65 kg (10 stone) and is 1.7 m (5 ft 7 in) tall is: 65 divided by (1.7 x 1.7) = 22.5. This weight would fall within the normal range (see below for explanations of different readings).

## What it means

- **BMI under 17** You may have difficulty conceiving. If you are poorly nourished when you become pregnant, your baby

**Above:** Keep a plate of fruit in the refrigerator for a healthy way of relieving those hunger pangs.

may lack nutrients before the placenta is fully developed and capable of supplying him from your blood.

- **BMI 17–19** You are a little underweight, but if you gain at a reasonable rate your baby should be fine.
- **BMI 20–25** This is the optimum weight range, associated with fewest problems during pregnancy.
- **BMI 26–30** You are a little heavy, so are more likely to suffer discomforts such as heartburn, varicose veins, tiredness, breathlessness or skin irritation caused by friction and perspiration.
- **BMI over 30** Women in this band tend to suffer from health problems that can complicate pregnancy, such as high blood pressure and diabetes. Medical procedures such as fetal heart monitoring and epidurals can be more difficult, and the baby may be slightly heavier than average.

# Weight gain **common questions**

**Q** What causes weight gain during pregnancy, except for the growing baby?

**A** Part of the weight you gain during pregnancy is directly associated with the baby, the placenta, extra fluids and so on. The rest consists of the amount of fat you add to your body. Overall weight gain in pregnancy averages 12 kg (27 lb), but anything between 5 and 15.5 kg (11 and 34 lb) is considered to be normal.

**Q** Under what circumstances might I expect to put on more than the average weight gain?

**A** You may put on more weight than average during pregnancy if you are tall and heavily built, if your baby is large or if you are expecting more than one baby. If you have a sedentary job you may not burn off calories as easily as someone who is more active – for example, someone who looks after small children. On average, women expecting their first baby gain an extra 0.9 kg (2 lb) compared with those who are on their second or subsequent pregnancies. This may be because they are more likely to have high blood pressure, which tends to be associated with fluid retention, or because their metabolism may be less efficient than in later pregnancies.

**Q** Everybody jokes about 'eating for two' when you are pregnant, but how much should I really be eating?

**A** Nobody needs to 'eat for two' during pregnancy. Most women find that their instinctive appetite is a guide to how much food they need, and you would do better to concentrate on increasing the nutritional quality of the food you are eating and not the quantity.

**Q** Is there any wisdom in going on a slimming diet during pregnancy?

**A** Pregnancy is not a good time to go on any kind of diet, as it could make it difficult for your baby to receive enough essential nourishment. Nutrients work together to build a healthy baby: for example, vitamin C helps you to absorb iron and protects your supply of vitamins A and E, but it needs replacing frequently as very little is stored. Slimming diets put your baby on a diet too, which could lead to poor health or growth. Concentrate instead on eating a healthy balanced diet (see Diet during pregnancy, pages 92–101) and taking gentle exercise (see Exercise and pregnancy, pages 102–109). Make sure that you get sufficient rest so that you are not tempted to fill up on cake or crisps to give you an energy boost.

# Diet during pregnancy

A healthy diet is important for everyone, but even more so when you are pregnant. Your body needs the right fuel to function efficiently and to cope with the demands of your growing baby. Don't attempt to 'eat for two', but rather try to have a diet that includes all the food groups described here, as well as a good range of vitamins and minerals (see page 94). On average, a pregnant woman needs to increase her daily calorie intake from 2000 to 2200 calories only in the last three months.

**Above:** Lentils, beans and nuts are a convenient source of protein for vegetarians.

# A balanced diet

In order to maintain a balanced diet, your daily food intake should consist of these food groups in the proportions given:

## Fats

Fat should provide no more than 30 per cent of your total daily calories. However, many products, including some so-called health foods, contain well over this amount. Also, most of the fat in processed foods, snacks and sandwiches is saturated or hydrogenated, and worse for your health than unsaturated fats. Found in foods like sunflower or olive oils, fresh nuts and oily fish, unsaturated fats contain essential fatty acids. If these are missing from your diet your baby will grow because your body supplies the best substitute available, but development may not be as good as it could be. (It is advised that you do not eat more than two portions of oily fish per week.)

## Dairy products

Eat 2–3 portions of dairy products a day. Dairy products, such as milk, yogurt and cheese, contain small amounts of zinc and some B group vitamins, and are also rich in protein and calcium. Although your body becomes more efficient at absorbing calcium from foods when you are pregnant, you should take care to include a variety of dairy products in your diet, especially towards the end of pregnancy.

## Proteins

Aim to eat 2–3 portions a day. Found in foods such as fish, meat, poultry, game, eggs, dairy

**Above:** Broccoli is a good source of folic acid, important for cell growth in early pregnancy.

products, lentils, pulses, beans, soya products, nuts and seeds, proteins are essential for the maintenance and repair of your cells and the growth of new cells in your baby.

## Fruit and vegetables

Eat 5–8 portions of fruit and vegetables a day. Fruits and vegetables supply valuable vitamins and minerals (see page 94) as well as dietary fibre, which helps to ease the constipation that a large proportion of women experience during pregnancy. Bear in mind that vegetables frozen on the day of purchase may contain more vitamin C than 'fresh' vegetables that have taken days to reach the shop.

## Complex carbohydrates

These should make up one-third of your daily calories. Starchy foods, such as breads, grains, cereals and potatoes, should be the mainstay of anyone's diet, but it is particularly important during pregnancy that you obtain most of your energy from these foods rather than from fats or sugar. These carbohydrates are broken down and released into the bloodstream slowly, providing energy steadily through the day. This helps avoid tiredness and may relieve nausea.

# Diet **Common questions**

**Q** I am only 12 weeks pregnant and I feel hungry all the time – is this normal?
**A** Lots of women feel hungry in the first few weeks, when their metabolism is increased, and often find that eating little and often helps to keep pregnancy nausea at bay. It is important that you eat a healthy, balanced diet. You should not worry about weight gain as long as you are eating healthily – pregnancy really is not the time to start dieting.

**Q** I am falling into bad habits with my diet, snacking on chocolate and crisps the moment I feel hungry, and eating my toddler's leftovers when I know my supper is an hour away. I quite often feel bloated and tired. What can I do to improve things?
**A** First, try to avoid snacking all day and aim not to miss any meal, as this can cause your metabolism to fluctuate. Try to include pasta or potatoes in your meals, which will give you more energy and satisfy your hunger for longer. If you get really hungry between meals, nibble on pieces of raw vegetables or fruit instead of chocolate, which tends to give your blood sugar levels a short-term boost, but leave you hungry again shortly afterwards. If you still tend to eat for a quick energy fix, try a few early nights instead, or scale down any extra commitments you have taken on so that you can cope more comfortably.

# Diet during pregnancy
## Vitamins and minerals

| Vitamin/mineral | What it does | Found in |
|---|---|---|
| Vitamin A | Promotes bone growth, healthy eyes, skin and gums; helps mucous membranes to resist infections. | Carrots, green leafy vegetables, broccoli, milk, cheese, salmon, halibut, apricots, peaches. |
| Vitamin B-complex | Promotes healthy nervous system, tissues, skin, red blood cells; helps to metabolize foods to release energy. | Red meat, yeast extract, dairy produce, eggs, nuts, beans, bananas, pulses, rice, bran, wholemeal bread, potatoes. |
| Vitamin C | Promotes healthy skin, bones and joints; increases iron absorption; helps recovery from stress; fights infection | Citrus fruits, blackcurrants, green peppers, broccoli, cabbage, potatoes |
| Vitamin D | Promotes strong bones and teeth; regulates absorption of phosphorus and calcium. | Eggs, dairy produce, margarine, oily fish (herrings, kippers, salmon, mackerel, sardines and tuna); exposure to sunlight. |
| Vitamin E | Promotes circulatory, nervous and reproductive systems; strengthens muscles and aids stamina; lowers blood pressure. | Almonds, Brazil nuts, olive oil and sunflower oil, eggs, dairy produce, wholegrain cereals, broccoli, carrots, celery, apples, avocados. |
| Vitamin K | Produces blood-clotting substance that prevents haemorrhage. | Lean meat, broccoli, spinach, tomatoes, nuts, oatmeal, avocados. |
| Calcium | Strengthens bones and teeth; promotes immune system; helps muscle contraction, blood clotting, and hormone release. | Dairy produce, green leafy vegetables, oranges, white bread, sardines, soya, wheatgerm, yeast extract, molasses, raisins, prunes, almonds, Brazil nuts. |
| Iron | Combines with protein to form haemoglobin which carries oxygen around the body; helps muscle contraction; prevents fatigue. | Red meat, molasses, sardines, dried fruit, asparagus, wholegrains, beans, lentils, almonds, wholemeal bread, cocoa, potatoes, broccoli. |
| Zinc | Essential to over 100 enzymes that process nutrients in the body. | Cheese, chicken, turkey, lamb, eggs, peas, carrots, seafood, wholegrains. |
| Magnesium | Promotes healthy tissues, muscles and nerves; deficiency may contribute to miscarriage and premature birth. | Nuts, seafood, meat, eggs, dairy produce, dried apricots, green leafy vegetables, wholegrains, hard water. |

# Diet **Common questions**

**Q** Can I improve my diet by taking dietary supplements?

**A** As a general rule, vitamins and minerals are better absorbed and used by the body in the natural combinations present in food. A poor diet plus a pill or a vitamin-fortified drink is not the same as a good, balanced diet. However, supplements can sometimes be valuable. They may provide a temporary boost if you are unable to eat balanced meals because of your work or travel schedule, if you are recovering from an illness or if you suffer from severe pregnancy sickness.

Check with your doctor or pharmacist before you self-prescribe any vitamin or mineral supplements other than folic acid, as they can interact with other medications. In addition, an excess of some nutrients can be harmful.

**Above:** Carrots are a great source of carotene, which is used by the body to make vitamin A.

**Q** Why do pregnant women need to take folic acid supplements?

**A** This B vitamin is found in dark green leafy vegetables, yeast extract, nuts, eggs, oranges, Cheddar cheese, bananas, lettuce, broccoli, Brussels sprouts, haddock and salmon. It is important for cell division, reproduction and for the formation of red blood cells. A deficiency prevents the baby's neural tube from forming, which can lead to defects such as spina bifida. You are advised to take a folic acid supplement (400 mcg) for at least three months before and after conception, because some women carry a gene that prevents them from using folic acid well even if they eat healthily. There is some evidence that supplements may increase the multiple birth rate slightly; and if you use medication for epilepsy you should consult your doctor before taking them.

**Q** Why do some women get food cravings? Is it harmful to succumb to them?

**A** If you are poorly nourished your baby will quickly use up your reserves. Cravings for strange things such as chalk may indicate a lack of nutrients, but if you generally eat healthily a passion for chocolate or citrus fruit is more likely to indicate that your body needs energy, or extra vitamin C to counteract symptoms of stress. Exhaustion makes many women turn to snacks that provide a quick energy boost, but these are often high in sugar and fat and may take away your appetite for healthier food. Getting extra rest is a more effective strategy.

# Diet during pregnancy
## Special diets

If you have a restricted diet, either by choice or for medical reasons, you will probably be more aware than most people of what you eat. However, you may need to make some changes when you are pregnant to ensure you obtain the correct nutrients in the correct proportions to meet the nutritional needs of yourself and your baby.

## Vegetarians and vegans

If you are vegetarian or vegan, you will, like any pregnant woman, need a balanced diet that supplies all the nutrition you and your baby require, and you only need to make a few changes to your normal eating habits. Meat, fish and dairy foods supply protein, vitamins, minerals and essential fatty acids. To get the correct balance from a vegan or vegetarian diet simply takes a little ingenuity.

- **Essential amino acids** Proteins are made up of substances called amino acids, eight of which – the essential amino acids – cannot be manufactured in the body. Vegetarians who eat dairy products and eggs will get all eight from these foods. Apart from buckwheat, quinoa, amaranth, soya beans and soya-based products such as tofu, no single plant source of protein contains all the essential amino acids, so non-dairy vegetarians and vegans need to eat a mixture of each type every day.

**Above:** Boost iron absorption by consuming iron-rich foods with foods rich in vitamin C, like oranges.

- **Iron** You can boost your iron absorption from plant sources, such as beans, lentils, nuts, breads, fortified breakfast cereals, pasta, spinach, watercress and dried fruit, by eating them with foods rich in vitamin C, such as a glass of orange juice. Eggs also contain iron.
- **Essential fatty acids** Sesame, sunflower and pumpkin seeds, linseed (flax seed) and walnuts are all rich sources of omega-3 fatty acids for vegetarians. Sesame and sunflower seeds, linseed and walnuts also provide omega-6 fatty acids.
- **Vitamins and minerals** By eating a balanced vegetarian or vegan diet you

should get enough vitamins and minerals. If you are unsure, ask your midwife or doctor, who may suggest a suitable supplement to take during pregnancy. Choose cereals and breads that are fortified with vitamins and minerals. If you are not eating dairy foods, you must obtain sufficient calcium elsewhere – try fortified soya milk, soya yogurts and tofu instead. Vitamin B12 is difficult to obtain in a vegan diet so eat foods such as yeast extract and fortified breakfast cereals and soya products, or ask for a supplement with vitamin B12.

## Food safety

During pregnancy, changes take place in your immune system so that it does not reject your baby's DNA. This leaves you more at risk from food poisoning, which could put your baby at risk. As well as avoiding any foods that may be unsafe (see pages 98–101), you should also make sure that your own kitchen is a safe, hygienic place for food preparation.

All food-preparation areas should be kept scrupulously clean. Use separate chopping boards for cooked meat, uncooked meat and vegetables. Wash all equipment in hot soapy water after use and wash knives between cutting meat and vegetables. Change tea towels and dish cloths daily and wash them at the highest temperature possible.

You should wash your hands before and after preparing food and after handling raw meat or eggs. Always wash vegetables, fruit and salads, and rinse rice and pulses (dried and canned) before use.

Only buy food you will eat before its best-before date. Rewrap foods if necessary and put them into the freezer or refrigerator as

# Special diets
# Common questions

**Q Is it possible to pass a food allergy on to my baby?**
**A** If you suffer from a food allergy or intolerance, you should avoid eating the food in question while you are pregnant or breastfeeding because you could pass on the allergy to your baby. If the baby's father, anyone in your immediate families or any of your older children has eczema, asthma, hay fever or a medically diagnosed food allergy, avoid peanuts and foods containing them while you are pregnant or breastfeeding. For other foods to avoid, see the guidelines on pages 98–101.

soon as possible. The coldest part of the refrigerator should be no higher than 5°C (40°F) and the freezer should be set to -18°C (0°F) or lower. Wrap raw meat and store it on a plate at the bottom of the refrigerator, and keep eggs separately. Do not put milk and dairy products in the door. Store cooked and uncooked foods in different parts of the refrigerator and ensure that everything is kept covered.

Throw away any food that has been in the freezer for longer than the manufacturer's guidelines. Always defrost food on a plate in the refrigerator. Never cook food that is not totally defrosted, unless the instructions say it may be cooked from frozen.

# Diet during pregnancy
## Food guidelines

| | Foods you can eat | Foods to avoid | Risk |
|---|---|---|---|
| Cheese | Hard cheeses: (in moderation) Asiago, Austrian smoked, Caerphilly, Cheddar, Cheshire, Derby, double Gloucester, Edam, Emmental, feta (made with pasteurized milk), Gloucester, Gouda, Gruyère, haloumi, Jarlsberg, Lancashire, mozzarella (made with pasteurized milk), paneer, Parmesan, pecorino (hard), provolone, Red Leicester, Port Salut and Wensleydale.<br><br>Soft cheeses: Bel Paese, Boursin, cottage cheese, cream cheese, curd cheese, fromage frais, mascarpone, Monterey Jack, Philadelphia, processed cheese spreads, petit-suisse, quark and pasteurized ricotta | All soft, mould-ripened cheeses, even those made with pasteurized milk, such as Brie, blue Brie, Cambozola, Camembert, Chaumes, crottin, Lymeswold, Pont l'Evêque, Tallegio, vacherin, unless thoroughly cooked.<br><br>Blue-veined cheeses, such as Bavarian blue, blue Cheshire, blue Shropshire, Blue Vinney, blue Wensleydale, Danish blue, dolcelatte, Gorgonzola, Roquefort and Stilton, unless thoroughly cooked. Avoid unwrapped cheeses from the delicatessen. All unpasteurized cheeses, such as fontina, especially soft ones. | Listeriosis<br><br><br><br><br><br><br>Listeriosis or salmonellosis |
| Milk, cream, yogurt | Pasteurized, sterilized or ultra-heat treated (UHT) cows', goats' and sheep's milk and products made from them. | Untreated cows', goats' and sheep's milk, and products made from them. | Salmonellosis, E. coli 0157, toxoplasmosis, brucellosis |
| Ice cream | Pre-packed ice cream and ice lollies kept in the freezer. Home-made ice cream and sorbets containing no egg white or yolk. Ice cream from ice-cream parlours. | Home-made ice cream and sorbets containing egg white or yolk. Soft-whipped ice cream from kiosks or ice-cream vans. | Salmonellosis |

|  | Foods you can eat | Foods to avoid | Risk |
|---|---|---|---|
| Eggs | Bought mayonnaise, salad cream and mayonnaise-based dressings made with pasteurized dried egg. Freshly cooked hard-boiled eggs. Well-cooked omelettes and scrambled, poached and fried eggs where both yolk and white are set through. Pasteurized dried egg white and whole egg. Shop-bought egg sandwiches and salads, and Scotch eggs. | Foods containing raw egg, for example, home-made mayonnaise, Béarnaise and Hollandaise sauces, mousses and uncooked home-made cheesecakes. Soft-boiled eggs and undercooked omelettes and scrambled, poached and fried eggs. Lightly cooked egg dishes, for example, tiramisu, zabaglione, crème brûlée and soft meringues. | Salmonellosis |
| Meat | Well-done meat. Cured meats if cooked, but only in moderate quantities as many contain high levels of salt. | Raw and undercooked meat, including dishes such as steak tartare and carpaccio of beef. | Toxoplasmosis |
|  |  | Pre-cooked meat from the delicatessen. | E. coli 0157 |
|  |  | Uncooked cured and smoked meats, such as bacon and hams, for example, Parma ham and other forms of prosciutto, sausages such as salami, mortadella and chorizo, and air-dried meat. Cold meat sold loose from the delicatessen. | Toxoplasmosis |
|  |  | Liver and liver-based products, for example, pâtés and liver sausage (Leberwurst). | High levels of retinal, a form of vitamin A considered harmful to unborn babies. |

# Diet during pregnancy
## Food guidelines

| | Foods you can eat | Foods to avoid | Risk |
|---|---|---|---|
| **Poultry and game** | Thoroughly cooked poultry or game. Cooked and thoroughly reheated poultry or game. Pre-packed cooked chicken only if thoroughly reheated. Home-cooked chicken in sandwiches, salads and picnics, if kept chilled before eating. | Raw or undercooked poultry or game. Cold poultry or game if sold loose from the delicatessen. | Salmonellosis, listeriosis |
| **Fish** | Properly cooked fish. Guidelines suggest no more than two portions of oily fish (mackerel, herrings, pilchards, sardines, salmon or trout) a week. Tuna – no more than two steaks or four cans per week. Shop- or restaurant-bought sushi and sashimi that has been frozen beforehand. Cooked smoked fish. Smoked salmon. | Raw or undercooked fish, for example, in dishes such as carpaccio of tuna, as well as home-made sushi and sashimi. | Toxoplasmosis |
| | | Shark, swordfish and marlin. | Excessive mercury levels |
| | | Uncooked smoked fish, for example, mackerel pâté, taramasalata and gravadlax. | Toxoplasmosis |
| | | Fish oil supplements. | High levels of retinal (see page 99) |
| **Shellfish** | Freshly and thoroughly cooked shellfish as part of a hot meal. Pre-cooked shellfish eaten cold, if kept chilled beforehand and used within sell-by date. | Raw shellfish, for example, fresh oysters. | Salmonellosis |
| | | Any shellfish with no sell-by or use-by date. | Campylobacter |

| | Foods you can eat | Foods to avoid | Risk |
|---|---|---|---|
| Pâté | | Avoid all. | Listeriosis |
| Cook-chill foods | Foods that have been thoroughly reheated until piping hot all through. (Take extra care with dishes containing chicken, eggs or seafood.) Quiches, if reheated until piping hot. Pre-packed pies, pasties and pastry slices, if chilled and stored correctly. | Foods that have not been reheated.<br><br>Cold quiches.<br><br>Cold items from the delicatessen, for example slices of meat pie. | Listeriosis<br><br>Salmonellosis<br><br>Listeriosis |
| Fruits and vegetables | Raw or cooked, if peeled and rinsed or scrubbed clean under running water. | Unwashed fruits and vegetables | Toxoplasmosis |
| Salads | Freshly made salads from well-washed ingredients. Dressed salads prepared immediately before eating (see mayonnaise under Eggs, page 99). Pre-prepared bagged salads if thoroughly re-washed just before eating and eaten before use-by date. Ready-made dressed salads, for example, bean or potato salads or coleslaw, if eaten within use-by date. | Pre-prepared bagged salads if not rewashed | Listeriosis, toxoplasmosis |

# Exercise and pregnancy
## Where to start

Most women benefit from gentle, non-competitive exercise during their pregnancy. Exercise improves fitness, boosts your feel-good factor, and can help to reduce mood swings and depression. Even a short session can help you to get a better night's sleep, and increasing your strength and postural awareness also helps you to avoid injury.

## Get motivated

Strength, suppleness and stamina are important when you are pregnant. Strong muscles support and protect ligaments that are softened by hormones. Suppleness allows your body a full range of mobility so that you can move with less effort and adopt useful positions when you are giving birth. Stamina provides the sustained energy you need to cope with the demands of pregnancy or an extended labour.

Discuss a suitable exercise regime with your midwife or doctor. Many of the forms of exercise you take already will be fine: gentle aerobics, badminton, cycling and jogging can all continue during pregnancy. Particularly good for building strength and flexibility are yoga, Pilates and swimming. You will find many classes with qualified instructors at your local health and leisure centre.

**Above:** Gentle stretching increases your suppleness in preparation for the challenges of labour and birth

## Listen to your body

- Never force your body in any way – the key to exercise is little and often.
- If an exercise feels too strenuous, makes you light-headed or causes any other problem, leave it out.
- Drink plenty of water so that you don't become overheated.
- If you feel tired or under the weather, stop exercising until you feel better.
- If you cannot complete an exercise session, just do as much as you feel able.

# Exercise **Common questions**

**Q** I do very little exercise as a rule, but am keen to make an effort. What is the best way to start?

**A** If your job and lifestyle are sedentary and you take no regular exercise, you will benefit greatly from regular gentle activity. Start by looking for opportunities to walk instead of driving or using public transport. If you work on the upper floor of a building, try walking down the stairs instead of taking the lift, then move on to climbing up them. Within a short period you will find that you start to feel more energetic and less tired at the end of the day, and you can progress to moderate exercise as your pregnancy advances.

**Q** What is the best form of exercise ?

**A** Your body has many physical changes to accommodate during pregnancy, so moderate, low-impact exercise is more suitable than competitive sport or activities where you risk overstretching or have to work hard to keep up. Most women are able to adapt their usual activities, but ask your coach, midwife or doctor for advice if you are in any doubt.

**Q** I have heard that dancing is very good for pregnancy, but I have never done it before. Is this a good time to start?

**A** Dancing is great exercise and a wonderful mood lifter. However, it may be better to continue with a familiar sport or activity rather than trying something completely different during pregnancy. If you do try a new form of exercise, make sure that your instructor knows you are pregnant and is able to advise you.

**Q** Why is stretching such a good idea?

**A** Suppleness is very important in pregnancy. If your range of movement is restricted, even simple tasks that involve reaching or twisting – such as getting in and out of a car or putting a toddler in a highchair – become more difficult. A good level of suppleness also enables you to be comfortable in positions that make giving birth easier. Some women find that they are naturally supple, while others have more stamina or strength. Regular stretching will enable you to get to know what your body is capable of and help you to accept both its abilities and its limitations.

*'I've been doing yoga on and off for years to tone and balance my body. When I have not done any stretching for a few days I notice how stiff I am, mentally and physically. I get tired more quickly now that I am pregnant, especially after working all day, but then I cannot ease my back or fasten my shoes as I can when I practise regularly. I feel so much better when I make myself practise.'*

*Sally, 28 weeks pregnant*

# Exercise and pregnancy
## Keeping fit

If you are reasonably active and want to improve your fitness, try to fit in three 15- to 20-minute sessions of moderate exercise into your schedule each week. You will really feel the benefits.

**Above:** Pregnancy keep-fit classes are a great way of exercising regularly and safely.

## What to do

You could buy a pregnancy exercise video or look for details of special classes for pregnancy on the noticeboard at your local leisure centre or hospital. Pregnancy exercise classes are also useful for making contacts with other mums-to-be in your area. Before joining a general exercise class, make sure that the teacher knows you are pregnant.

If you take part in competitive games, or sports that involve rigorous training or tempt you to push yourself, talk to your coach about the appropriate level of training. You may need to ease up or take special precautions. It is very unwise to strive to win, to finish a routine when you are exhausted or to push yourself to the point of being more than a little breathless when you are pregnant.

## Walk to fitness

You may be suprised at the benefits you can gain simply from walking. Regular walking strengthens your legs, improves your flexibility and is easy to monitor. It provides good aerobic exercise, helping your lungs to take in more oxygen with less effort and also increasing your stamina. If you do not generally take much exercise, you will soon see an improvement in your fitness if you walk for just 20 minutes, three times a week, and keep a record of your pulse rate.

# Keeping fit **Common questions**

**Q** I have started a regular walking regime and it requires me to check my pulse rate. How do I work it out?

**A** Whatever your activity, you can check that you are exercising within safe limits by finding your maximum safe pulse rate in beats per minute. Subtract your age from 220 and multiply the result by 0.6 for the lower end of your range, and by 0.85 for the upper end. Walk for 10 minutes, and then check your pulse rate. If you find it is near the lower end of your range, your speed is about right; if not, slow your pace down. As your fitness improves, your pulse rate will go down while you walk at the same speed or maintain the same level of activity. Some authorities suggest that during pregnancy an upper pulse rate of 140 is desirable, regardless of age.

**Q** I have always had an active sports life and regularly cycle and go running. Are there any sports I should avoid?

**A** You might want to avoid sports such as skiing or horse-riding, where there is a risk of accidental injury, but in general most activities can be continued during pregnancy provided you listen to your body and make sensible adjustments. For example, jog on grass in trainers that prevent jarring; use an exercise bike, or cycle on quiet roads; when you play tennis or badminton, ask your partner to send shots you can return with ease.

**Q** I have heard that swimming is a good exercise for pregnant women. Is this true?

**A** Swimming provides excellent exercise, increasing strength, stamina and suppleness. However, arching your back to keep your head out of the water and kicking in breaststroke may make your back and pelvic ligaments ache. Change your leg movement if you feel any pain in your groin after you have been swimming breaststroke, or use backstroke or front crawl to avoid strain.

# Seven tips for **exercising safely**

1 If you have had a recent miscarriage, have high blood pressure, or you smoke and your BMI (see page 90) is over 30, check with your doctor before taking up exercise.

2 Your pulse rate should always stay under 140 and your temperature under 38°C (100°F).

3 Keep strenuous activity to a maximum of 15 minutes per session. Avoid it in hot or humid weather, or if you feel unwell.

4 If you are a competitive athlete, discuss the appropriate level of training with your coach.

5 Never push your body to win a race or complete a training routine.

6 Avoid anything that causes strain or feels uncomfortable.

7 Seek advice from your doctor or midwife if you have any unusual symptoms.

# Exercise and pregnancy
## Yoga and Pilates

The gentle stretching of yoga and Pilates is particularly beneficial, improving posture, strength and suppleness, and encouraging you to work with your body. Always tell your teacher you are pregnant in case exercises should be adapted, or join a special pregnancy class.

## Yoga

Yoga comes high on the recommended list of appropriate regimes for pregnant women. It combines movement and meditation to

**Below:** Pilates exercises are particularly good for helping with backache during pregnancy.

*'I practise Astanga yoga, which is quite physical, and I've been told that women who do this kind of yoga can have difficult labours and births. Apparently, having very strong pelvic floor muscles is a problem, because the muscles find it hard to relax and let go during labour. I am joining a yoga for pregnancy class, so that I can carry on practising, following a more suitable routine.'*

*Donna, nine weeks pregnant*

promote the wellbeing of body, mind and spirit. The exercises improve posture, muscle tone, breathing and blood circulation. The emphasis on breathing, concentration and visualization will benefit you not only during your pregnancy, but also throughout labour, helping you to relax and focus throughout the contractions.

A well-balanced yoga session helps with lymphatic drainage and keeps the endocrine system (the hormone-control system) toned and healthy. It also focuses on good posture and muscle tone. As a result, women who practise yoga tend to look more toned than other mothers-to-be. They are also less bothered by oedema (fluid retention) and swollen joints and suffer fewer cellulite problems. Yoga practice is also a great confidence booster and many women benefit emotionally as well as physically. For some it may be the only session of total 'me-time' an expectant mother gets all week.

## Pilates

Pilates is an ideal form of exercise to make your pregnancy and the birth more comfortable, and to help your body recover afterwards. It comprises a series of gentle exercises designed to strengthen core strength, the pelvic floor and your muscles, without putting stress on your joints. It focuses on the centre of the body – the area from the hips to the bottom of the ribs.

As well as building your strength and stability, Pilates also boosts your balance and coordination and improves the circulation of your blood. It also enhances concentration and encourages you to develop a special relationship with your body as you exercise. This is particularly relevant during pregnancy and as a preparation for labour.

# Yoga and Pilates
# Common questions

**Q Is it safe for anyone to do yoga?**
**A** If you have a history of prolapsed (slipped) discs or have suffered a whiplash injury or a fall, visit an osteopath or chiropractor before you engage in any yoga practices. If you have any doubt about your condition, check with your health professionals and let them know what practices you are planning to use. If there is any show of blood you must stop immediately and seek medical advice.

**Q I've never done an exercise class before. Should I be starting something like Pilates while I'm pregnant?**
**A** Pilates is perfectly safe even if you've never done it before, but you should check with your midwife before starting any new exercises. Make sure you enrol with a qualified Pilates instructor who has experience in running classes for pregnant women. Your instructor should take you through a series of exercises to assess your fitness levels before you start.

With its emphasis on developing good posture and central stability, which are easily underminded during pregnancy, Pilates will help to prevent backache and neck tension. It is also very useful for strenghtening the pelvic floor muscles and other muscles that you will use during labour and birth. The focus on using specific breathing sequences as you exercise will also help you to use breathing to relax during labour.

# PELVIC FLOOR EXERCISES

## The pelvic floor

**The pelvic floor consists of a 'hammock' of muscles and ligaments, resembling a figure of eight, and stretches from your pubic bone (at the front) to the bottom of your backbone.**

The muscles and ligaments of the pelvic floor 'hammock' play an essential role in holding your bladder, bowel and uterus in place, as well as helping to close the outlets of the bladder and bowel. These muscles also have an important function in love-making, because their contractions increase the pleasure for both you and your partner.

These pelvic muscles and ligaments come under particular strain during pregnancy and childbirth. As the weight of your baby becomes greater, an increasing strain is placed on the muscles, while at the same time the pregnancy hormone relaxin softens and stretches them. In consequence, if you already have any weakness in your pelvic muscles, you may find that you begin to leak urine – particularly whenever you cough, laugh, sneeze or exercise.

## The importance of these exercises

It is crucial that you do exercises to maintain the strength of your pelvic muscles. Prolonged or repeated stretching of the pelvic floor muscles can result in permanent damage. If you ignore any weakness in your pelvic floor, you may develop conditions such as a prolapsed vagina, rectum, bladder or uterus. This is where the muscles fail to support the organs and start to 'drop', bulging into the vagina. This can result not only in urinary incontinence but also in lack of control over bowel movements. Surgery may be necessary to repair this.

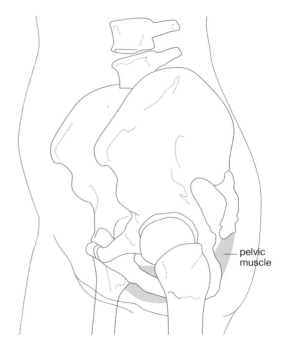

pelvic muscle

**Above:** Regular exercise of the pelvic floor muscles will help with problems such as stress incontinence.

# When to start

There is no reason why you should not start doing these exercises as soon as you find out that you are pregnant. It is important to continue these exercises, not only during your pregnancy but also after the baby is born, in order to help yourself to regain the muscle tone. Do not leave exercising until after the birth because then you will not be able to feel the muscles as well as you can now. In fact, it is recommended that all women do these exercises throughout their lives to guard against stress incontinence.

*'I have only just realized that my pelvic floor muscles have been weakened – almost six months after the birth – because I've gone back to work and promptly caught a cold ... and every time I sneeze, I leak!'*
*Cecilia, mother of Joshua*

## How to do these exercises

Sit comfortably, with your back straight and knees relaxed and held slightly apart.

- Imagine that you are trying to avoid breaking wind, or that you are 'holding on' to a desperate need to open your bowels. As you squeeze the muscles around your back passage you should feel the muscles move. Do not lift your buttocks or move your legs.
- Imagine that you are sitting on the toilet to pass urine. Clench the muscles you would use to stop the stream of urine and imagine drawing them up, like a rising elevator.
- Imagine that you are trying to grip a tampon in the vagina using your pelvic floor muscles.

In each case, relax the muscles quickly and then repeat the exercise. Try to combine the three exercises. Pull up the muscles quickly several times and then do the exercises again slowly. Think about the position of the different muscles and how they feel. Imagine the muscles as an elevator – rising three floors and stopping at each one. When they are on the top floor, lower them in stages, stopping at each floor! Repeat the exercises 10 times, five times per day.

Check that you are doing the exercises properly by putting a finger into your vagina and feeling the muscles tighten as you clench. Develop an awareness of how your muscles feel when they are relaxed. This is important in the second stage of labour, when you are pushing out your baby. Tighten the muscles of your pelvic floor as you breathe in and then, with each outward breath, slowly relax the muscles as much as possible.

Try to associate the exercise with another activity, for example when you have a drink or after you have passed water. It does not matter what position you are in – you could be standing, sitting, squatting or lying down. The great thing about these exercises is that you can do them anywhere and at any time and no one else will be any the wiser about what you are doing!

# Alternative therapies

There are a range of alternative therapies for different conditions experienced during pregnancy. Many midwives are qualified in complementary therapies, such as aromatherapy, massage and reflexology. Ask what is on offer when you go for your check-up.

**Above:** Essential oils have a powerful effect on body and mind and should be handled carefully.

## Reflexology

Reflexology is beneficial for emotional wellbeing and safe during pregnancy, provided you are treated by a qualified reflexologist. It works on the principle that the feet are a map of the body, and different areas of the feet correspond to particular parts of the body. Therefore, 'treating' the feet benefits these areas of the body. A reflexology treatment is similar to a foot massage – your feet may feel tender at times, but it should be very relaxing.

Stress and anxiety cannot be alleviated by one session, so you may need regular sessions over some weeks. If you have a complicated pregnancy, reflexology should only be done by a member of your maternity team, such as your midwife or doctor (if they have been trained in the technique).

## Aromatherapy

In aromatherapy, essential oils, which are extracted from plants, are applied to the skin or inhaled. Some of these oils have an energizing effect on the mind and body, while others are relaxing. This is due to the scent of the oil and its effects on the skin. Oils are usually mixed with a 'carrier' oil, such as grapeseed oil, or added to water. Such essential oils are powerful agents that should be handled with care; they should not be used before week 12 of pregnancy.

### Using essential oils

Always dilute oils in water or a carrier oil and do not use them more than three times a week. For a footbath, add 2–3 drops of essential oil to a bowl of warm water; as an inhalation, add 3 drops to warm water and inhale the vapour; in a bath, stir 4–6 drops of oil into warm water (do not use soap and do not stay in the bath for more than 20 minutes); for a massage, mix 5 drops of essential oil with 25 ml (1 fl oz) of grapeseed oil.

## Oils to choose

- **From 12 weeks** Use citrus oils for revitalization (you should avoid going out in sunlight if citrus oil has been applied directly to the skin).
- **From 24 weeks** Use chamomile oil for relaxation and treating insomnia.
- **From 28 weeks** Use lavender oil for relaxation and treating insomnia.
- **Final weeks** Use neroli oil for relaxation and treating insomnia.

## Oils to avoid

- **During pregnancy in general** Cajuput, celery seed, cinnamon leaf, citronella, clary sage, fennel, jasmine absolute, lavandin, lavender (before 28 weeks), marjoram (sweet), may chang, myrrh, niaouli, rosemary, spike lavender, tagetes, yarrow.
- **If you have high blood pressure** Do not use rosemary or thyme (red).
- **If you have a family history of allergy, asthma or eczema** Any nut or wheatgerm oils should be avoided.

# Homeopathy

Homeopathy works holistically, so you need to match the remedy to your personal characteristics and symptoms. Follow the instructions on the pack. You should avoid strong flavours such as peppermint or coffee, as they impair the remedies' effectiveness. Stop treatment as soon as there is an improvement. If the remedy does not help, consult a qualified homeopath.

# Medical herbalism

Make a herbal tea using a tea bag or a teaspoonful of dried herb per cup of boiling water. Leave it to stand for 10 minutes and

# Alternative therapies
# Common questions

**Q** Can essential oils be used throughout the nine months of pregnancy?

**A** It is best not to use any essential oils during the first three months of pregnancy, and some oils should not be used at all (see opposite). Before using any oil, do a patch test on your arm to check for any adverse skin reactions. If you have any doubts about the suitability of an oil, consult a qualified aromatherapist.

**Q** What are Bach flower remedies?

**A** Bach flower remedies are used to treat emotional states rather than physical symptoms and many women use them to relieve stress. The best known is Rescue Remedy, a composite of five others: Star of Bethlehem for shock, Rock Rose for terror and panic, Impatiens for mental stress and tension, Cherry Plum for desperation and Clematis for feeling withdrawn or distant. There are 38 individual Bach flower remedies, all widely available in healthfood stores and pharmacies.

drink it on its own, or with milk and honey. Try chamomile to relax your nervous system and your digestion; lemon balm and linden blossom (lime flowers) promote mental relaxation and help calm the body.

More potent, a herbal infusion is steeped for longer. To help you sleep, leave a handful of Californian poppy or elder flowers in 600 ml (1 pint) of boiling water for 30 minutes, then strain into a hot bath.

# RELAXATION TECHNIQUES

## Resting your mind and body

**Pregnancy is the ideal time to start learning relaxation techniques, as they will benefit not only you, but also your baby.**

### Relaxation step by step

Relaxation simply involves recognizing tension and consciously letting it go. Try this exercise every day for two weeks, keeping the sessions short (5–10 minutes each). With a little practice, you will only need to check through the groups of muscles to stay relaxed.

1 Sit in a comfortable chair or lie down, whichever you prefer.
2 Tighten up one leg as much as possible, notice what this feels like, then let go and feel the difference. Then tighten and release in turn: your other leg, lower back and buttocks, abdomen, shoulders, arms and hands, neck, jaw, cheeks, lips, eyes and finally your forehead.
3 Go around your body again. This time tighten each group of muscles very slightly, letting go as soon as you are aware of tension.
4 Go around your body a third time, simply checking that each muscle group is completely relaxed. If not, release the tension. When you are fully relaxed, observe how gentle your breathing has become.
5 When the session is over, stretch, wriggle your fingers and get up slowly. Deep relaxation can lower your blood pressure and if you jump up suddenly you may feel dizzy or light-headed.

Relaxation is more than just resting. It is possible to rest physically but still be alert mentally, perhaps thinking about your long list of 'things to do'. It is important that you recognize how to clear your mind and truly unwind. Relaxing is a skill that can benefit anyone at any time of life, not just during labour. The techniques can lower your blood pressure and increase the oxygen supply to your baby, helping her to thrive.

## Breathing awareness

Breathing and relaxation go hand in hand: when one changes, so does the other. If you are breathing in a panicky, jerky fashion you will straightaway start to feel tense – notice the effect on your shoulders and arms. Equally, tensing your muscles deliberately while breathing gently is difficult, because your whole body wants to let go.

Staying relaxed during labour allows your uterus to work efficiently and makes the whole experience easier. When you are in labour, you should aim to make your breathing as quiet and effortless and your muscles as relaxed as possible. The secret is to recognize slight tension in your body or changes in your breathing at the earliest moment and then readjust them consciously before they have a chance to take hold.

**Above:** During your pregnancy, allow yourself quiet times when you can let go of all your worries.

# Deep relaxation

Once you are confident that you can relax at will, try the following methods to help you enter a deeper state of relaxation. You may find that one or other of these practices will enable you to let go more easily, or may work better on certain occasions.

- **Special place** Choose a place that you already associate with feeling relaxed, indoors or out, real or imaginary. Visualize it vividly – think about what you can see, the sounds, the smells, the colours, the weather, the time of day and so on. Allow your mind to play freely, but try to place yourself within the scene, rather than being a bystander who is observing yourself from the outside.

- **Descending steps** Imagine that you are standing at the top of a flight of 10 steps. Descend slowly, counting from 10 down.

*'I live life at breakneck speed and I was shocked by how much pregnancy slows you down. I got so overtired that I had difficulty sleeping and then I worried about not getting the sleep I needed for work. The more anxious I was the less I slept, until it became a vicious circle. My doctor told me to slow down and gave me two weeks off work. I bought a relaxation tape and had some reflexology sessions to get me back into a sleep routine. Now if I feel tired I go through my relaxation routine before stress gets a grip on me.'*

*Sally, 31 weeks pregnant*

With each step you take, pause for a moment to let the tension go, so that when you reach the bottom step – if not before – you are deeply relaxed.

- **Sounds** When you are in peaceful surroundings, focus your attention on the sounds that enter the room or space. Identify each sound and decide whether it is welcome or unwelcome to you. If your mind wanders off the task, gently bring it back and consciously relax your face muscles. Many people find that they can relax best when listening to certain types of music, or to the recorded sound of water, leaves rustling or bird song.

## Massage in pregnancy

Massage is not just for labour, it is a way of helping you to get in touch with your body, release tension and clear your mind. Massage is also useful for giving your partner a chance to help and feel more involved in your pregnancy. Let him know what feels good, play some relaxing music and light some candles.

## When and where to massage

Ask the person who is massaging you to concentrate on areas other than your bump, which should be given no more than a light stroking.

- **Weeks 1–12** Head or face massage can soothe away headaches. The body should not be massaged.
- **Weeks 13–28** Indigestion and insomnia are common, and massage of the back, shoulders and buttocks will help with relaxation and sleep. The abdomen can be massaged during this time, but only with light, gentle strokes.
- **Weeks 29–40** Massage should now concentrate on the back, neck, shoulders and particularly the legs to relieve fatigue. The lower back and buttocks can be massaged during labour to help the process along.

## Neck and lower back massage

These areas may be the weakest and most troublesome, and muscle tension here often leads to the shoulders being held unnaturally high by the end of the day. Ask the person who is massaging you to follow this step-by-step guide to a neck and lower back massage:

1 Starting at the lower back, with your hands flat on either side of her spine, glide them

**Left:** Allowing your partner to give you a relaxing massage is a way of involving him in the pregnancy.

up her back, across her shoulders and return to the starting position. In all back massage, the pressure is on the up stroke. Repeat this three to five times. Work up her back again, making small circles in opposite directions, until you reach the shoulders. Return as before. Repeat three to five times.

2 Working on one side at a time glide across her shoulder blade. Then separate your hands, bringing one around the shoulder and the other around the armpit, pulling back gently as you return to your starting position. Repeat this three to five times and then move to the other side.

3 Bring your hands gently down to her shoulders and rest them there for about 30 seconds. Then, with your thumbs on the muscle at the back of the neck and your fingers over the front of the shoulders, begin to squeeze the shoulder muscles between the heels of your hands and your fingers, working outwards towards the tops of her arms and then back in. Repeat this three to five times.

4 Splaying your fingers slightly, rest them on either side of her breastbone (sternum), at the top of the breast tissue. With the pads of your fingers, massage the muscle between the upper ribs, working out from the breastbone to the edge of the ribcage. Repeat each stroke three to five times, then move up to the next rib muscle. Ask her to take a few deep breaths between strokes.

# Massage
# Common questions

**Q** Are there any safety precautions I need to be aware of?

**A** You can massage the face and head up to week 12, but should not massage the body at all, and do not use essential oils in any form during this time (see pages 110–111). Do not use intense pressure or vigorous strokes, especially on the abdomen, inner thigh and groin. Do not apply pressure around and across the top of the ankles, because these points relate to the ovaries and the womb. Do not massage varicose or spider veins. Use less pressure over joint areas and work along either side of the spine, not directly over it. You should avoid lying on your back in late pregnancy.

**Q** What are the best positions for receiving a massage?

**A** As your pregnancy progresses, you will need to adopt different positions in order to receive massage, using pillows for support. For a back massage, you may feel more comfortable straddling a straight-backed chair (using a pillow to make yourself comfortable) but, by the fifth month, lying sideways is advisable, with plenty of pillows around your stomach area and under your upper legs. This position is also useful for massage during the early stages of labour.

# Sex during pregnancy

Continuing to have sex during pregnancy is healthy: it helps to exercise your pelvic floor, relaxes you and, if you orgasm, exercises the muscles of the womb. Your baby is safe in the bag of fluid and neither you nor your partner can hurt her.

## What to expect

It is normal to feel more sensual at certain times in your pregnancy than others. Most women find that they experience a sexual peak during mid-pregnancy. This is partly the result of hormones and not having to worry about contraception, and partly because your body feels more voluptuous.

Orgasm can make your uterus contract, so you may feel slightly uncomfortable, but this will not harm your baby. Increased discharge may make your vagina slippery, which can make it harder for your partner to reach orgasm.

In early pregnancy, your breasts may be particularly tender; if that is the case, tell your partner so that he can avoid touching them when you are having sex.

## Three great positions for sex

1 He can be on top, so long as his weight is held off your abdomen.
2 Lying side by side, with your legs over your partner, avoids putting pressure on your bump but enables you to face each other.
3 Kneeling on all fours, with your partner entering you from behind, puts no pressure on your bump, but still provides an opportunity for foreplay.

## True story

**Sexual difficulties**

'After we found out that Martha was pregnant we had a fantastic sex life and were simply overwhelmed with happiness. But when Martha started to show – and I hate to say this – I lost sexual interest in her for a while.

'It wasn't that I didn't love or even fancy her. During the day I was oozing with pride about the size of her bump and how cute she looked waddling around. It made me want to cuddle her all the time. But sexually? I couldn't go there. I made the mistake of likening it to me developing a huge beer belly, and asked her if she would still want to make love to me then. This didn't go down well.

'We know that we're not meant to admit it – and it's probably best that we don't – but looked at dispassionately, the increase in size of your partner is pretty shocking.'

*Greg, partner of Martha, 28 weeks pregnant*

# Sex **Common questions**

**Q** Is it normal to go off sex during pregnancy?

**A** We are all different and, for every woman who goes off sex while she is expecting a baby, there will be another one who feels particularly sensual. Your feelings might change at different times of your pregnancy, too. In the early stages, women sometimes feel too tired and nauseous to enjoy sex and then, later on, when they are feeling better, they find that their bump becomes uncomfortable and not conducive to an active sex life. There are other ways for the two of you to make love apart from sex. Give each other a massage or a cuddle. You will both want to feel loved and give love, so find the most suitable ways of being intimate together.

**Q** When is it not safe to have sex?

**A** If you have a history of miscarriages, premature labour or bleeding in pregnancy, it may be advisable not to have sex, so check with your midwife or doctor first. It is advisable not to have sex if you have a condition called placenta praevia, in which the placenta is lying close to the cervix (see page 130). However, for the majority of women, it is perfectly safe to have sex throughout the pregnancy.

**Q** What are the best positions for sex?

**A** As you get bigger, you will probably need to experiment with positions because you will not want your partner resting on your bump or breasts. Pregnancy is the perfect opportunity to become more adventurous. It is important to

keep a sense of humour because your baby may become active at the most inappropriate moment! As your bump grows you might find it more comfortable being on top of your partner.

**Q** Is it true that sex can trigger the start of labour?

**A** Sex can help to get you into labour towards the end of your pregnancy, but only if your body is ready to do so. Semen contains the hormone prostaglandin, which is the same as the synthetic hormone used to induce labour. Also, when you are aroused, your body releases the hormone oxytocin, which helps to stimulate your uterus and can start contractions.

**Right:** You and your partner can continue to express yourself sexually during pregnancy.

# YOU AND YOUR PARTNER

## Involving your partner

**Some men are fascinated by pregnancy and want to be involved at every stage, while others find it difficult to relate to the unseen changes happening in their partner's body.**

However interested your partner may be in the developing baby, he can only experience this pregnancy through you. Even if he is less than enthusiastic about having a baby, he will probably want to share decisions about antenatal care, tests and the place where your baby will be born. As your pregnancy progresses he may become more actively involved, encouraging your efforts to get fit, or helping to gather information and make decisions about the birth. He may rethink his attitude to work or life in general, make changes in his commitments or start to notice small jobs around the home that have been ignored for months.

## How does your partner feel?

He may feel detached at the beginning of the pregnancy, because he is not experiencing any of the signs or symptoms that, for you, make the pregnancy real. It may be that your partner needs something more tangible before he can really know and accept the pregnancy. You will not look any different and so, in some cases, it is only when he has seen an ultrasound image of the baby, or heard the heartbeat, that the reality will hit him.

Your partner will also have his own concerns about the pregnancy and birth, and about the idea of becoming a parent. He may be anxious about whether he can provide financial security for his family, particularly if you are planning to give up work. Some men might also worry about whether they will be a good father, perhaps because they had a difficult relationship with their own father.

Some men react by withdrawing to ground where they feel more confident; for example, by taking on extra work or spending more time with their friends. If your partner resists taking

## Two tips for **strengthening your relationship**

1 Set aside half an hour a week, with five minutes each to express your feelings without interruption and 20 minutes to discuss anything else that comes up. You will learn about each other and build a framework that makes it easier to deal with issues before they threaten your relationship.

s Taking pleasure in your partner's company helps to fan the flames of love. Try to find activities that you both enjoy, can do together and can keep up after your baby arrives. Family life is challenging; pregnancy is an opportunity to deepen your understanding of each other's needs and strengthen the bond between you.

an active interest in the baby, do not pressure him. He may well change his mind in time: many fathers become less anxious as the pregnancy advances and they begin to adjust to their new role.

## Your relationship

The relationship between you and your partner is bound to alter as you adjust to your new roles. Many couples are concerned about this, but change is not necessarily negative. Pregnancy may bring you and your partner closer together, as you share new and exciting hopes for the future. Many fathers-to-be are both practically and emotionally supportive. However, if your partner seems bewildered or unhelpful try to discuss his worries with him. He may not understand your needs or why you feel the way you do.

Your partner may find It hard to adjust to your pregnancy. You become the focus of everyone's attention and he is expected to support you, but he may be caught up in his own worries. Some men feel proud of their partner's pregnancy, but are still ambivalent about becoming a father.

## His view of sex

Some men are reluctant to make love during pregnancy for fear of hurting the baby. However, it is perfectly safe for most women to have sex throughout their pregnancy, and your partner may need to be reassured that his penis does not go further than the vagina, and that the baby will not be affected.

The arrival of your baby will inevitably change your relationship in some ways and for some couples it is important to spend some quality time together before they become a family. If possible, plan a holiday together before the birth.

**Below:** Feeling the movements of the baby will help your partner begin to bond with his child.

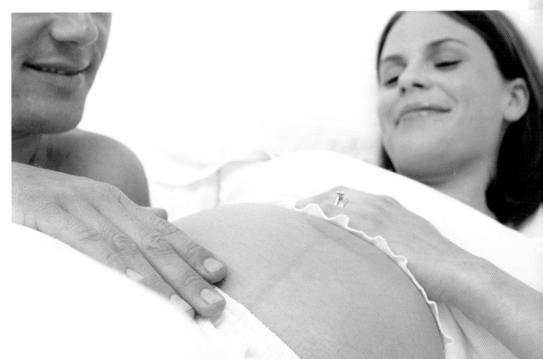

# Travel and pregnancy

The thought of a holiday appeals to many first-time pregnant women because this may be the last chance for time alone together with their partner for some years. Most women feel at their best during mid-pregnancy, when fatigue and nausea are less likely, so this is the ideal time to take a break if work commitments and money allow. Wherever you are going, whether abroad or nearer home, you should take a copy of your antenatal records with you.

## A checklist for travelling abroad

If you are travelling to a foreign country, take a few common sense precautions:

- Ask your doctor whether you need any vaccinations for your destination and which ones are suitable during pregnancy.
- Make sure that your travel insurance covers you for pregnancy-related cancellation and health problems.
- Take a copy of your medical notes with you, including a record of your blood group and any allergies, and contact numbers for your midwife or doctor.

## Deep vein thrombosis

**Pregnant women are at increased risk of deep vein thrombosis (DVT, see pages 132–133). On a long flight you should get up and walk around every couple of hours. Ask for an aisle seat if possible, so that you can stretch your legs and leave your seat easily. You can also wear supportive flight socks that reduce the risk of DVT. Drink water to prevent dehydration and wear slipper socks, as your feet will inevitably swell during the flight. If you are suffering from pregnancy sickness, ask for a seat over the wings as the ride is less bumpy there.**

- Where food and drink are concerned, be absolutely scrupulous about hygiene. Drink bottled water if you have any doubts about the tap water – and remember to avoid ice for the same reasons.
- You may not be able to tolerate the heat as much during pregnancy, so stay in the shade during the hottest part of the day and drink plenty of water to prevent dehydration and keep your body temperature down.

**Below:** A relaxing break may be just what you need – but don't overdo the sun.

# Travel **Common questions**

**Q** Is it safe to continue driving during pregnancy?

**A** It is safe to continue driving while you are pregnant but, as always when travelling long distances, take a break after a couple of hours and walk around. The seatbelt might feel more uncomfortable but it is still important to wear it. Ensure the diagonal strap goes between your breasts and the lap strap goes across the lower part of your hips, flat on your thighs – not across your bump.

**Q** How far into a pregnancy is it safe to fly?

**A** Most airlines will not accept women after 34 weeks of pregnancy onto flights, but check with the individual airline. In some cases it may not be advisable to fly during pregnancy, for example, if you have a history of high blood pressure or premature labour, so check with your doctor first. Also, it is unwise to fly in an unpressurized aircraft because this can significantly reduce the oxygen supply to you and your baby.

**Q** I have always suffered from travel sickness and am used to taking medication for it. Is this safe during pregnancy?

**A** Although some travel sickness medicines are safe for most pregnant women under medical supervision, you may prefer to do without them. 'Travel bands' – stretchy bands worn on the wrists – work on the acupressure point to reduce nausea.

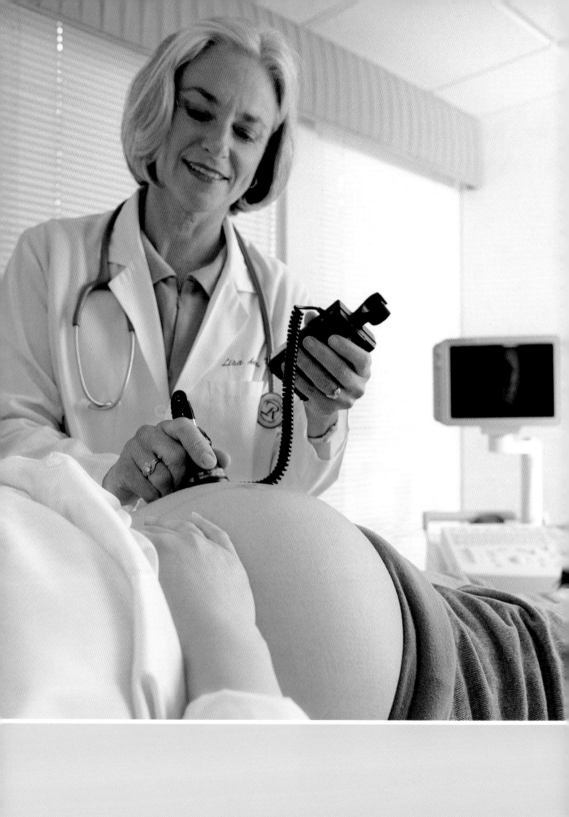

# 5

# complications and common complaints

# Avoiding risks

Being pregnant makes you suddenly very conscious of all the everyday items that might be hazardous to your baby while he is at such a crucial stage of his development. It is obviously good to be concerned about your baby's welfare, but if you become too anxious about everything, you will find it difficult to relax and enjoy your pregnancy.

**Above:** Consult a pharmacist or doctor to check that your medication is safe to use during pregnancy.

## Over-the-counter and prescription drugs

You are just as likely to suffer from everyday illnesses, such as coughs, colds and tummy upsets, when you are pregnant than at any other time, and you may hear conflicting advice about which over-the-counter (OTC) or prescription drugs are safe. If you are in any doubt, check with your pharmacist or doctor, who will be able to give you the most up-to-date advice. Always tell them that you are pregnant, particularly in the early stages, when your pregnancy may not show or may not be in your medical notes.

## Drug treatments for ongoing conditions

With many conditions, for example, diabetes, epilepsy or depression, the most important consideration during pregnancy is that your health should be as good as possible, because your health is vital for the health of

your baby. For this reason, your doctor will always weigh up whether it is better for you to continue with your current medication, to change drugs, or to come off them entirely, and he or she will make the best decision for your particular situation.

## Infectious diseases

You should avoid coming into contact with infectious diseases, especially rubella, chickenpox and mumps. However, the majority of pregnant women are immune to these diseases – you can ask your doctor or midwife to do a blood test if you have any doubt about your own immunity. Apart from fever affecting your baby's development, these diseases carry a number of particular risks: chickenpox may cause fetal malformations in early pregnancy and problems in the newborn; mumps is associated with a slight risk of miscarriage in

# Avoiding risks **Common questions**

**Q** I read that cannabis is one of the few recreational drugs you can use during pregnancy. Is this true?

**A** No. All recreational drugs have potential side-effects and should be avoided at all costs. For example, cannabis affects the production of male sperm for up to nine months after use, and hard drugs (for example, cocaine and heroin) can damage the chromosomes in the sperm and egg, leading to abnormalities in the baby. Sharing syringes also increases the risk of contracting HIV or hepatitis. Use of recreational drugs during pregnancy can cause such problems as miscarriage, low birth weight, congenital abnormalities and even babies born with addictions.

**Q** I am epileptic. What implications will this have on my pregnancy?

**A** If you are epileptic, it is vital to see your doctor for advice before you try to conceive. He or she may advise a change of medication because some drugs have been more thoroughly tested for pregnant women. However, the most important thing for you and your baby is to make sure your seizures are kept to a minimum, so this will be taken into consideration when giving you advice. Your doctor will also advise you to take extra folic acid, as epilepsy drugs can affect your ability to absorb it. You will be carefully monitored throughout your pregnancy to ensure that both you and your baby are fine.

**Q** I suffer from depression and regularly take antidepressants. Can these be harmful to my baby?

**A** Check that your antidepressants are suitable for use during pregnancy. The majority of women who take antidepressants during pregnancy go on to have healthy babies, and drugs are now available that are considered safe for use during pregnancy. Your doctor will be able to advise you on the best way to change or manage your medication to ensure that both you and your baby are protected.

the first 12 weeks; rubella is associated with malformations, such as deafness, blindness and heart disease, especially during the first three months of pregnancy.

## Chemicals

We use an enormous number of chemicals at work and at home and they are not usually harmful if we follow the manufacturer's instructions. However, these chemicals may have a cumulative effect, so it is best to restrict their use during pregnancy, especially during the first three months. Where you can, it is a good idea to use natural cleaning agents – bicarbonate of soda, salt, vinegar and lemon juice – or eco-friendly products. Avoid inhaling vapours from, for example, glue, petrol, paint, oven-cleaners, cleaning fluids and air-fresheners, and use pump-action sprays rather than aerosols.

# Miscarriage

The term 'miscarriage' refers to a pregnancy that is lost before 24 weeks of gestation. Miscarriage occurs after approximately 50 per cent of conceptions. However, in many cases it is not recognized because it happens very early on, within a fortnight of conception, when it is often interpreted as a late period. Miscarriage is clinically diagnosed in only about 15 per cent of pregnancies.

## What happens?

Miscarriage involves the opening of the cervix and a considerable amount of bleeding. There are two types of miscarriage: complete miscarriage, in which the products of conception are completely expelled; and incomplete miscarriage, in which some of the products of conception are retained. In rare cases, these will become infected (septic) and the infection may spread, causing peritonitis and septicaemia.

## Treatment

In some cases, miscarriage can be allowed to progress on its own with no further intervention. If treatment is required, this can be either through the use of drugs to encourage the uterus to expel the products of conception or through an operation, which is called an ERPOC or evacuation of retained products of conception.

**True story**

**Overcoming miscarriage**

'Looking at the rose tree in our garden – planted in memory of the baby we lost – takes me back to when I first discovered I was pregnant. I'd had severe vomiting from early on, but I'd heard that sickness was often a good sign, so I wasn't concerned.

'By my 12-week scan I was feeling a bit better and really excited. My husband, John, and my mum were with me. The screen was facing away from us as the radiographer, who was very quiet, asked me if I was sure about my due dates.

'Then she gave me an internal scan, which I thought was unusual. I was completely unprepared when she said, "I'm really sorry, Cheryl, but it's not good news. The pregnancy isn't viable, I can't find a heartbeat." I remember saying, "but I'm still being sick", and being told that this was because I hadn't expelled the baby, so my body still thought I was pregnant.

'I had to have an operation to remove the lining of the womb, which was really traumatic because I had to have a general anaesthetic, and it took three weeks for the bleeding to stop. But as soon as I'd had a normal period, I was on a mission to get pregnant again.'

*Cheryl, mother of Patrick and Adam*

# Miscarriage **Common questions**

**Q What causes miscarriage?**
**A** Over 50 per cent of miscarriages in early pregnancy are a result of the baby having abnormal chromosomes. There are also a number of less common maternal factors. These include infection, for example, listeriosis, cytomegalovirus or rubella; an underlying medical disorder, for example, thyroid disease or systemic lupus erythematosus; smoking; alcohol; older age of the mother.

In rare cases, miscarriage is caused by a congenital abnormality of the uterus or cervix. A miscarriage in mid-pregnancy may be due to the cervix dilating unusually early (cervical incompetence), possibly caused by previous cervical surgery, for example a large cone biopsy after abnormal smear tests.

**Q What is meant by recurrent miscarriage and why does it happen?**
**A** This is the term used to refer to three or more consecutive miscarriages. Recurrent miscarriage happens in 1 per cent of women. If you suffer from the condition, the underlying causes will need to be investigated. Possible causes of recurrent miscarriage include genetic abnormality in either parent; abnormality of the uterus; chronic illness, for example, thyroid disease or diabetes (see pages 136–139); raised levels of testosterone or luteinizing hormone (LH); cervical incompetence (see above); or the blood-clotting disorder antiphospholid syndrome.

Another cause is polycystic ovary syndrome (PCOS), which is common, affecting 1 in 10 women at one stage, and characterized by multiple small cysts within the ovary. It features irregular periods and reduced fertility, as well as excessive hair growth and acne. The condition is associated with being overweight.

**Q How soon after a miscarriage can I start to try again?**
**A** There are no strict rules about when to try for another baby. Many women are advised to wait for a few months, mainly so that their cycle can return to normal and to make it easier to know how many weeks pregnant they are when they manage to conceive.

**Below:** Discussing feelings openly can help both parents deal with the trauma of miscarriage.

# Ectopic pregnancies

An ectopic pregnancy occurs when a fertilized egg implants outside of the uterus, usually in the Fallopian tube or, more rarely, in the ovary or abdominal cavity. Ectopic pregnancy can be life-threatening. The main danger arises when the pregnancy occurs in the Fallopian tube and causes a rupture, in which case major internal bleeding, shock and collapse can ensue.

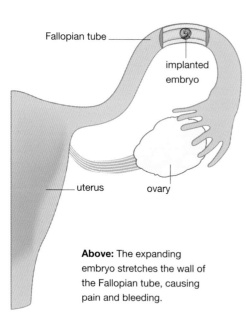

Fallopian tube

implanted embryo

uterus          ovary

**Above:** The expanding embryo stretches the wall of the Fallopian tube, causing pain and bleeding.

## Symptoms

Most women with an ectopic pregnancy complain of a missed or abnormal last period, vaginal bleeding or abdominal pain. However, not all women have these classic symptoms. Therefore an ectopic pregnancy should be suspected in any woman of reproductive age who has abdominal pain.

## Diagnosis

Early diagnosis is vital whenever an ectopic pregnancy is suspected, for example, when the uterus is found to be empty or, in some cases, when a mass is seen next to the uterus. Investigations such as an ultrasound scan – which is often performed transvaginally – and blood tests are useful in diagnosis. Carrying out a laparoscopy will enable the obstetrician to inspect the Fallopian tubes and pelvis and will confirm the diagnosis.

## Five risk factors for an **ectopic pregnancy**

1 A previous ectopic pregnancy.
2 A history of pelvic inflammatory disease (for example, chlamydia infection).
3 Previous tubal surgery (for example, reversal of a sterilization procedure).
4 Conception while on the mini-pill or with a coil in place.
5 Fertility treatment (for example, ovulation induction or in vitro fertilization).

# Ectopic pregnancies **Common questions**

**Q** What is the procedure if an ectopic pregnancy is detected?

**A** Treatment of an ectopic pregnancy is aimed mainly at preventing major haemorrhage and most commonly involves an operation that is performed on the affected Fallopian tube. It may be necessary to remove the tube, or the ectopic pregnancy itself can be removed while preserving the tube. Nowadays, this can often be done by using keyhole surgery, but it may be necessary to make an incision (usually just below the bikini line) in the abdomen, particularly if the ectopic pregnancy has ruptured the Fallopian tube. If the tube ruptures, a blood transfusion may be required.

In some cases, it may be possible to treat a small ectopic pregnancy with powerful drugs designed to stop it growing, thereby avoiding the risk of it rupturing or the need for surgery.

**Q** What are the consequences of an ectopic pregnancy? Will it happen again, for example?

**A** The conditions that originally gave rise to the ectopic pregnancy, and its treatment, may affect subsequent fertility. Approximately 65 per cent of women are pregnant again within 18 months of an ectopic pregnancy. In subsequent pregnancies, women who have had a previous ectopic pregnancy will usually be advised to have an early ultrasound scan, at about seven weeks gestation, in order to determine whether the pregnancy is within the uterus or not.

**Q** Will a pregnancy test show positive in ectopic pregnancy?

**A** A urine home pregnancy test will be positive in almost all instances of ectopic pregnancy, but it might be only weakly positive. A blood test will always be positive in an ectopic pregnancy.

*'Having reported a minor pain in my abdomen and the passing of a little blood to my doctor, I was referred to hospital. After an internal scan and a blood test I was told that I had an ectopic pregnancy and that I would have to have it surgically removed that day. The procedure itself was relatively simple – keyhole surgery under general anaesthetic to remove the pregnancy and part of my now damaged Fallopian tube – but I was not prepared for the shock of emergency surgery, losing part of my reproductive system (could I conceive again?) and of going into the hospital six weeks pregnant and coming out not pregnant the following day.'*

*Sally, mother of Sam*

# PLACENTAL PROBLEMS

## Knowing what to look for

**The placenta is vital to the baby's continuing wellbeing in the uterus (see pages 56–57). Problems concerning the placenta can therefore have important consequences for the baby, during both the pregnancy and the birth.**

### Placenta praevia

This occurs when the placenta is situated in the lower part of the uterus. The main danger is major bleeding, which normally occurs after about 30 weeks. Although the 20-week scan often shows the placenta to be 'low-lying', in most cases the placenta moves upwards, out of the way of the cervix. As a result, by late pregnancy, fewer than 1 per cent of pregnancies show placenta praevia. Risk factors include:

- Previous placenta praevia
- A previous caesarean section
- A larger than usual placenta (for example, twin pregnancies).

### Symptoms

Classic symptoms include recurrent episodes of painless, heavy vaginal bleeding. It's not known why this happens before labour. During labour it is the result of the placenta lying over the dilating cervix and coming away from the uterine wall.

### Diagnosis

Diagnosis may be achieved through an ultrasound scan or, particularly when the placenta is at the back of the uterus, a transvaginal scan, which will show how close the leading edge of the placenta is to the cervix. Another indication, apart from bleeding,

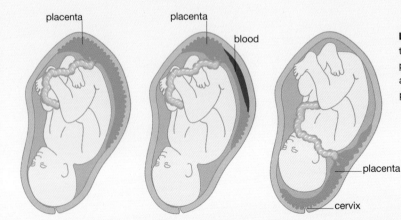

placenta

placenta

blood

placenta

cervix

**Left:** From left to right: the placenta in a normal position; placental abruption; and placenta praevia.

is the baby's failure to engage into the pelvis. Instead, she adopts a variety of positions (an unstable lie, see page 205) because the placenta prevents her from adopting the 'head-down' position of late pregnancy.

## Treatment

A blood transfusion may be necessary if bleeding is excessive. The mother may be advised to rest and avoid sexual intercourse. A placenta that is very close to the cervix will prevent a normal birth, so a caesarean section will be advised.

# Placental abruption

This happens when the placenta detaches from the uterus wall. It occurs in about 1 per cent of pregnancies and results in bleeding, which may not be apparent, depending on how close to the cervix the placenta is situated. Risk factors include:

• Previous placental abruption
• High blood pressure
• Abdominal injury
• Smoking
• Use of cocaine
• Pregnancy later in life
• Several previous pregnancies.

## Blood clotting

Any major haemorrhage can disturb the blood-clotting system. These disturbances are more common after a placental abruption because the amount of bleeding may be very much greater than that revealed. Other conditions, such as pre-eclampsia (in which abruption can occur), can also directly affect the mother's blood-clotting system.

## Symptoms

Symptoms of placental abruption include severe abdominal pain and bleeding. With a severe abruption the uterus will be tender and rigid. The amount of blood lost through the vagina may not accurately reflect the true amount of bleeding, as blood can be concealed within the uterus. This is a risk to the baby and also to the mother, who may develop major problems with blood clotting.

## Treatment

This depends on the abruption's severity. A mild abruption may only require a period of observation in hospital. Severe cases may require resuscitation of the mother and early delivery by caesarean section.

# Retained placenta

The third stage of labour is the delivery of the placenta. In 1–2 per cent of pregnancies the placenta fails to come out, despite carefully pulling on the umbilical cord. In these circumstances, the mother is at risk of post-partum bleeding because the uterus is unable to contract properly.

## Treatment

A short wait of an hour or so may resolve the problem. If not, it may be necessary to remove the placenta manually. This is done under anaesthetic (usually an epidural or a spinal). The obstetrician gently uses fingers to separate the placenta from the wall of the uterus. Once the placenta has been removed, the mother will be given oxytocin intravenously to help the uterus contract and thus reduce further blood loss. Antibiotics will usually be recommended because of the increased risk of infection.

# Special-care pregnancies

Pregnancy imposes many stresses and strains on healthy women. However, if you already have a condition such as high blood pressure, heart disease, thyroid disease or asthma, you will be naturally concerned about the effects of the condition on your pregnancy and also about the effects of your pregnancy on the condition.

## High blood pressure

Some women already have high blood pressure (or hypertension) when they become pregnant. Others may be diagnosed as having hypertension during the pregnancy. The main problems that are associated with hypertension during pregnancy are the increased risks of developing pre-eclampsia, reduced blood flow through the placenta, affecting the growth of your baby or having a placental abruption (see page 131).

## Deep vein thrombosis and pulmonary embolism

During a normal pregnancy, the mother's blood clots more easily than it would do if she were not pregnant. This is so the amount of blood lost at birth is reduced. Having slightly thicker blood puts all pregnant women at risk of clots in the legs (deep vein thrombosis, or DVT) or lungs (pulmonary embolism, or PE). There are additional factors, as well as pregnancy, that

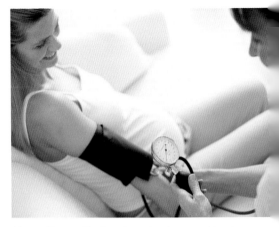

**Above:** If you suffer from hypertension, your blood pressure will be closely monitored.

## HIV/AIDS

In most countries pregnant women are encouraged to have an HIV test. If a woman accepts screening, she is talked through the procedure and the possible consequences, and asked to give her consent. If the results of the test are positive, she will be offered counselling. The aim of treatment is to lower the chances of HIV infecting the baby. Giving the mother antiretroviral drugs during the last few months of pregnancy reduces the risk of the baby acquiring the infection. HIV-positive pregnant women will normally be advised to have an elective caesarean section and to bottle- rather than breastfeed.

All babies born to HIV-positive mothers start life with HIV antibodies, but this does not automatically mean that they are infected, as these are the mother's antibodies. The baby will be given a series of tests over the ensuing months to monitor the levels of the virus in the bloodstream.

# Special-care pregnancies **Common questions**

**Q What causes high blood pressure and can it be treated?**

**A** In most cases, the cause of the hypertension is unknown (referred to as essential hypertension) while a minority of women have an underlying cause, for example, kidney or heart disease. If you are already taking antihypertensives, your obstetrician will advise you whether to continue taking your medication. If you are not, he or she will decide whether your blood pressure is high enough to warrant starting medication. It can be stabilized with drugs known as antihypertensives, the dosage of which may be adjusted according to the stability of your blood pressure. A close eye will be kept on your blood pressure throughout your pregnancy, and you will be given extra scans to monitor your baby's growth. Raised blood pressure can be an indicator of pre-eclampsia (see pages 142–143).

**Q Can deep vein thrombosis be treated?**

**A** Deep vein thrombosis (DVT) and pulmonary embolism (PE) are potentially life-threatening complications. If you are at risk, your doctor may advise you to take blood-thinning drugs during and immediately after your pregnancy to prevent a clot developing. If your doctor suspects a blood clot, you will be referred to hospital for tests to confirm the diagnosis. If a clot is found, you will be given drugs (usually by an injection into the skin but sometimes through a vein) to prevent the clot worsening.

**Q What happens if I am diagnosed with heart disease?**

**A** If you become pregnant and have significant heart disease, your doctor will refer you to a specialist clinic where you can receive the best advice and appropriate tests, such as an echocardiogram (an ultrasound of your heart). Your condition will also be monitored regularly.

increase the risk of blood clots. These factors include obesity, greater age, having a caesarean section, a history of a previous blood clot, pre-eclampsia, immobility (for example, during long-haul flights), and thicker blood caused by a tendency to excessive blood clotting (or thrombophilia).

The symptoms of a DVT are swelling, redness, pain and tenderness in the calf muscle, while breathlessness, chest pain on breathing in, a cough and coughing up blood may indicate the presence of a PE.

## Heart disease

In a normal pregnancy, significant changes occur in the cardiovascular system. These include an increase in heart output of almost 50 per cent; an increase in heart rate of up to 20 beats per minute; and a lowering of blood pressure in early and mid-pregnancy. These changes often lead to the discovery of an innocent heart murmur, which can be heard through a stethoscope thanks to increased blood flow. Labour places an additional strain on the heart.

# Special-care pregnancies

## Thyroid disease

It is normal for the thyroid gland, which is situated at the front of the neck, to increase in size during pregnancy. This is due to the increase in blood flow that occurs during pregnancy. However, the gland can cause problems if it is overactive (hyperthyroidism) or underactive (hypothyroidism).

## Sickle-cell anaemia

Sickle-cell anaemia is a genetic disorder that mainly affects people of Afro-Caribbean origin, as well as some people from the Mediterranean region, the Middle East and Asia. People who suffer from sickle-cell anaemia have abnormal haemoglobin that becomes distorted (sickle-shaped) under conditions of stress, blocking small blood vessels and causing severe pain and sickle-cell crises. The stress of pregnancy may be sufficient to trigger a sickle-cell crisis.

## Asthma

During normal pregnancy, your body's demand for oxygen is increased. Breathing increases by approximately 50 per cent, usually as a consequence of breathing more deeply rather than more quickly. As a result, you may experience slight breathlessness. However, respiratory diseases, such as asthma, can also cause you to feel breathless, and this can lead to difficulties in diagnosis. Asthma also causes coughing, wheeziness and chest tightness, often in response to allergens, such as pollen, or after exercise. Asthma does not usually cause any significant harm to the pregnancy, although severe asthma may restrict the baby's growth or cause premature labour.

## Thalassaemia

Thalassaemia is a genetic disorder that causes abnormality of the proteins making up the respiratory pigment haemoglobin. There are two types of thalassaemia: alpha thalassaemia, which is common in women from southeast Asia; and beta thalassaemia, which is common in women from Cyprus and Asia. If only one of the genes for haemoglobin is faulty, then the condition is known as a thalassaemia trait. This may be detected for the first time during your pregnancy, when you are given a routine blood test for anaemia.

*'I've had asthma since I was a small child. I use inhaled steroids twice a day and I also have a ventolin inhaler. When I became pregnant my doctor lowered my dose but at 20 weeks I caught a chest infection and had to go back onto my normal dose. I was worried Ben would be affected but he was absolutely fine.'*

Sam, *mother of Ben*

## Special-care pregnancies **Common questions**

**Q** I have read that treatments for thyroid disease can be potentially harmful for the baby. Is this true?

**A** If you have hyperthyroidism, your doctor will prescribe antithyroid drugs. These can cross the placenta and cause fetal hypothyroidism, so the lowest possible doses of the drug must be used. Your paediatrician should be made aware of your condition so that your baby can be checked after the birth. It is usually safe to breastfeed. Hypothyroidism is treated with thyroxine, and very little of this crosses the placenta so your baby would not be at risk of side-effects.

**Q** What is the treatment for thalassaemia?

**A** If you have the thalassaemia trait, you may need iron and folate supplements throughout your pregnancy, particularly if your ferritin levels (a measure of your iron levels) are low. If your partner also has the trait, you should be referred for further tests because there is a risk that your baby may have the more serious condition, known as thalassaemia major.

**Q** What risks are involved with sickle-cell anaemia and how is it treated?

**A** Pregnant women with sickle-cell anaemia have an increased risk of miscarriage, premature labour, stillbirth and pre-eclampsia, as well as deep vein thrombosis, pulmonary embolism, urinary tract infection and puerperal sepsis. The baby is also more likely to suffer from growth restriction and fetal distress. If you have sickle-cell anaemia, you should be referred to an antenatal clinic that is used to dealing with high-risk pregnancies, where there are obstetricians and haematologists at hand.

**Q** What happens if I develop obstetric cholestasis?

**A** If you are diagnosed as having OC, your baby should be monitored at regular intervals. You may be offered vitamin K to reduce the chance of bleeding. You may also be given antihistamines to relieve the itching, although ursodeoxycholic acid, which reduces the level of bile acids circulating in the blood, is more effective. It is usually advisable to induce labour at 37–38 weeks. The likelihood of OC recurring in future pregnancies is about 90 per cent.

## Cholestasis

Obstetric cholestasis (OC) is characterized by severe itching that normally affects the arms and legs, particularly the palms of the hands and soles of the feet, and the trunk. It develops during the last three months of pregnancy. Blood tests usually show abnormalities in liver function and an increase in bile acids, but other causes of itching, such as hepatitis or gallstones, need to be excluded. In OC, the mother is at increased risk of bleeding after the birth and the baby is more likely to be stillborn or suffer from fetal distress.

# Diabetes in pregnancy
## Pre-existing diabetes

Diabetes is a disorder that prevents the body from using food properly. Normally, the body's principal source of energy is glucose. After being digested in the stomach, the sugars and starches found in your diet enter the bloodstream in the form of glucose, a sugar that becomes a source of energy. The body utilizes the hormone insulin to get the glucose from the bloodstream to the muscles and other tissues of the body. If you have diabetes, the body either does not produce enough insulin or is resistant to it.

## The role of insulin

Insulin is manufactured by the pancreas, a gland lying behind the stomach. Without insulin, glucose cannot get into the cells of the body, where it is used as fuel. Instead, high levels of glucose accumulate in the blood, from where the glucose spills into the urine via the kidneys. This condition is known as diabetes. The common symptoms of diabetes include frequent passing of urine, exceptional thirst and a dry mouth.

If you have diabetes before pregnancy (that is, pre-existing diabetes), it will be one of two types:

• **Type 1** or insulin-dependent diabetes mellitus (IDDM), which was formerly called juvenile onset diabetes. This results from the failure of the pancreas to produce enough insulin.

• **Type 2** or non-insulin-dependent diabetes mellitus (NIDDM), formerly called maturity onset diabetes. This is caused by the body becoming resistant to insulin so that it cannot use it efficiently. It is much more common than type 1 diabetes.

## Effect of pregnancy

Pregnancy itself makes the body resistant to insulin because of the anti-insulin effects of the pregnancy hormones released from the placenta. In normal pregnancy, the body produces almost double the amount of insulin. However, if the pancreas fails to produce enough insulin, pre-existing diabetes can become worse or diabetes can develop for the first time (for more on gestational diabetes, see pages 138–139).

## Management of pre-existing diabetes

If you have pre-existing diabetes, your doctor should refer you to a specialized clinic, where you will be able to see an obstetric/diabetic team. This team will comprise an obstetrician, a midwife, a diabetic physician, a diabetic nurse, a dietician and an ophthalmologist (who will check for any diabetic damage to the retina of the eye).

The main aim of any treatment is to achieve near-normal glucose levels. This will entail:

• Frequent monitoring of your blood glucose, which you will be able to carry out at home.

**Above:** A diet low in sugar and fat and high in fibre helps prevent blood glucose levels falling too low.

- Changes in your insulin dosage, if this is thought necessary.
- The avoidance of oral diabetic drugs during pregnancy, because these can produce low blood glucose levels in your developing baby.
- Paying particular attention to your diet: a low-sugar, low-fat, high-fibre diet with regular snacks can prevent your blood glucose levels falling too low.

## Scans

If you have pre-existing diabetes, you will also be given a series of scans:
- An early scan to date the pregnancy.
- A detailed anomaly scan at 20 weeks to check your baby for any structural abnormalities.
- Serial scans to check your baby's growth and the amount of amniotic fluid surrounding your baby. (The quantity of amniotic fluid sometimes becomes increased in diabetic pregnancies, a condition known as polyhydramnios.)

## Risks of poorly controlled diabetes

Poorly controlled diabetes during pregnancy can have adverse effects on mother and baby.
- **Risks to the mother** There is an increased risk of miscarriage, pre-eclampsia (see pages 142–143) and infection, particularly of the urinary tract and respiratory system. In addition, the high-risk nature of these pregnancies increases the likelihood of a caesarean section being necessary.
- **Risks to the baby** Excess glucose from blood of a mother with pre-existing diabetes can cross the placenta and enter the fetus, causing abnormalities, particularly during the first three months, when most of the organs are forming. Common abnormalities include heart, skeleton and neural tube defects (for example, spina bifida). Fetuses of diabetic women are often larger but their growth may be restricted. There is also a five to tenfold increased risk of the baby dying during late pregnancy and the few weeks after the birth, which is why it is important that diabetes is monitored and well controlled. In addition, newborn babies sometimes suffer from complications, for example, respiratory distress syndrome and jaundice.

## Birth

If you have pre-existing diabetes, the birth will usually be planned for 38–39 weeks, with the options of induction of labour or caesarean section. You may be given intravenous infusions of insulin and dextrose during your labour to control your blood glucose levels.

# Diabetes in pregnancy
## Gestational diabetes

About 5 per cent of women, especially those from the Indian subcontinent and southeast Asia, develop diabetes for the first time during pregnancy. As well as the implications for the pregnancy, women with gestational diabetes have a 50 per cent chance of developing type 2 diabetes within the next 10–15 years.

## Management

Many units screen women who are at particular risk, such as those with a personal or family history of gestational diabetes, a previous large baby or a large baby in the current pregnancy, unexplained stillbirth, obesity, high levels of glucose in the urine (glycosuria) and excess amniotic fluid (polyhydramnios). If it is thought that you have gestational diabetes, your midwife or doctor will arrange a 'glucose tolerance test' to establish the diagnosis. This test measures your blood glucose levels after you have taken a sweet glucose drink.

In most cases, gestational diabetes will respond to a low-fat, increased fibre diet and altered carbohydrate intake. Avoiding sugary foods can lead to improvements, although an insulin dosage may become necessary. Regular scans to check your baby's growth are advisable.

**Below:** A glucose tolerance test is used to establish a diagnosis of gestational diabetes.

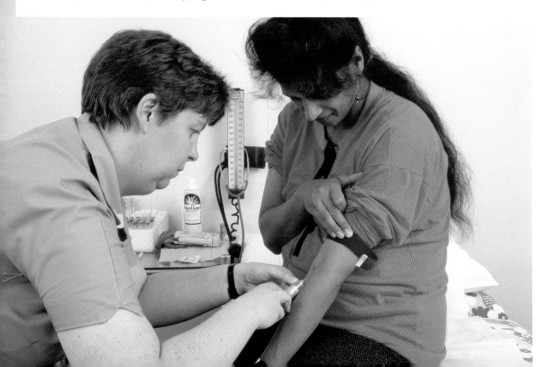

# Diabetes **Common questions**

**Q** I have pre-existing diabetes. Should I talk to my doctor about having a baby before I try to conceive?

**A** Yes, if you have diabetes and are planning to become pregnant, you should talk to your doctor first. He or she can explain about any possible risks and can arrange for you to receive the best advice and care both before and throughout your pregnancy. It is very important to get counselling about good diabetic control when you are planning to become pregnant. This can significantly reduce the risk of your baby having a congenital abnormality, as well as improving the outcome of your pregnancy. Talk to your doctor about improving the management of your diabetes and, as in all pregnancies, take folic acid to reduce the risk of spina bifida.

**Q** How will I know if I have developed gestational diabetes?

**A** At antenatal checks, your midwife will test for sugar in your urine. If she suspects you might have developed diabetes, she will refer you for a glucose load, or tolerance, test. This involves having a series of blood tests and taking a very sweet glucose drink, to determine the body's ability to break down sugar in the blood. The diagnosis will be made after an abnormal result of such a test.

**Q** I am diabetic. Will this have an effect on my baby?

**A** Babies of diabetic mothers are more likely to be large (9 lb/4 kg and more). Women with poorly controlled insulin-dependent diabetes run a higher risk of having a baby with congenital abnormalities, such as a heart defect, and those with gestational diabetes are more likely to develop pre-eclampsia. Overall, however, most women with diabetes have a normal pregnancy and a healthy baby.

**Q** Will I need to have a caesarean section?

**A** The growth of your baby will be closely monitored, and if it is thought that she is very large, your labour may be induced. If this is the case, the risk of a caesarean increases. Some women may be advised to have a caesarean if it is felt they will not respond favourably to an induced labour. This is a major operation, so the decision to do it will not be taken lightly.

**Q** What happens once the baby is born?

**A** Some insulin-dependent diabetic women find it takes a few days for their baby's blood sugar levels to stabilize. These newborns may need to go to the special-care baby unit for observation, particularly if labour was induced before 37 weeks. Most women with gestational diabetes find it disappears once the baby is born, but you will have a check-up three months later. The risk of developing type 2 diabetes increases in women who have had gestational diabetes, so they will be advised to stick to the diet and exercise regime that was recommended in pregnancy.

# RHESUS DISEASE

## Development of Rhesus incompatibility

**If you develop antibodies to the Rhesus factor after giving birth, fetal anaemia can result in a subsequent pregnancy.**

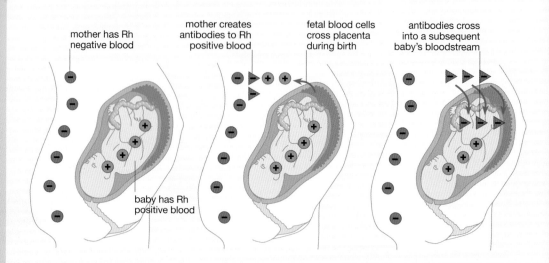

mother has Rh negative blood

mother creates antibodies to Rh positive blood

fetal blood cells cross placenta during birth

antibodies cross into a subsequent baby's bloodstream

baby has Rh positive blood

Everyone is born with a certain blood type (A, B, AB or O) and Rhesus factor (Rh positive or Rh negative). If both you and the father are Rh negative, there is no danger of your developing Rhesus incompatibility, because your baby will also be Rh negative. However, if you are Rh negative but the father is Rh positive, your baby may be Rh positive and you may become sensitized to the Rhesus factor in your baby's blood.

This can happen if some of the baby's blood cells cross the placenta and enter your bloodstream during birth. If you are not given an Anti-D injection within 72 hours of the birth, you may develop antibodies to the Rhesus

**Above, left to right:** The development of Rhesus incompatibility.

factor – to your baby's red blood cells. These antibodies may also be produced during miscarriage or termination.

Developing antibodies to the Rhesus factor during a first pregnancy is not usually a problem. However, in any subsequent pregnancies, if the baby is again Rh positive, the antibodies to the Rhesus factor in your body can cross the placenta and destroy your baby's red cells, leading to fetal anaemia. After the birth, the destruction of red blood cells results in high levels of bilirubin (a yellow pigment produced by the breakdown of the blood cells). As well as making your baby appear jaundiced, this can also be harmful to his brain.

## Symptoms and diagnosis

The severity of Rhesus disease depends on the quantity of the baby's blood cells that have been destroyed by antibodies. The condition ranges from mild disease, in which the baby is found to be slightly anaemic at birth, to severe disease, in which the baby suffers heart failure in the uterus.

A warning sign of Rhesus disease is the presence of Anti-D antibodies in the mother's blood. If you are found to have high levels of Anti-D antibodies, your obstetrician will recommend regular ultrasound monitoring of your baby to keep an eye on his progress.

## Treatment

If your baby has Rhesus disease, he can be treated either while he is still in the uterus or after the birth:

- **In the uterus** If your baby seems to be anaemic, a fetal blood sample can be taken. If this confirms anaemia, he can be given a blood transfusion. This procedure may need to be repeated until he is developed enough for birth.
- **After the birth** Treatment depends on the severity of your baby's jaundice and anaemia. In mild cases of jaundice, bilirubin levels may respond to light therapy (phototherapy). In more severe cases, an exchange blood transfusion may be considered necessary.

In former years, if there was any suspicion that a baby might be suffering from anaemia, an amniocentesis was performed. Nowadays, this procedure has largely been replaced by the use of a cerebral Doppler to measure the blood flow to the baby's brain. A very high blood flow is an indication that the baby may be anaemic.

Recently, it has become possible to tell whether a baby is Rhesus positive or negative from a blood sample taken from the mother. If, for example, Rhesus disease is suspected, discovering that the baby is Rhesus negative is very reassuring.

## Prevention

One of the greatest success stories in obstetrics is how rare Rhesus disease has become. The condition now appears much less frequently, as a result of the increased use of injections of the blood product Anti-D in Rh negative women who are considered to be at risk of Rhesus disease. Anti-D injections successfully prevent Rhesus disease by destroying any fetal cells that enter the mother's circulation before she has a chance to produce any antibodies.

Anti-D is routinely given to the mother after the birth (within 72 hours) if the baby is shown to be Rh positive. In recent years, Anti-D injections have also been advised at 28 and 34 weeks. Anti-D is recommended for pregnant Rh negative women after certain events (for example, miscarriage, threatened miscarriage – if this occurs after 12 weeks – or 'trauma' to the abdomen, such as a fall or car accident), and following certain procedures that carry a risk that fetal blood could cross the placenta (for example, amniocentesis or chorionic villus sampling, see pages 194–195).

# Pre-eclampsia and eclampsia

Pre-eclampsia occurs only during pregnancy (generally after 20 weeks) and during the period just after the birth. It can affect both the mother and the unborn baby. It is a complication of around 1 in 10 pregnancies overall and affects 1 in 50 severely. Pre-eclampsia is a major cause of growth restriction in the uterus and perinatal mortality.

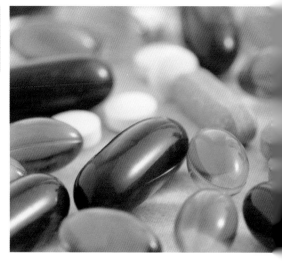

**Above:** Pre-eclampsia may be averted by low doses of aspirin and some vitamins. Consult your doctor.

## What happens?

A small proportion of women with pre-eclampsia (2 per cent) go on to develop convulsions, known as eclampsia. Risk factors for pre-eclampsia include:

- A first pregnancy
- Being pregnant with twins or triplets
- A new partner (pre-eclampsia is thought to be caused by a defect in the placenta, which may be affected by the genetic make-up of the fetus)
- Previous pre-eclampsia or a family history of pre-eclampsia (for example, in a sister or mother)
- A pre-existing medical problem, for example, high blood pressure (see page 132) or diabetes (see pages 136–137).
- Maternal age of over 40 or less than 18 years.

## Screening

All pregnant women should have their blood pressure monitored regularly and their urine tested. Women who are at particular risk of developing pre-eclampsia may be offered extra tests, for example, blood tests to check kidney and liver function, and blood counts. Ultrasound scanning of the uterine artery (by Doppler measurements) can detect any abnormalities in blood flow at 20–24 weeks. Women with a decreased blood flow are at greater risk of developing disease.

*'I went to see my midwife as my legs were so swollen I couldn't get my shoes on. I had no other symptoms, so was horrified when she said, after checking my blood pressure, that she thought I had pre-eclampsia and that I would need to be admitted to hospital immediately.'*

*Angela, mother of Matthew*

# Pre-eclampsia **Common questions**

**Q What are the causes of pre-eclampsia?**

**A** Although the exact causes of pre-eclampsia are not fully understood, current understanding suggests that the placenta is mainly responsible. Failure of the fertilized egg to implant properly in the uterus results in the placenta receiving less blood from the mother's uterine arteries. This triggers a sequence of events that can harm the mother, especially her cardiovascular, urinary and central nervous systems and her liver. It also affects her blood-clotting mechanism, can adversely affect the growth of the fetus and increases the risk of placental abruption (see page 131).

**Q Are there any specific symptoms?**

**A** Symptoms include visual disturbance (such as flashing lights), headache, upper abdominal pain, vomiting and rapidly worsening swelling (for example, of the legs and ankles). However, most women do not complain of symptoms when the condition first arises, so diagnosis depends on the vigilance of the midwife or doctor. Therefore, pre-eclampsia is more commonly diagnosed when classic signs of high blood pressure, high levels of protein in the urine (proteinuria) and swelling appear. Pre-eclampsia is an enigmatic condition that presents itself in a great variety of ways, so it is not always easy to spot. Blood tests are also useful in diagnosis.

Eclampsia is diagnosed when convulsions (fits) occur alongside symptoms of pre-eclampsia. Of these seizures, 44 per cent occur post-natally, 38 per cent before birth and 18 per cent during birth.

**Q How is pre-eclampsia treated?**

**A** The only cure for pre-eclampsia is birth of the fetus and placenta. However, for women with only mild disease, the course of action is usually to continue the pregnancy until it is safe to deliver the baby. On the other hand, if the condition is severe or life-threatening, which unfortunately can occur early in pregnancy, there may be only a few hours in which to act. Treatment therefore depends on the severity of the disease and the length of time for which the baby has been developing.

Blood pressure treatment is sometimes advisable, either in the longer term in mild disease (for example, with oral medication) or in the short term (often with intravenous drugs), as part of an intensive treatment regime aimed at stabilizing the mother's condition before birth. In severe cases, intravenous magnesium sulphate is commonly used in order to prevent eclampsia occurring.

**Q How can I prevent pre-eclampsia?**

**A** Low doses of aspirin (75 mg/day) – or calcium, vitamins C and E and folic acid – may help to prevent pre-eclampsia in women who are particularly at risk. However, you should always consult with a doctor before taking any course of action.

# Common complaints during pregnancy

Changing hormone levels and your growing baby can have unexpected effects on your appearance and how you feel. The following charts feature brief descriptions of the common and less common complaints that women experience during pregnancy, together with practical suggestions for coping with them. This is only a guide. If in doubt, always consult your doctor or midwife.

| Complaint/condition | Description | Action |
| --- | --- | --- |
| **Skin conditions** | | |
| Heat rash | Heat rash, especially under the breasts and in the groin, is common. Most pregnant women sweat more, and sweat trapped in the glands gives rise to itchy pimples. | • Wear a support bra.<br>• Wash regularly and dust with unscented talcum powder.<br>• Try moisturizers and avoid excessive weight gain if possible. |
| Itchy stomach | Nearly all women get an itchy stomach, caused by skin stretching and becoming thinner, resulting in loss of moisture and dryness.<br>    Other common skin conditions that may coincide with pregnancy, or be aggravated by it, include eczema, urticaria and scabies. | • Use gentle soap and massage your skin with a mild moisturizing lotion to soften it.<br>• To relieve itching, try a simple moisturizer or a safe anti-itching remedy. A cool bath may help.<br>• Mention the itchiness to your midwife if it persists. |
| Pigmentation changes – general | A general increase in pigmentation is normal. More marked in dark-haired women, it mostly affects the nipples, genital area and abdomen. Some changes are permanent.<br>    Freckles and moles may darken, often fading back to normal soon after the birth. The number and size of moles may increase. | • If you notice any new mole, or any change in the appearance of existing moles, including size, shape and colour, or itching or bleeding, you must see your doctor immediately. |

| Complaint/condition | Description | Action |
|---|---|---|
| Pigmentation changes – chloasma | Also known as the 'mask of pregnancy', this butterfly-shaped pigmentation appears on the face of 70 per cent of pregnant women. It sometimes appears as small blotches but almost always fades after the birth. Chloasma is caused by a combination of oestrogen, other hormones and sunlight. | • If the marks bother you, use concealer make-up that matches your skin tone. Do not try to bleach dark marks: it is unlikely to work and it is best to avoid chemicals during pregnancy. |
| Pigmentation changes – linea nigra | This is a dark line that appears down the centre of the abdomen and usually fades after the birth of your baby. It is caused by increased levels of hormones and is nothing to worry about. | None |
| Polymorphic eruption of pregnancy (PEP) | Some women get itchy pimples in their stretch marks. This usually occurs in the last three months of a first pregnancy or, more rarely, shortly after birth. The pimples disappear after birth and are less severe in subsequent pregnancies, if they recur at all. | • Your doctor may prescribe a cream to ease the problem. |
| Red or itchy palms or soles of the feet | Some women develop red, itchy palms and some get red itchy soles to their feet. This is a side-effect of oestrogen in the blood (but see also Cholestasis, page 135). | • Always tell your midwife or doctor so they can rule out the possibility of cholestasis.<br>• Moisturize your hands and wear rubber gloves for housework. |

| Complaint/condition | Description | Action |
|---|---|---|
| Skin dryness | Many women with dry skin find that it gets even drier during mid-pregnancy. This is an effect of increasing oestrogen levels.<br><br>Ultimately, changes to the skin will depend on your individual response to the different pregnancy hormones in your body. | • Drink plenty of water.<br>• Air conditioning and central heating can be very drying to the skin. Hang humidifiers from your radiators and make sure that you get fresh air every day.<br>• Use a gentle face wash instead of soap. At night, use a rich moisturizer designed to work on your skin while you sleep. |
| Skin oiliness | It is fairly normal to suddenly develop spots during mid-pregnancy. This is due to pregnancy hormones increasing the production of sebum (an oily substance with antibacterial properties that is secreted onto the skin's surface), which can make your skin oily and prone to spots. | • If you are already taking any oral drugs for acne, you should stop as they could affect your baby's development. Some topical treatments are safe but check with your doctor or pharmacist.<br>• Drink plenty of water and eat a balanced diet containing plenty of fresh fruit and vegetables.<br>• After 12 weeks of pregnancy, you can dab spots with dilute tea tree oil whose antiseptic properties should help to reduce the inflammation.<br>• Use a gentle cleanser and toner regularly. Change to a light, unperfumed moisturizer designed for oily skin. Exfoliation can help. |
| Skin tags | Tiny, floppy growths develop on the underarms, face, neck and breasts in mid- to late pregnancy. They are nothing to worry about and usually shrink after the birth. They are probably caused by hormones. | • Show your doctor or midwife at your next visit. Unsightly skin tags can be easily removed with simple surgery. |

| Complaint/condition | Description | Action |
| --- | --- | --- |
| **Stretch marks** | Approximately 50 per cent of women develop these pink or red marks, which fade to a shiny silver after the birth. They may be itchy (see pages 144–145). Stretch marks seem to be more common in younger women and in women who are overweight, although they also occur in women who gain very little weight. They are thought to be caused by the skin stretching rapidly as you gain weight and causing ruptures in your skin structure. There may also be a genetic element involved | • If your skin is supple and you do not gain too much weight, stretch marks may be less of a problem.<br>• Moisturize well, particularly on your breasts, thighs and bump. After 12 weeks of pregnancy, try 4 drops of mandarin oil in 25 ml (1 fl oz) of carrier oil, such as baby oil. (Avoid creams that claim to prevent stretch marks, as they have no scientific basis.) |
| **Hair problems** | | |
| **Changes in texture** | Hair often appears to be thicker than usual during pregnancy, and individual hairs become coarser. This is because pregnancy hormones slow down the rate of hair loss, although the hairs will eventually fall out after the baby is born. Hair may also become dry, limp and unmanageable, and curly hair may frizz out of control. In late pregnancy, many women find that their hair becomes greasier. This probably results from increased production of sebum (see Skin oiliness, page 146). | • Experiment with shampoos to suit your hair condition. Do not have highlights, a perm or a relaxer, or use bleach, as chemicals may be absorbed through your skin. Hair dyes will not harm your baby, but your skin may be more sensitive, resulting in allergic reaction.<br>• Try a different hairstyle to make your hair more manageable before your baby arrives. |
| **Extra facial hair** | Some women notice more hairs on their body and face, which may be darker and thicker than normal. Others find that they have less body hair. This depend on the body's response to pregnancy hormones. | • Do not bleach dark hair growth as chemicals may be absorbed through your skin. Pluck hairs that bother you.<br>• Consult your doctor if the additional hair growth seems to be excessive. |

| Complaint/condition | Description | Action |
|---|---|---|
| **Breasts** | | |
| Blocked milk ducts/mastitis | Blocked milk ducts are more common after the birth but can occur beforehand. They take the form of small, painful lumps, often with red streaks radiating out from them – a condition that is known as mastitis.<br><br>Blocked milk ducts are the result of infection and can be caused or aggravated by wearing an under-wired bra or one that presses on the underside of the breast, or by pressure from car seat belts on a long journey. | • Wear a correctly fitted bra.<br>• Talk to your midwife, who can advise you how to get rid of the lump. See your midwife or doctor if you develop mastitis. This must be dealt with promptly to avoid infection spreading further. |
| Leaky nipples | From the fourth to fifth month of pregnancy onwards, your breasts may begin to secret colostrum. This is quite normal. | • Buy some breast pads to slip inside your bra if the leakage is marking your clothes. |
| Prominent glands in the areola | This is a sign that your breasts are preparing for breastfeeding and is quite normal. | None |
| Prominent veins | Spider veins, or thread veins, are quite normal and often disappear after the birth. | • They are caused by the action of oestrogen on the blood vessels.<br>• Use concealer make-up if these veins bother you. |
| Tenderness | Tender breasts are one of the early signs of pregnancy.<br>The tenderness is caused by stimulation of the milk-producing glands and, as the pregnancy progresses, expansion of the milk ducts as they prepare for lactation. | • Wear a support bra throughout your pregnancy. This will also help to prevent your breasts sagging when you stop breastfeeding.<br>• Try wearing a sleep bra if you are uncomfortable at night. |

| Complaint/condition | Description | Action |
|---|---|---|
| **Digestive system** | | |
| Constipation and wind | Constipation (the passing of hard, infrequent, dry stools) can occur from conception onwards and may be accompanied by other digestive disturbances, such as wind. From the early stages of pregnancy, the hormone progesterone relaxes your muscles, including those of the large intestine. This makes your digestive system sluggish, so that you may not have a bowel movement for several days. In addition, your bowel absorbs more water than usual, adding to the problem. Taking iron tablets may make the symptoms worse. | • Drink at least 2 litres (3½ pints) of water a day. Eat more fruit, vegetables and high-fibre foods. • Take light exercise, such as walking or pregnancy yoga, to improve your general circulation. • Remember that some over-the-counter laxatives are not safe to use because they reduce the amount of nutrients that you absorb. Always ask your midwife or doctor for advice. |
| Dental problems | Pregnant women can suffer from bleeding or swollen gums and loose teeth. This is caused by the action of the oestrogen hormone on the tissues of the mouth. | • Brush your teeth at least twice a day, using a softer toothbrush if your gums bleed. Floss regularly to remove any food that has settled between your teeth. • Make sure you see your dentist during pregnancy, because your teeth and gums may need some extra attention. |
| Food aversions | Many women develop an aversion to certain foods during pregnancy. This may be associated with a changing sense of taste. Some of these aversions may be protective because certain naturally occurring bitter substances can be harmful to the developing baby. | • If you cannot bear to eat certain foods, be sure to consume other foods that provide the same nutrients. For example, if you cannot stomach red meat, eat more poultry, fish and dairy products instead. |

| Complaint/condition | Description | Action |
|---|---|---|
| Food cravings | Some women develop cravings for particular foods, regardless of how healthy they are. | • If you crave unhealthy foods, prepare a plan of daily meals and stick to it as far as possible.<br>• Buy fewer unhealthy foods so you cannot easily snack on crisps and biscuits at home. |
| Food cravings – pica | Pica is the technical term for the desire to eat strange things, for example, coal, rubber bands – even mud! It may be caused by a nutritional deficiency. | • Tell your doctor, who may prescribe a nutritional supplement for you. |
| Heartburn | This unpleasant burning sensation occurs when stomach acids leak into the oesophagus. This is common during pregnancy because progesterone relaxes the valve that normally prevents heartburn from occurring. This pregnancy hormone also reduces the tone and activity of the stomach muscles, so that it takes longer to empty the stomach of its contents.<br><br>Also, in late pregnancy, the uterus presses upwards on the stomach, squeezing out the stomach acids. | • Eat little and often, and never late at night. Avoid spicy foods if you are not used to them. Drink milk or peppermint tea, and have a glass of milk at bedtime. Avoid drinks with a high sugar content, which may slow down the emptying of the stomach.<br>• Improve your posture because slouching can make the problem worse. In bed, either prop up your shoulders with pillows or prop up the head of the bed using a couple of bricks.<br>• If these measures do not help, ask your doctor to prescribe suitable medication. |

| Complaint/condition | Description | Action |
|---|---|---|

### Pregnancy sickness

| | | |
|---|---|---|
| 'Morning sickness' | This is often one of the first symptoms of pregnancy and affects roughly 70 per cent of women. It occurs mostly in the morning, but for many women can happen at any time in the day. Altered taste and smell sensations can make nausea worse. The sickness usually improves at around 14 weeks but sometimes continues throughout pregnancy, or disappears but then reappears towards the end.<br><br>Pregnancy sickness is thought to be linked to the pregnancy hormone human chorionic gonadotrophin (HCG). Levels in the blood drop at around 12 weeks, when other hormones begin to take over, which is why sickness and nausea are more common in early pregnancy.<br><br>The hormone oestrogen can lower blood pressure, as well as slowing the action of the digestive system, which in turn can cause nausea. | • Eat little and often. Choose foods that are high in protein and complex carbohydrates (for example, brown rice, pasta) and avoid fatty foods.<br>• Have a snack at bedtime and another at least 20 minutes before you get up. Take healthy snacks, such as dried fruit or rice cakes, with you when you go out.<br>• If you are vomiting, replace lost fluids. Avoid caffeinated drinks, which are dehydrating. Instead, drink vegetable or fruit juices as well as water, and eat fresh, juicy fruit. If drinking water makes you feel ill, try sipping water between meals, sucking ice cubes or eating ice lollies. Some women find that fizzy drinks help.<br>• Avoid smells and foods that trigger your nausea.<br>• Try to get more sleep and relax for short periods during the day. Morning sickness is often worse when you are tired or stressed.<br>• Keep occupied to take your mind off the nausea.<br>• Ask your doctor whether you need a general vitamin supplement (some women with pregnancy sickness lack vitamin B6).<br>• Travel bands, which are worn on the wrist and work by exerting pressure, have been shown to reduce nausea and sickness in pregnancy. |

| Complaint/condition | Description | Action |
|---|---|---|
| **Pregnancy sickness – severe** | Approximately 2 per cent of women suffer from a severe sickness (hyperemesis gravidarum) that is very different from normal pregnancy sickness. They are unable to keep down fluids and can become dehydrated. Severe sickness during pregnancy can also be a sign of a urine infection so this should always be excluded.<br><br>Symptoms include extreme weight loss, passing of small amounts of very concentrated urine, and dry, less elastic skin.<br><br>This sickness can also be a feature of a twin pregnancy or a 'failed' pregnancy or a rare condition known as a hydatidiform mole, when there is distorted growth of the placenta. In this case, the nausea and vomiting may be accompanied by vaginal bleeding, excessive enlargement of the uterus, increased HCG levels, early raised blood pressure and lack of fetal movement or heartbeat.<br><br>Consult your doctor who can find out whether the sickness is due to a urine infection. | • If you become very weak, you may be admitted to hospital for intravenous fluids and regular injections of antiemetics to prevent further vomiting.<br>• If your doctor suspects a failed pregnancy, he may recommend an early ultrasound scan.<br>• Consult your dentist for advice on the effects of the acid from vomiting and the possibility of the erosion of tooth enamel. |
| **Salivation and drooling** | Increased salivation or drooling seems to accompany pregnancy sickness and should diminish after the first few months. On rare occasions, it is caused by an increase in the amount of saliva. Sometimes it is due to a reluctance to swallow as a result of nausea. | • Chew mint-flavoured gum or use a mint-flavoured mouthwash. |

| Complaint/condition | Description | Action |
|---|---|---|
| **Respiratory system** | | |
| Breathlessness | Breathlessness in early pregnancy is usually caused by progesterone hormones stimulating the brain's respiratory centre, increasing your rate of breathing.<br><br>In late pregnancy, your baby is pressing on your diaphragm, which restricts your breathing. Your lungs are unable to expand fully due to the increasing size of the uterus and the difficulty of carrying the combined weight of the developing baby, the placenta, amniotic fluid and uterus.<br><br>If breathlessness is accompanied by fatigue and palpitations, this may be a sign of anaemia (see page 160). | • Sit up straight, not slumped. Try propping yourself up with a couple of pillows at night.<br>• If you show signs of anaemia, see your doctor or midwife.<br>• If you develop unexpected and severe shortness of breath, rapid breathing, blue lips and fingers, and a rapid pulse or chest pain, get medical attention immediately. |
| Sinusitis | Sinusitis affects the mucous membrane lining the cavities around the eyes, cheeks and nose (see also Nosebleeds, page 161). Symptoms include pain above and below one or both eyes, apparent toothache and thick, discoloured mucus. It often follows a cold and is caused by an infection. | • If you think you have sinusitis, tell your doctor, who may prescribe a safe antibiotic or decongestant. Do not use any over-the-counter decongestants as some may have adverse effects on your baby. |
| Stuffy or blocked nose | Many women feel particularly 'snuffly' during certain stages of pregnancy, for example, from 9–12 weeks. This can also cause headaches. It is the result of nasal congestion caused by swollen mucous membranes. | • Avoid getting dehydrated as, in theory, this can make nasal secretions even thicker.<br>• Nasal strips can hold your nostrils open if you are having problems breathing at night. These may also help if you snore. Do not use over-the-counter decongestants. |

| Complaint/condition | Description | Action |
|---|---|---|
| **Aches and pains** | | |
| Backache | As your pregnancy progresses, you may become more susceptible to back pain, especially if you are already prone to it. This is usually the result of poor posture. As your baby grows and your uterus expands, you may find you are not standing so upright. This can increase the curve in the small of your back, adding to the strain in an area that is already carrying more weight than normal. | • Watch your posture and try not to arch your back. Avoid standing for too long or sitting hunched over your desk. Be careful when lifting objects and always carry them close to your body.<br>• Replace your mattress if it is very old. If back or pelvic pains are severe, see a specialist pregnancy physiotherapist who may give you a 'bump support'. |
| Braxton Hicks tightenings | These mild, irregular tightenings are present from the beginning of pregnancy but you do not usually become aware of them until about the beginning of late pregnancy.<br>   These tightenings are named after the doctor who discovered their purpose, and they are a normal part of pregnancy. They squeeze blood out of the uterine veins, enabling them to fill with fresh blood, and help to stretch the lower part of the uterus, preparing it for labour. They may be triggered by having sex or an orgasm, but this does not mean that you are going into labour. | • If contractions become frequent, regular or painful, contact your midwife or doctor to rule out the possibility of an early labour. |

| Complaint/condition | Description | Action |
|---|---|---|
| Carpal tunnel syndrome | These pains in the hands generally occur in mid- and late pregnancy and usually disappear within a couple of weeks of the birth. The thumb, index and middle fingers and half of your ring finger may feel numb and/or get pins and needles, and there may be pain in the fingers that travels up to the wrist and the forearm. The symptoms tend to be worse at night and may be accompanied by a weakness in the movement of the thumb.<br><br>The condition is caused by swelling in the part of the wrist through which the median nerve to the fingers runs. | • Rest your hands on a separate pillow rather than sleeping with your head on your hands.<br>• Try to disperse the swelling by gentle exercise, for example, circling and flexing your wrists and putting them in cold water. Exercise can in general help to improve your circulation.<br>• Drink plenty of water.<br>• Ask your doctor to refer you to a physiotherapist, who can give you some exercises that may help. If the condition does not improve, you may be given a splint to support your wrist. An osteopath may be able to manipulate the wrist to help with the drainage.<br>• Occasionally, a steroid injection around the nerve can be given during pregnancy. |
| Headache | Many pregnant women get headaches. These are usually the result of hormone changes but can also be caused by anxiety and tiredness, low blood sugar or dehydration. They can also be a sign of high blood pressure, particularly after 24 weeks of pregnancy (see page 132). | • Wrap some ice in a flannel and hold it against your forehead.<br>• Alternatively, buy cooling gel strips from your pharmacist. |

| Complaint/condition | Description | Action |
|---|---|---|
| Leg cramps and restless legs | About 50 per cent of pregnant women suffer from night cramps in their legs at any time from 14 weeks of pregnancy. According to one theory, this is related to iron deficiency in areas of the brain, so iron supplements may help.<br><br>Restless legs (Ekbom syndrome) is a relatively common feature of pregnancy but usually settles down after the birth. This burning or twitching feeling in the legs is accompanied by an irresistible urge to move the legs, which can bring some relief. It can be very distressing and may severely interfere with sleep. | • Drink enough fluids. Increasing the calcium in your diet may help.<br>• Wear support tights and rest several times a day with your legs raised. Try leg stretches a few times during the day, or take several short walks.<br>• To relieve leg cramp, straighten your leg and point your toes towards your head, or pull your toes up towards your ankle to stretch the leg muscle. Breathe deeply to encourage the muscle to relax. If it works, apply gentle heat and gentle massage. If it doesn't, do not apply heat or massage, but tell your midwife or doctor as there is a slight risk of a thrombosis (see also Varicose veins, page 162). |
| Ligament pain | Ligaments are bands of tough fibrous tissue that connect bones and cartilage, control joint movement and support muscles. They loosen and stretch during pregnancy and cause a variety of aches, particularly around the sides of your stomach and your pelvis. This is usually nothing to worry about unless accompanied by other symptoms. | • Mention the problem to your doctor or midwife at your next antenatal appointment. |
| Pins and needles | Pins and needles or numbness in hands and feet are common (see also Carpal tunnel syndrome, page 155). The cause may be excess fluid (oedema) pressing on nerve endings (see Swelling, page 162). | • Sit with your feet up if possible. |

| Complaint/condition | Description | Action |
| --- | --- | --- |
| Rib pain | This is usually caused by your baby's feet lodging between your ribs. | • Try persuading her to move with a very gentle prod.<br>• If the pain is severe or constant, contact your midwife. Epigastric pain caused by inflammation of the liver sometimes occurs in pre-eclampsia. |
| Sciatica | This is a sharp pain that starts in the lower back, buttock or hip and radiates down one leg, usually during late pregnancy.<br>   It is caused by the uterus pressing on the sciatic nerve that runs from the middle of the back, through the buttocks and down each leg. | • Gentle stretching exercises and heat therapy may ease symptoms. |
| Stomach cramps | See Braxton Hicks tightenings and Ligament pain (pages 154 and 156). | • If cramps are accompanied by bleeding, fever or chills, faintness, increased vaginal discharge, or other unusual symptoms, see a midwife or doctor immediately. If they become more painful or occur frequently, contact your midwife or doctor. |
| Symphysis pubis dysfunction (SPD) | This condition can cause a lot of discomfort during pregnancy. It affects the pubic area or sometimes the lower back, and can start as early as the 12th week of your pregnancy. The pain may continue post-natally, but will eventually get better. It is caused by the joints in the pelvis parting slightly, because of hormones stretching and softening the ligaments (see Ligament pain, page 156). | • Your midwife should refer you to a physiotherapist, who can assess the extent of the problem and may give you a support belt to wear around your stomach. Rest is often advised and you should be taught how to get in and out of bed, keeping your knees together, and on how to get up and down stairs. |

| Complaint/condition | Description | Action |
|---|---|---|
| **Urinary tract system** | | |
| Urine infections | The risk of urinary infections in pregnancy is increased by diabetes. Progesterone relaxes the bladder and ureter muscles, which allows urine to collect and stagnate in the bladder. It sometimes passes back into the kidney, increasing risk of infection. | See below for specific urinary complaints. |
| Cystitis | The bladder is the commonest site affected by a urinary tract infection. Inflammation of the bladder (cystitis) produces symptoms that may include a burning sensation when urinating, a frequent urge to urinate that only produces a small amount, and general pain in the pelvic area. Sometimes urine is cloudy, with traces of blood and an unpleasant smell. If there are no symptoms, infection may be diagnosed during a routine screening. The condition can be recurrent. | • Drink plenty of water, as well as barley water and cranberry juice, to flush out your kidneys, ureters and bladder. Pass water immediately after sexual intercourse and wipe from front to back after using the toilet.<br>• Avoid over-the-counter remedies, which contain lots of salt. Consult your doctor, as antibiotic treatment is vital to avoid the infection reaching the kidneys (see below) |
| Kidney infections | Kidney infections are more serious. The symptoms are similar to those of cystitis but may be accompanied by fever, backache, chills and nausea or vomiting. If untreated, high fever can lead to premature labour. | • If you develop symptoms, call your doctor immediately. You may need to be admitted to hospital for intravenous antibiotics. |
| Increased urination | If there are no signs of urinary tract infection, this is normal. In early pregnancy, changes in circulation and muscle tone lead to a congested feeling in the pelvic area. Also, your bladder is squashed by the growing uterus until the 12th week. In late pregnancy, the engagement of your baby's head places pressure on your bladder. | • In late pregnancy, avoid standing for prolonged periods. |

| Complaint/condition | Description | Action |
| --- | --- | --- |
| Stress incontinence | During the last 12 weeks of pregnancy, you may leak urine when you cough, sneeze or laugh. This is caused by the pressure of your uterus and baby on your bladder, and possibly by the effects of hormones on the pelvic floor. | • Practise pelvic floor exercises (see pages 108–109). |
| **Reproductive system** | | |
| Bleeding/ spotting | There are many causes, from the minor (cervical erosion, where the surface of the cervix becomes fragile under the influence of hormones) to the serious (sexually transmitted diseases, ectopic pregnancy, miscarriage or cervical cancer). In late pregnancy, bleeding may indicate problems with the placenta (see pages 130–131), but sometimes no cause is found. | • Tell your midwife or doctor about any bleeding immediately, especially if it is accompanied by any pain. |
| Candida (thrush) | Pregnant women are prone to this infection, which is caused by a yeast (candida). Symptoms include a white, itchy discharge and vaginal soreness, and sometimes itching of the anus and pain on urination. Recurrent thrush can be a nuisance but is not harmful to the baby. However, it may be an indication of diabetes (see pages 136–139). | • Your midwife will take a swab to confirm the discharge's cause. Candida is easily treated with pessaries and creams. <br> • If your partner shows symptoms, he should be treated, too. <br> • Reduce the chance of recurrence by washing the affected area only with plain water. Avoid scented bath products and tight clothing. |
| Increased/ changed vaginal discharge | Normal in pregnancy, an increased vaginal discharge is usually caused by the effects of hormones on the tissues of the cervix and vagina. More serious causes are sexually transmitted diseases and candida (see above). | • If the discharge is excessive, itchy, smells bad or is coloured, tell your midwife or doctor, as some vaginal infections can provoke labour or be transmitted to the baby. |

| Complaint/condition | Description | Action |
|---|---|---|
| **Blood and circulation** | | |
| Anaemia | Women are usually checked for anaemia at their first midwife appointment, but iron-deficiency anaemia may develop at any time during pregnancy, particularly after the 20th week when the amount of iron required by your baby soars.<br><br>Symptoms include pallor, exhaustion, breathlessness, palpitations and fainting. | • Eat plenty of iron-rich foods (but not liver) with fresh fruit and vegetables (the vitamin C they contain will aid iron absorption).<br>• Ask your doctor or midwife whether you need an extra iron supplement. They may offer you another blood test and give you iron supplements if anaemia is suspected. |
| Blood pressure – high (hypertension) | About 10 per cent of women experience high blood pressure, especially towards the end of their pregnancy. Blood pressure is recorded as two measurements, systolic and diastolic. Systolic is the pressure as the heart beats and diastolic the pressure as it relaxes. | • Make sure that your midwife takes your blood pressure regularly. Have periods of rest and use breathing exercises as an aid to relaxation.<br>• Avoid too much salty food. |
| Blood pressure – low | In early pregnancy, blood pressure falls as your circulatory system expands to include the enlarging uterus and placenta. Blood pressure is lowest in mid-pregnancy and gradually increases towards pre-pregnancy levels at term.<br><br>The most noticeable symptom is dizziness when you stand up rapidly. You may also notice shaky fingers and a raised heart rate (see also Anaemia, above).<br><br>Fainting is a defence mechanism when the brain is not getting enough blood. It restores the brain's blood supply because blood no longer has to flow 'uphill'. | • Stand up slowly, especially after sitting for a long time.<br>• Make sure you do not go for too long without food.<br>• If you feel faint, lie flat on the floor and raise your legs above hip level. If you are very pregnant, lie slightly to one side rather than flat. If lying flat is not practical, sit down so you cannot fall and put your head between your knees as low as possible until you recover. A drink or a light snack may help.<br>• If you have not fainted before, ask your doctor to check possible causes. |

| Complaint/condition | Description | Action |
|---|---|---|
| **Haemorrhoids (piles)** | Piles are similar to varicose veins (see page 162) but they occur in the anus. They are painful, especially during or after opening your bowels, when they sometimes bleed, and often itchy.<br><br>In most cases, piles disappear a few weeks after the birth, although they may worsen in the short term after labour.<br><br>Piles are aggravated by the weight of the baby and uterus on the pelvic veins and by constipation with straining. | • To allow the piles to shrink and settle, try to avoid constipation by drinking plenty of fluids to avoid dehydration and eating lots of fruit and fibre-rich foods.<br>• Try not to strain when passing a stool: relax your pelvic floor muscles and breathe deeply. If necessary take a recommended stool-softening laxative.<br>• Avoid standing for too long, especially in late pregnancy. Lie on your side instead of your back.<br>• Take regular gentle exercise to improve your circulation: swimming is good.<br>• If the piles are uncomfortable or have prolapsed (are outside the anus), ask your doctor for a cream to reduce the swelling. They can be surgically removed if they persist. |
| **Nosebleeds** | These may occur more frequently during pregnancy due to dilation and congestion of the fine blood vessels causing the lining of the nose to become fragile and bleed more readily. This is especially the case if you are already suffering from a stuffy nose (see page 153). | • Do not blow your nose too hard because this may damage the walls of the blood vessels. Gently clear your nostrils alternately.<br>• To stem a nosebleed, lean forward slightly and pinch just below the bridge of your nose for five minutes. If necessary, repeat twice more or until the bleeding has stopped. Avoid blowing your nose. If the bleeding does not stop, recurs or is heavy, tell your doctor or go to the outpatients department of your local hospital. |

| Complaint/condition | Description | Action |
|---|---|---|
| Swelling | Puffiness of the ankles and wrists is common during pregnancy and is caused by the accumulation of fluid (oedema). This is probably related to expansion of the blood vessels near the skin, which increases the blood flow and encourages fluid to move into and remain in the tissues. In most cases this is uncomfortable rather than serious.<br><br>However, any new or rapidly worsening swelling, particularly later in pregnancy, may be an indication of pre-eclampsia (see pages 142–143), so you should tell your midwife or doctor.<br><br>In the legs, the pressure of the pregnant uterus slows the rate of blood flow in the small blood vessels, effectively squeezing out fluid into the tissues. | • Drink plenty of fluids.<br>• To alleviate discomfort, wear support tights or stockings instead of tight socks, and wear open-toed flat sandals, low mules or loosely laced trainers rather than tight shoes.<br>• Take short brisk walks and put your feet up when sitting down. If possible, lie down for short periods on your left side during the day. |
| Varicose veins | Varicose veins vary in severity from faint bluish lines to bulging veins that protrude from the skin. They ache and are sometimes very painful, as well as producing a feeling of heaviness. They are caused by a restriction in the flow of blood back to the heart. The veins dilate to accommodate the extra blood. The problem seems to be hereditary and may be exacerbated by excess weight.<br><br>Any tenderness in your calf or thigh, accompanied by swelling, inflammation, an increased heart rate or a raised temperature may indicate a thrombosis. | • Prevention is key. Do not sit with your legs crossed and raise your legs while you are seated. Avoid standing for long periods of time. Daily exercise, such as walking, swimming or yoga, helps by improving circulation.<br>• Massage your legs gently to prevent varicose veins, but do not massage the area once they appear.<br>• Wear support tights. Ideally, put them on before you get up.<br>• If veins are painful and itchy, apply an ice pack. Tell your doctor immediately if you suspect a thrombosis. |

| Complaint/condition | Description | Action |
|---|---|---|
| Vulval varicose veins | Varicose veins (see page 162) sometimes develop in the vulva during pregnancy, particularly as the baby becomes heavier. They can cause an uncomfortable feeling of heaviness that aches, particularly towards the end of the day. | • Wear a thick sanitary towel to support the affected area.<br>• Apply an ice pack to reduce the swelling. Avoid standing for long periods. |

### Energy and sleep

| Complaint/condition | Description | Action |
|---|---|---|
| Fatigue | Extreme fatigue is especially common during early and late pregnancy. In early pregnancy, fatigue is caused by increased amounts of hormones, particularly progesterone, which also helps you to sleep. Also, your metabolism is working overtime, your heart is beating faster and your baby is developing at an amazing rate. All this, combined with nausea, can make you feel completely drained.<br><br>In later pregnancy, especially during the last few weeks, the extra weight that you are carrying will make you tired and a variety of factors (for example, pressure on your bladder, heartburn, aches and pains) may make sleeping difficult. Excessive tiredness may be due to anaemia (see page 160). | • Do what your body tells you and get as much rest as you can. Learn how to relax (see pages 112–113) and set aside times each day to do this. Pace yourself: when you have the energy, use it.<br>• Drink plenty of water and do not go too long without food. Eat little and often to maintain your blood sugar level. Avoid sweet food and drinks.<br>• Try gentle exercise, which will give you more energy and improve your circulation.<br>• If you have any symptoms of anaemia (see page 160), tell your midwife or doctor. |

| Complaint/condition | Description | Action |
|---|---|---|
| **Emotional and mental** | | |
| Depression | Mild depression is common – perhaps more common than post-natal depression – and it is just as important as physical complaints. The symptoms include mood swings, lethargy, irritability, lack of interest in anything and an inability to concentrate. | • Ignore anyone who tells you to 'snap out of it'. Talk to your midwife or doctor, who should be able to refer you to a therapist.<br>• Look after yourself: eat healthily, get enough sleep and ask for help if you need it.<br>• Make time to do the things you enjoy. Exercise in particular can help you to feel better. |
| Mood swings | Although mood swings, irritability and weepiness may be difficult for you and those around you to deal with, they are very common during pregnancy. They are simply the result of the natural rollercoaster of emotions that accompanies pregnancy. | • Avoid foods that give an initial high, then have a rebound effect, such as sugar and coffee.<br>• Indulge yourself: spend quiet time alone; try a pedicure or massage; take up relaxation techniques and yoga, Pilates or gentle exercise. |
| **Miscellaneous** | | |
| Dizziness | Feelings of light-headedness often occur during early or mid-pregnancy because of low blood pressure. Later, it may be caused by the pressure of the uterus on the vessels carrying blood back to the heart. Other possible causes include anaemia (see page 160) and low blood sugar levels. | • Avoid standing for long periods and never take hot baths.<br>• Tell your midwife or doctor if you get recurring dizziness. |
| Ear blockage | Women may get partial deafness (as if they have cotton wool in their ears), and 'popping' (as in an aircraft). This is due to congestion of the tissues lining the Eustachian tubes, which run between the back of the throat and the inner ears. | • Block one nostril with your finger and blow gently through the other nostril. Repeat with the other nostril. Do not stick cotton buds into the ear canal. |

| Complaint/condition | Description | Action |
|---|---|---|
| Eyesight changes | Many women find that they become either short- or long-sighted during pregnancy. This is because the extra fluids in the body cause the eyeball to change shape. The tear ducts secrete less fluid and the eyes are drier.<br><br>These changes may make hard contact lenses uncomfortable and result in tired eyes or headaches after watching the television, reading or working at a computer, but should return to normal within a few months.<br><br>Headache and visual disturbances (for example, blurring, dizziness, floaters or spots), late in pregnancy in particular, may indicate high blood pressure (see page 132). | • Get your eyes tested to see whether you need a pair of glasses for a while.<br>• If you wear hard contact lenses, you may have to switch to soft lenses or glasses.<br>• Tell your midwife or doctor if you have any unusual symptoms. |
| Fingernail and toenail changes | Some pregnant women find that their nails grow more quickly. Others find that their nails become softer, develop grooves and break or split easily. | • Keep your nails short, wear gloves to wash up and moisturize your nails at least once a day.<br>• If you notice discoloration, you may have an infection and this should be treated by your doctor. |
| Raised temperature and increased sweating | Many women find that they are constantly warm, particularly in their hands and feet, and have a permanently shiny face. This is because your basal metabolic rate increases by about 20 per cent during pregnancy. This increases the amount of body heat that you generate. Some of this heat is dissipated through the skin by means of increased blood flow, making the hands and feet warmer. | • Wear loose clothing made from natural rather than synthetic materials.<br>• In winter, wear layers so that you can peel them off as necessary.<br>• If your underarms are working overtime, have wipes and an antiperspirant to hand. You'll be more aware of any problem than people around you, so try not to get stressed as this will make it worse. |

# STRESS AND PREGNANCY

## The causes of stress

**Having a baby is a huge life-changing event, which will inevitably cause some degree of stress, even if your pregnancy is planned and your baby is much wanted.**

**Above:** Talking over your concerns with a midwife, doctor or friend can help you cope with stress.

It is natural that, at some point during your pregnancy, you will have worries, feel emotional or be overtired because of the demands of everyday life. If you feel excessively worried or tired for any length of time, however, you may need to look at ways of reducing your stress levels. Emotional stress has a negative effect on your body and mind and may even influence the development of your baby. If stress causes blood pressure to rise, this can result in a reduced blood flow to the baby and may affect growth. It has also been suggested that the stress hormone, cortisol, may cross the placenta during pregnancy and lead to anxiety in children.

Stress levels need close monitoring, but the problem is often that you will not even recognize that you are suffering from it (see the box opposite for some signs of stress).

## Ways of coping with stress

Whether you find it helps you most to talk about things or simply switch off for a bit, there are many ways in which you can help yourself cope. If you are stressed, consider the following ideas:

**1 Accept help** If you feel stressed you will certainly benefit from more support and you should accept offers of help gladly.

If you have other children and a friend or family member offers to have them for a couple of hours, seize the opportunity to give yourself a rest. If you have to stay in hospital for a few days after the birth, you will feel better knowing that they are already comfortable being with someone else when you are not around.

2 **Talk** Discuss your feelings with others, including your midwife or doctor. As well as wanting to monitor how you feel, they may be able to put you in touch with local women's groups.

3 **Exercise** You do not have to belong to a gym to get sufficient exercise – even taking a brisk walk in the fresh air is good for you. Exercise makes the body release endorphins, the natural 'feel good' chemicals, and also makes you feel more energetic.

## Some signs of stress

- **Reduced concentration**
- **Irritation**
- **Withdrawal**
- **Disturbed eating patterns (reduced appetite or overeating)**
- **Insomnia, fatigue**
- **Feeling low or anxious**
- **Inability to relax**
- **High blood pressure**
- **Aching muscles**

4 **Make time for yourself** Treat yourself to a good book, favourite magazine or that DVD you've always wanted to watch, and remember to make space for some quiet moments to yourself each day. If the prospect of an uninterrupted bath seems blissful, switch off the telephone, shut the door and relax.

5 **Massage** Ask your partner to give you a massage (see pages 114–115). Letting him give you a soothing massage has the added benefit that he will feel that he is doing something practical to help you cope with your pregnancy.

6 **Eat well** Your diet can have a huge influence on how you feel. Be sure to include lots of fresh fruits and vegetables and do not snack on high-energy foods, such as biscuits and sweets. They may provide a 'quick energy fix', making you feel better for about 10 minutes, but when your blood sugar level falls sharply after eating, you will feel no more energetic, and perhaps even more lethargic. Yo-yoing energy levels may also make any mood swings that you are suffering worse. You may find that it suits you better to have several small, healthy meals a day instead of three larger ones, as this will help to keep your blood sugar levels more even. If you find your energy levels are dropping between meals, snack on a rice cake, cereal bar or piece of fruit. (See pages 92–101 for more information about diet during pregnancy.)

# antenatal care

# Choice of care

There are various options open to you when it comes to choosing who should look after you while you are pregnant as well as where to have your baby. You need to consider whether you want to give birth at home or in hospital. If you are thinking about a hospital birth, there may be several options in the area in which you live and different types of care, ranging from birthing centres to consultant-led units, may be available.

## Midwife-led care

Where care is midwife led, midwives provide all your antenatal care and, as long as your pregnancy continues to be straightforward,

## Private care

Some women employ an independent midwife to provide all of their care. They like to feel that there is a guarantee that they will have the same midwife providing continuity of care throughout their pregnancy, birth and also post-natally. Statistically, independent midwives have a high proportion of home births. You could also pay to see an obstetrician privately for your antenatal care, or choose to give birth in a private maternity unit.

a midwife will also provide your labour and post-natal care. How this care is provided depends on where you live and what is available in the area. Your community midwife can provide your antenatal checks, either in a clinic or in your home. You may see various midwives who are part of a team, or you may have one named midwife throughout your pregnancy. There may be a domino scheme, where your midwife accompanies you to hospital when you are in labour and discharges you home soon after the birth.

## Shared care

This is where antenatal care is shared between the midwife, doctor and a consultant obstetrician at the hospital or maternity unit. Shared care is usually recommended if your pregnancy falls into a 'higher risk' category –

**Left:** Your midwife will be happy to talk through all your antenatal care options with you.

# Choice of care **Common questions**

**Q** My doctor has talked about a local 'midwife unit', and says that it might be a suitable option for me. What exactly is it?
**A** This is usually a much smaller, often stand-alone unit or birthing centre, where midwives and health care assistants provide the care. Women are encouraged to have an active birth and a birthing pool is usually available. This type of unit is more suitable for women with uncomplicated pregnancies who do not anticipate any problems in labour as there are no facilities for administering epidurals and no special-care baby unit.

**Q** Why do some women decide to have a home birth?
**A** Some women would prefer to give birth at home, where they feel comfortable and with their family close at hand, rather than in the unfamiliar, more clinical surroundings of a hospital. If your pregnancy is uncomplicated then statistically it is just as safe to give birth at home as in hospital. The reality is that women who give birth at home need less pain relief,

experience less intervention, are more likely to know the midwife who looks after them, and feel more in control throughout the birth.

**Q** What happens if I opt for a home birth in early pregnancy but change my mind later?
**A** Circumstances may change during your pregnancy which influence your decision. There is no contract to sign and no one will chastise you for changing your mind.

**Q** What will happen at my first check-up?
**A** This will probably be the longest check you have, because your midwife will need to take details of your medical, obstetric and family history and current circumstances. It also offers the first real opportunity for you to meet your midwife and ask any questions you have, for example, about the availability of antenatal classes or how to get comfortable at night. You will be weighed and your blood pressure taken. The midwife will give you general advice on health, for example, diet and exercise, and take blood tests as necessary.

for example, if you have a complicated obstetric or medical history, if you are pregnant with twins or if you have diabetes. Your midwife will explain why a recommendation for shared care is being made, but ultimately the choice is yours.

## Hospital (consultant unit)
Consultant units have obstetricians on their staff, as well as the facilities to deal with any

complications that may occur during the birth. If your labour is straightforward you will have a midwife caring for you in labour and during the birth. However, if there are any problems, an obstetrician will be available to carry out an assisted birth (forceps or ventouse) or a caesarean section. You will also have the option of the full range of pain relief, including an epidural, which would be administered by an anaesthetist.

# Hospital birth

For many women, having a baby is their first experience of being in a hospital. Suddenly finding yourself in an unfamiliar environment, with strange equipment all around, can be very unnerving. Ideally, part of your antenatal care should include a tour of the maternity unit where your baby will be born if you choose a hospital birth.

## Six questions to ask about the **labour ward**

**1** How many birth partners can you have?

**2** What use can you make of the furniture in the room you will be in during labour? Does the bed have multiple positions? Is there room for a large beanbag or rocking chair? Can you bring your own birthing ball?

**3** What is the hospital's rate of births by caesarean section compared with normal vaginal births?

**4** Is there a lot of intervention (such as monitoring and episiotomies)?

**5** Is there a birthing pool? What percentage of the midwives attend water births?

**6** How do you gain access to the maternity unit at night? (Hospital security procedures may mean that the door you would normally use is locked.)

**Above:** Hospital birth does not mean labour in bed; you are free to move around the room.

## What to expect

Most hospitals provide tours of the labour suite, often at evenings or weekends so that partners can attend. Such a visit is worth making so that you can learn what facilities are available and the various instruments that might come into use. You can also take this opportunity to find out whether your hospital is geared more towards a 'hi-tech' or 'low-tech' birth, or somewhere in between (see page 174). If you do not discover this until you are in labour you will be too preoccupied to ask questions that could help reduce any anxiety.

You also take a look at the equipment that is available. Many labour suites are able to

# Hospital birth **Common questions**

**Q** Is intervention inevitable if I opt for a hospital birth?

**A** Intervention is a matter of judgement and depends partly on the philosophy of the hospital and its staff. Some hospitals advocate intervention before any problem occurs, in the hope of preventing a difficult or dangerous situation arising. Others favour watching carefully but not intervening unless a problem is manifest. The technology is there for them to use if needed.

**Q** What role do student midwives play? Will one be present at the birth of my baby?

**A** Student midwives always work under the close supervision of a qualified member of staff, and your permission will be asked if a student wishes to be present during the birth. Women often imagine that there will be a crowd of students gathered in the delivery room, but this is no longer the case. At most you can expect a student midwife or student nurse who can offer additional support. By staying with you during labour, a student midwife offers continuity of care, and this has been shown to have a positive effect on a woman's ability to cope.

provide birthing aids such as large beanbags, birthing balls, rocking chairs and even essential oils or CDs. These all assist in creating a more relaxing atmosphere.

## Who's who on the labour ward?

With a low-risk pregnancy, there is no need for anyone other than the midwife to care for you. The midwife is qualified to care for you during pregnancy, normal labour and birth. After the birth she helps you to feed and care for your new baby. There are occasions when you will meet other staff on the labour ward, and they may include:

- **An obstetrician** A doctor specializing in the care of women experiencing complications during pregnancy, labour or the post-natal period.

- **An anaesthetist** A doctor specializing in anaesthetics, who would put an epidural in position, or be part of the team if you needed a caesarean section.
- **A paediatrician** A doctor specializing in babies and child health, who will check your baby after the birth. A paediatrician would be present at instrumental deliveries or if any problem was anticipated with your baby, for example, premature labour.
- **Other staff** There will be a number of other people on the ward, such as health care assistants, porters and theatre staff.

# Hospital birth
## High-tech and low-tech

**Above:** Ask your hospital about equipment, such as a birthing ball, that they may be able to provide.

*'The hospital staff were fantastic. As I'd had a caesarean after a 20-hour labour, I was given my own room – so I could finally get some rest. I can never thank the doctors and midwives enough for looking after us.'*
Val, mother of Harry

A high-tech birth might involve you sitting in bed with a hormone drip to control the contractions, a fetal monitor to record your baby's heartbeat and perhaps an epidural to numb sensation. A low-tech approach involves no active intervention, so long as you and your baby are both fine. You could cope with contractions using relaxation and breathing techniques, but pain relief is always on hand if you need it.

## What do you prefer?

Most hospitals adopt a mixed approach that is basically low-tech, but involves protocols regarding, for example, when a drip should be used to speed up labour or how long the second stage of labour should continue before you require an assisted birth. If this is your first baby you may not necessarily know the level of intervention that you would prefer for labour and birth (assuming that there are no complications).

To find out which kind of birth would suit you best, try answering the following questions. The more questions you answer 'No' to, the more likely you are to feel reassured by using birth technology. The more questions you answer with a 'Yes', the more likely you are to prefer a natural approach.

• Do you mind the idea of being wired to machinery during labour?

# Hospital birth **Common questions**

**Q** Why should I consider a hospital birth?

**A** Hospital is the safest place for expectant mums who are considered high risk. This could include women who have a medical condition, such as a heart problem, insulin-dependent diabetes, or problems during pregnancy, such as pre-eclampsia, or premature birth. If it is anticipated that a woman or her baby will need a high level of medical care or a special-care baby unit, a hospital is the appropriate place to give birth.

**Q** What are the advantages of a hospital birth?

**A** There are a number: obstetricians work in the hospital, which means that there are the facilities to look after women who need a higher level of intervention with their care; there is the facility to do instrumental deliveries or a caesarean; and the full range of pain relief options are available, including an epidural, which is sited by an anaesthetist. If you have other children at home, you may want a night or two away just with your new baby.

**Q** What are the disadvantages of a hospital birth?

**A** With a hospital birth, you are more likely to end up with interventions, such as an episiotomy, assisted birth, caesarean section, a drip to speed up contractions, pain relief, and also a higher risk of infection. Another drawback is that you are less likely to get one-to-one care from a midwife you know – midwives on the labour ward may have several women to look after.

**Q** How long will I have to stay in hospital?

**A** This depends on the sort of birth and how well you and your baby are. In most hospitals you can leave straight from the labour ward or stay for a few days after your baby's birth. Even with a first baby, many mothers go home within hours these days, and most leave within a day or two.

- Do you empathize with women who choose to give birth at home?
- Would you prefer to move around and choose comfortable positions?
- Do you believe that labour can be a natural event for most women?
- Do you believe that relaxing in familiar surroundings can make labour easier?
- Do you have any doubts that doctors and midwives always know what is best for you and your baby?
- Would you prefer to have no intervention as long as your baby is all right?
- Would you prefer to avoid drugs if this is at all possible?
- Do you disagree with women who want whatever drugs are available, as long as they do not have to feel anything?

# WATER BIRTH

## Easing your baby's passage into the world

**Women are often attracted to water during labour in the same way that they take a bath if they have menstrual pain or backache or feel stressed.**

The idea of a water birth was originally explored by the Russian Igor Tcharkovsky in the early 1970s. He discovered that newborns have a so-called 'dive reflex': like dolphins, they start trying to breathe only when they are brought to the surface of the water and come into contact with the air. Therefore, a baby can stay under water safely for the first few seconds of its life.

**Below:** Water birth is safe because your baby will not breathe until he reaches the surface.

# Advantages of a water birth

The use of water during labour can have many benefits. Studies have shown that it helps you to relax, which reduces pain. Being in a room with a pool is often a less clinical experience, and you may find that you get one-to-one care with the midwife. If necessary, you can still use gas and air in a pool, although you cannot use any other form of pain relief.

Not all women would be encouraged to use a birthing pool but, if you are considered low risk and have good midwifery care, it carries no more risks than a conventional birth. Even if you do not like the idea of giving birth in the water, it is worth trying the pool for labour and then getting out for the birth. A flexible attitude is important, as every birth is unpredictable.

If you would like a water birth, consider hiring a birthing pool, which can be either used at home or taken to the maternity unit if it does not already have one. Plan ahead as hospital birthing facilities are subject to availability.

The basic criteria for having a water birth are as follows:

- You have to be at least 37 weeks pregnant. Premature babies may still be underdeveloped and should not be born in a pool.
- Your baby should be lying head down because this is the easiest and safest position for his descent into the water.
- If you are carrying twins, you would normally be advised against a water birth because of the risk of complications.
- You will not be able to use the pool if you have had an epidural or pethidine (these pain relief options are not available for a water birth). You can, however, still use gas and air.

## Five reasons for considering a **water birth**

1 Water encourages relaxation, greater mobility and calmness, all of which help you cope better with pain. It also supports your body, making it easier to change position and move around the pool.

2 Water can help prevent or lessen the risk of tears, by helping the vagina to stretch and soften, easing your baby into the world.

3 It can speed up labour by stimulating better hormone secretion. Immersion in water stimulates the production of oxytocin, which can bring about more powerful contractions and therefore a faster dilation of the cervix.

4 Water reinforces a feeling of privacy and personal space. Midwives often interfere less if you are in a birthing pool, although they do periodically check your blood pressure and your baby's heart rate.

5 The transition from the sanctuary of the amniotic sac to the dramatically different outside world is smoother and easier for a newborn if he first finds himself in a more familiar watery environment.

*'The water felt so fantastic. I stayed on my knees and leaned on the side of the pool, as this was the most comfortable position. I pushed out my baby in the water and steered him to the surface myself. It was just incredible. Barry cut the umbilical cord and held him.'*

*Jayne, mother of Gabriel*

# Home birth

The advantage of having a baby at home is that you are in a familiar, comfortable environment with none of the elements of uncertainty and fear that can inhibit labour in a hospital. You have the freedom to move around as you wish, and to have as many people with you as you choose. Women who have a home birth are more likely to feel in control and relaxed than those who give birth in hospital.

## What to expect

If you choose to have your baby at home, your midwife will generally bring the birth equipment to your house at around 37 weeks and leave it there. It will include gas and air and baby resuscitation equipment, all of which she will talk through with you.

There is little you need to do to prepare for a home birth. Think about how you might use the furniture during labour – you want to remain upright and be moving around. Have some plastic sheeting and old towels to hand. It is also useful to have a torch or desk lamp ready, so that the midwife can examine your perineum after the birth to see if you need any stitches.

A home birth will proceed much the same as it does in hospital. Once labour is established, your midwife will stay with you until the baby is born. You are free to do as you please in order to make yourself comfortable – walk about the room, meditate, take a bath –

**Above:** Giving birth at home can make you and your partner feel more in control and relaxed.

with your midwife observing you, checking your blood pressure and your baby's heartbeat. After the birth, she will clear up. She will then check over you and your baby, write her notes and, when you are settled and everything is tidy, leave a telephone number in case you need her. She will make routine visits to check you and your baby over the next few days, as you feel necessary.

# Home birth **Common questions**

**Q** Why should I consider a home birth?

**A** Evidence shows that, in a straightforward pregnancy, it is as safe to opt for a home birth as to have a hospital birth. Home is just as safe, and many would argue safer, because of the one-to-one care that you will receive from your midwife. Your midwife will be trained in resuscitation, and carries oxygen to administer to mother or baby in an emergency. She also carries drugs that will help control excessive bleeding that may follow the birth. With a hospital birth you are more likely to end up with interventions, and you have a greater risk of infection. Even if you are taken to hospital during labour, you are still less likely to have a caesarean section than someone booked for a hospital birth.

**Q** What are the advantages of having a home birth?

**A** There are several. In addition to being in a familiar environment, you reduce the elements of uncertainty than can sometimes occur in hospital, and which may inhibit or prolong your labour. You can have any number of birth partners, and your children can be with you if you wish. Likewise, you may prefer the intimacy of knowing that random members of staff are not going to walk in. You will also get one-to-one care from a midwife throughout your labour and, towards the end of labour, a second midwife will arrive to give extra support.

**Q** What happens if there is a complication?

**A** Midwives are trained and equipped to deal with any emergencies that may arise. However, if there are signs that all is not well during labour, your midwife may advise you to go to hospital. You should discuss any reasons that she might have for doing this beforehand. They will probably include your baby showing signs of distress during labour, including opening her bowels; very slow progress of labour; any bleeding during labour; high blood pressure; and signs of infection. If you are planning a home birth, it is a good idea to pack a bag for the hospital, just in case it is needed.

*'Last week I asked a woman in the clinic if she had thought about having a home birth. She told me that, because she had had a forceps birth last time, she didn't think it was allowed. I told her that the word "allowed" wasn't in my vocabulary and it shouldn't be in hers either.'*

*Anne, midwife*

# Pain relief

You can never judge in advance what pain relief, if any, you will want during labour, but it is important to be aware of the options and the effects they can have on your labour. Keep an open mind because many factors will influence your labour, including your baby's position, whether or not labour is induced, and even the shape of your pelvis.

## Natural pain relief

Giving birth is a natural process and, unless there are complications, the vast majority of women are physically capable of giving birth without medication. There are many different ways of dealing with contractions besides using drugs. Most of the techniques are based on tackling fear as much as the pain of the contractions (see the chart on pages 182–183). Fear has a negative effect on the body in labour, slowing down contractions, tensing muscles and increasing pain. Alternative forms of pain relief put a great deal of emphasis on relaxation with the release of endorphins – the body's natural painkiller.

## Medical pain relief

Even if you are planning to give birth using natural methods of pain relief alone, you should still find out about the various options for medical relief (see the chart on pages 184–185). You will have no idea of your pain

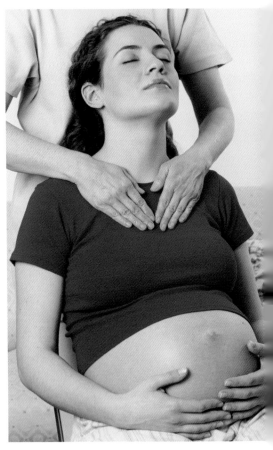

**Above:** Gentle massage relaxes the body and provides natural pain relief during labour.

threshold until labour starts, and it may be that the pain is simply too much for you to endure. You are not a failure if you opt for medical pain relief. The important thing is to feel in control of your labour. There are various options, and each has its disadvantages as well as its advantages. Gas and air (Entonox) makes some women feel nauseous or disorientated, while pethidine and other narcotic drugs can affect the baby. If you are certain from the outset that you do want to use drugs to control the pain, then an epidural may be the most effective method for you.

# Pain relief **common questions**

**Q** What is it like to use gas and air?

**A** Gas and air does not take the pain of the contractions away, but it will make you feel more removed from them. It takes about 30 seconds of breathing the gas for it to take effect, so it is important to start using it as soon as you feel a contraction building. It might make you feel woozy and light-headed, taking the edge off the pain, but will leave you conscious enough to be in control. It can give you a dry mouth, so make sure you sip plenty of fluids. Bear in mind that using gas and air will restrict your movements to some extent, because you have to stay near the supply, so it is wise to put off using it for as long as possible if you want an active birth.

**Q** Can I still have an epidural if I use gas and air?

**A** If you want to try some other pain relief, that is fine. Many women use gas and air while waiting for an epidural to take effect. If the epidural wears off close to the birth of your baby, you can use gas and air, which will help you feel more aware of your contractions.

**Q** When is the best time during labour to have an epidural?

**A** You should really be in established labour before having an epidural, and if you have remained mobile for some of your labour you will have helped the baby to descend lower into the pelvis. There is no 'cut off' point for an epidural, as such: for some women it is still appropriate to have one even if their cervix is 8 cm (3 in) dilated, because progress may have been slow and the baby may be in an awkward position. If you are in stage 2 of labour and it looks as though you are likely to have a forceps birth, a spinal anaesthetic may be suggested. This is similar to an epidural, but is given in a single dose. It takes around six hours to wear off, whereas an epidural wears off within an hour or two.

**Q** Are there circumstances under which I would be refused an epidural?

**A** An epidural is not recommended if you have a blood disorder that increases your chances of bleeding, or an infection. Some spinal conditions, such as scoliosis (curvature of the spine) make it difficult or impossible to position an epidural; a review during your pregnancy by the anaesthetist could help to clarify this.

# Pain relief
## The natural options

| | What to do | How it works |
| --- | --- | --- |
| Relaxation | Learn how to release the tension in your muscles by breathing (see pages 212–213). Relax your face, which will automatically relax your other muscles. Focus on some mental image or listen to a special piece of music to distract you from the contractions and help you relax through them. | Relaxing tense muscles encourages the body to produce endorphins, the natural painkillers. |
| Water | Relax in a warm bath. If you have backache, take a shower and aim the showerhead at the base of your spine. A hot-water bottle, or towels soaked in warm water, placed on your back may help, particularly if you have backache during labour. | The warmth relaxes the muscles, reducing tension and pain, and helping your body to produce natural endorphins. |
| Massage and aromatherapy | You will be reliant on your birth partner for this. Research suggests that just visualizing your partner's hand massaging you stimulates your body to release oxytocin, which helps the contractions to keep coming. Try putting a few drops of clary sage, jasmine or rose on a handkerchief to inhale during labour. | Massage is soothing and comforting, and it also helps in relaxing tense muscles. |
| Transcutaneous electrical nerve stimulation (TENS) | A TENS machine consists of a small portable handset and sticky electrode pads that you attach to your back. | With every contraction the machine releases small electrical impulses that block the pain and encourage the body to release endorphins. |
| Hypnotherapy | Courses are available in self-hypnosis and breathing techniques for labour and birth. (See Hypnotherapy, page 213.) | Uses self-hypnosis, deep relaxation, visualizations, anxiety management and breathing techniques to keep you feeling positive and in control. |

| Advantages | Disadvantages | Effectiveness |
|---|---|---|
| Safe for you and your baby. You can keep active. Even if you are having a vaginal examination, or waiting for an epidural or pethidine to take effect, it helps to know how to relax. | None | Relaxation will help you cope with pain. |
| Safe for you and your baby. Suitable either at home or in hospital. Water supports the weight of your body and you can change positions easily. | None | These measures will help you cope with pain by making you more relaxed, so the experience of pain is reduced. |
| Safe for you and your baby. Can work well in any position. Can be used with other methods of pain relief. | You may not feel like being touched when it comes to labour. Some essential oils should not be used during pregnancy – check with an aromatherapist. | Massage can be effective in helping you cope – particularly with backache during labour. |
| Safe for you and your baby. Can be used at home or in hospital. You are in control of its use and movement is not restricted. Easily removed if it does not work. | May need to be hired from a major drugstore or baby-care shop (not all maternity units have a machine, or they might be in use). Cannot be used in a birthing pool. | Reports vary. Some women find TENS irritating or inadequate. Others say they could not have managed without it. It may be most helpful during early labour. |
| Safe for you and your baby. Can be used at home or in hospital. You are in control. Movement is encouraged. No equipment is necessary. | Courses are not universally available and those that are may be expensive. | Users of the technique report less pain and stress, shorter labour, fewer complications and medical or surgical intervention, quicker recovery times and better bonding with their babies. |

# Pain relief
## The medical options

| | What happens | How it works | Advantages |
|---|---|---|---|
| Gas and air (Entonox) | A mixture of nitrous oxide and oxygen is inhaled through a mouthpiece or facemask. | Provides mild analgesia. Relieves tension. | Safe for you and your baby. You control its use. No restrictions on movement. Can be used in a birthing pool. Clears quickly from the system. Helps to establish a breathing pattern for each contraction. Can be used with other methods of pain relief. |
| Pethidine or meptazinol | Narcotic drugs are injected into the buttock or thigh by a midwife. They take 20 minutes to have an effect and last for up to three hours. | Mood-altering, producing relaxation and drowsiness. Relieves tension and anxiety, which can prolong labour. | Given by midwife, so readily available for use. |
| Epidural | Anaesthetic is introduced through a fine tube, inserted by an anaesthetist into the base of the spine. This can either be topped up by the midwife, as required, or given continuously through an infusion pump, which allows the numbing effect to last for as long as necessary. Once the epidural has been removed, the effects wear off quite quickly – usually within an hour. | Numbs the area from the top of the bump downwards. | Can lower blood pressure if it is very high. Will not affect the baby unless your blood pressure drops. |
| Spinal block | An anaesthetist injects anaesthetic into the fluid around the spinal cord and then removes the needles. This provides a dose of very effective pain relief that lasts for around five or six hours in total. | Numbs the area from the waist down. | Can lower blood pressure if it is very high. Will not affect the baby, unless your blood pressure drops. |

| Disadvantages | Effectiveness |
|---|---|
| May produce nausea. | Excellent for taking the edge off the pain – it will hurt, but you do not care so much. |
| Crosses the placenta and can make your baby sleepy even after birth, which can be serious if given close to birth. Baby needs to be closely monitored. May produce nausea, which can be counteracted by another drug. You may be confined to bed because of sleepiness, which can slow down labour. | Effective for women who are tense. Takes the edge off the pain. Some women find it a problem because they can feel the contractions but are too sleepy to do anything about them, such as change position. |
| Administered by an anaesthetist. You must keep still while it is administered, which may be hard during contractions. You may need to be catheterized. A drip must be set up in case blood pressure falls. Can slow contractions, so a drip may be necessary to speed things up. Movement is severely or totally restricted. You cannot feel contractions, so may need to be told when to push. Risk of severe headache if the needle accidentally pierces the sheath around the spinal cord. Increases the chances of an assisted birth (forceps and ventouse, see pages 230–231). | The most effective form of pain relief, which works in 90 per cent of cases. Unfortunately some women only feel the effects of an epidural down one side of the body. |
| Anaesthetist needs to be available and you must keep still. You are usually catheterized. Same risk of severe headache as epidural. Movement is restricted. Nausea is a common side-effect. Can take about five hours to wear off. | Very effective, fast pain relief for unplanned caesareans and some instrumental deliveries. |

# Birth plans

Drawing up a birth plan makes you consider the variety of options available, as well as think about what is important to you and your partner. A written birth plan acts as a communication tool between you and your midwife and helps to set the 'tone' of the sort of labour and birth that you are hoping for.

**Above:** Writing a birth plan is an effective way of communicating your wishes to the midwife.

## Where to start

To make choices, you need information, and it is never too early to start finding out what is available. Reading, talking to other women who have had babies, attending antenatal classes and chatting with your midwife should give you some idea of the sort of birth you would prefer.

## Birth plans
# Common questions

**Q** How should I present my birth plan?
**A** A letter is more personal and will give the midwife caring for you some idea of your personality. Put something of yourself into the plan and explain what you and your partner feel is important and why. Some antenatal notes have a space for you to write a birth plan, but you can always write one up separately.

## Birth plan checklist

Consider the following points:
- Do you want to know the midwife who cares for you in labour?
- Do you want to be encouraged to move about during labour?
- Have you considered all of your options for pain relief (see pages 182–185)?
- Do you want to avoid constant fetal monitoring, which would stop you moving about during labour? (See Monitoring the baby, pages 216–217.)
- What are your views on induced labour? (See Being induced, pages 224–225.)
- Under what circumstances would you be prepared to have an episiotomy? (See Episiotomy and tearing, pages 234–235.)
- Do you want to deliver the placenta without intervention? (See Stage 3 of labour, pages 222–223.)
- Does your partner want to cut the cord?
- Do you want your baby delivered onto your stomach?

# Birth partners

The greatest influence on your ability to cope during labour is the support that you receive. This will come not only from your midwife, but also from the person or people you choose to have with you at the birth. You need to feel confident that they will be able to give you the emotional support and practical care that you will need.

## Who to choose

Although most fathers want to be there at the birth, this is not right for everyone. Some men are not happy about seeing their partner in physical pain, while in some cultures men are discouraged from being present at a birth and two female relatives attend instead. You must trust the people you choose to stay with you and be honest about what you expect from them during your labour – but essentially they should want to be there.

## Birth partners **Common questions**

**Q** How many birth partners can I have?
**A** Most maternity units are happy for you to have two people with you during labour because research shows that continual support benefits mothers in a number of ways, such as feeling more in control of labour and more positive about the birth experience. Consider who would be best to provide this support. It may be your partner, a friend, a sister or your mother. Women who have had children before will not worry about seeing you in pain and are more able to reassure you that everything is completely normal.

**Q** My husband wants so much to be at the birth, but he is anxious about how he will cope with it all. How can I encourage him?
**A** Many men have fears about birth, the most common being concerns about seeing their partner in pain and not being able to 'cure'

them of it. Persuade your husband to attend antenatal classes with you. The opportunity to talk with other men in the group and discovering that he is not alone in his fears might make him more confident about being present at the birth.

**Q** What should a birth partner do?
**A** A birth partner can help you in a number of ways: he or she can time your contractions and help you to establish a good pattern of breathing, support you as you move around in labour and massage your back and shoulders. Once the midwife is with you, your birth partner can be your spokesperson if you do not feel up to it. He or she needs to listen to you and provide comfort and emotional support. During the last few pushes your birth partner can also encourage you by telling you the progress of the baby's head.

# Tests during pregnancy
## Antenatal check-ups

Pregnancy involves a lot of tests, not only to find out right at the start whether you are really pregnant or not but also, throughout your pregnancy, to check on your health and your baby's health. At each check-up, your midwife will add information to your antenatal notes. You may be given these, to take to other check-ups. You will obviously read them, so it is useful to know what the tests are for, what they involve and how to interpret the results that are recorded.

## Checks for the baby

- **Position and presentation** This refers to the way your baby is lying in the uterus and which way up he is.
- **Fundus** This refers to the height of your uterus. If you are 28 weeks pregnant and the midwife feels that the growth of your baby is right for the gestation, she will write: = dates, or = 28 cm. 'Weeks' refers to the duration of your pregnancy on the day of your check.
- **Fetal heart** The midwife listens to the fetal heart with a handheld Doppler or a pinnard, which looks like an ear trumpet.
- **Relation to the brim** Towards the end of your pregnancy the midwife will record how much of your baby's head can still be felt above the brim of the pelvis and how much has descended into the pelvis. This is expressed in terms of fifths.

## Antenatal check-ups
## Common questions

**Q What kind of blood tests are carried out?**
**A** You will be advised to have blood tests that check what blood group you are, and if any antibodies are present in your blood. They will also check whether you are immune to rubella, and will check for hepatitis and syphilis. Your haemoglobin will be checked to see whether you have anaemia. Some screening tests will also be offered to you (see pages 192–193).

**Q Why is it so important to keep an eye on my blood pressure?**
**A** High blood pressure (hypertension) can affect the growth of your baby and can also develop into a life-threatening condition called eclampsia (see page 142). Approximately 10 per cent of women develop pre-eclampsia during their pregnancy but, with careful monitoring, it does not become a problem.

**Q What is my urine tested for?**
**A** You should take a sample of urine with you to every check-up. The midwife tests it for sugar, which can show up if you have recently consumed a lot of sugary foods or drinks, but can also be a sign of diabetes; and protein, which can be a sign of pre-eclampsia when accompanied by a rise in blood pressure or oedema (swelling, see page 162). It can also sometimes be a sign of an infection. She may also test for ketones, which indicate that your body is short of sugar and are often found in women who have severe pregnancy sickness.

# What your notes mean

If there is anything you do not understand, it is better to ask than to go home and worry. Here are some common phrases and abbreviations:

## Your details

**Para 0/1/2 +1:** You have had 0, 1, 2 previous births. +1 means a miscarriage or termination after 24 weeks gestation

**LB or SB:** Live birth or stillbirth

**TCA 3/7 (4/52):** To come again in three days (or four weeks)

**Brim:** The inlet or upper rim of your pelvis

**Fundus:** The top of your uterus, which rises in your stomach as your baby grows and descends a little when the baby's head engages

**BP:** Blood pressure

**PET:** Pre-eclampsia (pre-eclamptic toxaemia)

**US or USS:** Ultrasound scan

## Urine

**NAD:** Nothing abnormal detected

**Alb/Tr Prot+ (or ++):** Albumin/trace of protein. The plus signs indicate the amount of protein found. This could signify the start of pre-eclampsia

**0 Gluc:** No glucose found in the urine. Two ++ or more glucose would be considered high

## Blood

**Bloods:** Blood tests done

**Hb:** Haemoglobin or blood count

**Fe:** Iron tablets. The prescription name may be recorded.

**WR:** Syphilis test **VDRL/TPHA** or **FTA-Abs** are alternatives

## Your baby's health

**FMF or FMNF:** Fetal movements felt, or not felt

**H:** Fetal heart. **H or NH** means heard or not heard. The heart rate (usually between 120 and 160 beats per minute) may be recorded. **FHHR** means fetal heart heard and regular.

## Your baby's position

**LOA/ROA:** Left (or right) occipito anterior (or **LOP/ROP** posterior). Presenting part, or the part of your baby nearest to the cervix and likely to emerge first

**Vx or Ceph:** Vertex or cephalic, meaning 'head down'

**Br/Tr:** Breech (bottom down)/transverse (lying across the uterus)

**Eng or E:** Engaged. This refers to how far down your baby's head is in your pelvis. When recorded in fifths it means the proportion of your baby's head above the brim of your pelvis. So 2/5 means the head is almost fully engaged, ready for the birth, while 4/5 means it has started to engage

**Neng or NE:** Not engaged

**Right:** Your midwife can check the baby's position by gently feeling your abdomen.

# Tests during pregnancy
# Ultrasound scans

Ultrasound can provide a detailed examination of almost all fetal structures and it is a useful diagnostic tool during pregnancy. It has been shown to be safe, and has become widely acceptable to mothers and an indispensable part of antenatal care.

## Uses of ultrasound scans

Ultrasound scans are used for a number of different purposes:

- **Monitoring fetal growth and wellbeing** Until 14 weeks, the size of your baby is measured by her crown-rump length. After this, fetal weight can be estimated by measuring the head circumference (HC), biparietal diameter (BPD – the width of the head), abdominal circumference (AC), and femur length (FL – length of the thigh bone). The amount of amniotic fluid (see page 57) is also important. A low amount may indicate that your baby is not getting enough nutrients.
- **Locating the placenta** If the placenta is too low and remains that way in late pregnancy (see Placenta praevia, page 130), you may need a caesarean section.
- **Guiding invasive procedures** Chorionic villus sampling and amniocentesis (see pages 194–195) are best performed under continuous ultrasound control. In this way, the needle can be safely guided to the sampling site without harming you or your baby.

## True story

**Testing for Down's syndrome**

'I was looking forward to the 20-week scan. We'd had a nuchal scan at 12 weeks, which was amazing. Plus we'd got a low-risk result for Down's. This time round, I noticed the sonographer kept looking at the same area. After the scan we were led into a room and a consultant was called. My heart was beating so rapidly that I could hardly breathe.

'We were told that our baby had a much higher risk of Down's syndrome than was previously thought. I had the choice of carrying on, with the fear that my baby might be severely disabled, or I could have an amniocentesis test to find out for sure, but possibly miscarry. It took us 10 days to decide to go ahead with the amniocentesis. I was convinced I was going to lose the baby.

'We had intended to get the results in person rather than over the phone, but when I called the day before to make sure they'd be in the nurse told me she had them already. I held my breath as she told me we were in the clear – and then I burst into tears.'

*Julia, mother of Ben*

# Ultrasound scans **Common questions**

**Q** What happens at an ultrasound scan?

**A** To start with, the person doing the scan will rub a special gel onto your abdomen to reduce any signal loss. He or she will then place a probe (a transducer) onto your abdomen. The transducer both emits and receives ultrasound waves. These reflected ultrasound waves are continuously assembled into a picture on a screen. This shows solid structures as white and liquid structures as black. Moving structures, such as the fetal heart, can be assessed, and freezing the picture enables accurate measurements of the fetus to be taken.

**Above:** An ultrasound scan allows parents-to-be to see an image of their baby for the first time.

**Q** What is ultrasound used for during early pregnancy?

**A** It is possible to use ultrasound to diagnose pregnancy from approximately 4–5 weeks after your last menstrual period, and detection of a fetal heartbeat at around 6 weeks will confirm the viability of your pregnancy. An early ultrasound scan can also confirm a multiple pregnancy and determine the number of placentas. The main purpose of the early scan (usually done at 10–12 weeks) is to establish the estimated date of delivery. If done between 11 and 14 weeks, it can screen the fetus for chromosomal abnormalities, such as trisomy 21 (Down's syndrome), by measuring the thickness of the fat pad at the back of the neck (nuchal translucency, see page 192).

**Q** What is the detailed scan at 18–20 weeks used for?

**A** The purpose of this scan is to check that your baby is developing normally. This scan carefully examines each part of your baby in turn and any problems are noted. It will detect even small abnormalities, such as a cleft lip or tiny holes in your baby's heart. If a problem is found, or suspected, you will be told at the time of the scan and an appointment to have another scan with a specialist should be made within 72 hours. Around 15 per cent of scans will need to be repeated for one reason or another; most problems that need repeat scanning are not serious.

# Tests during pregnancy
## Screening tests

The series of tests that you are given throughout your pregnancy help to ascertain whether you or your baby have any problems. They are designed to check the level of risk and include blood tests, urine tests and ultrasound scans. If a screening test indicates an increased risk for a condition, it will usually be followed by a diagnostic test (see pages 194–197), to determine whether or not the condition is present.

## What are the tests?

Some hospitals offer certain screening tests routinely to all women, while others offer them only to women in 'at-risk groups' of having or developing a particular condition that might require special care or intervention. Routine blood tests and ultrasound scans are among these screening tests (see pages 190–191), but there are a number of others:

- **Nuchal scan** This may form part of the routine ultrasound scan and is performed at 11–14 weeks. The fold of skin at the back of your baby's neck (the nuchal fold) is checked to see whether any excess fluid is present, which is a possible sign of Down's syndrome.

- **Serum screening at around 10 weeks** If you are at risk of having a baby with Down's syndrome, you will have a blood test to establish the levels of the fetal hormones plasma protein A and human chorionic gonadotrophin (HCG) present in your blood.

- **Serum screening at around 16 weeks** You will be given further tests to check the levels of fetal hormones in your blood at about 16 weeks. Depending on the hospital, this will be an AFP test (to check for alphafetoprotein, or AFP), a triple test (which also checks for HCG and oestriol), or a triple-plus or quadruple test (which checks for inhibin A, too). Abnormal levels of these hormones may be an indication of spina bifida or Down's syndrome.

- **Genetic screening** Your blood can also be tested for inherited conditions, for example, sickle-cell anaemia, haemophilia, thalassaemia and cystic fibrosis, according to your ethnic, family or geographical background. For conditions such as sickle-cell anaemia, your partner will also be screened if you test positive. It is important to remember that these tests only indicate the possibility of a baby inheriting a condition. If the results are positive, you will be offered diagnostic tests in order to investigate further.

# Screening tests **Common questions**

**Q** Under what circumstances might mine be considered an 'at-risk' pregnancy?
**A** There are several factors determining this. Among them are your medical history and any previous pregnancies, and your family history, for example, if there are inherited conditions such as cystic fibrosis among members of your family or your partner's family. Your ethnic group (and that of your partner) is also taken into account. (Higher rates of thalassaemia are found in people of Mediterranean origin; sickle-cell anaemia is mainly found among people of African descent, and cystic fibrosis occurs in white people of western European origin.)

**Q** What is an anomaly scan?
**A** This is the name given to the ultrasound scan you receive at 18–20 weeks (see pages 190–191). It also provides an opportunity to check for signs of spina bifida, changes that might be associated with Down's syndrome, and conditions that might require antenatal monitoring and neonatal care.

**Q** Is it up to me whether these tests are carried out?
**A** Yes it is, and there are a number of things you should consider when deciding whether or not to have any screening test. A low-risk assessment will be reassuring, while a higher risk assessment will give you the opportunity to decide whether to have follow-up diagnostic tests, so you can be fully prepared for your baby's arrival. Many women find the stress of screening very disturbing and they prefer not to have it done. Your midwife and doctor have your best interests at heart and should talk through the options of further tests with you. However, the decision rests with you. At this stage, it may be wise to start thinking about what you will do if the result is positive.

**Q** Are the screening tests accurate?
**A** Although the accuracy of detection rates has improved, no screening method is perfect. For example, raised levels of alphafetoprotein (AFP) in your blood may have other causes, such as a twin pregnancy. On average, only 1 in 20 women is assessed as being at high risk of carrying a baby with Down's syndrome and offered diagnostic testing. However, of these assessments, only 1 in 60 will be correct. Overall, screening tests will identify about 60 per cent of all cases of Down's syndrome.

# Tests during pregnancy
## Diagnostic tests

If the result of a screening test (see pages 192–193) indicates that your baby is at high risk of an abnormality, you will be offered a follow-up diagnostic test. These tests are not routinely available or performed as they are invasive and there is a risk of provoking a miscarriage in 1–2 per cent of cases. Usually, a fine needle or biopsy forceps will be guided by ultrasound to take a sample of placental tissue, amniotic fluid or fetal blood for analysis.

## Who is offered a test?

A diagnostic test is offered to women at risk of having a baby with a chromosomal abnormality. Risk factors include:

- Late age (late 30s and 40s)
- A history of a chromosome abnormality (for example, if you have a previous child with Down's syndrome)
- A family history of a genetic disorder like cystic fibrosis
- A problem seen on the ultrasound scan
- An increased serum screening risk or a raised nuchal translucency (see page 192).

## Chorionic villus sampling (CVS)

CVS is the removal and examination of a small amount of placental tissue (afterbirth), known as chorionic villi. Because the placenta and

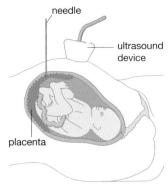

**Left:** Transabdominal CVS: a needle is used to take a sample of placental tissue.

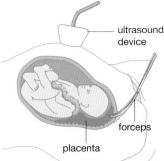

**Left:** Transvaginal CVS: a catheter or biopsy forceps pass through the cervix to take the placental sample.

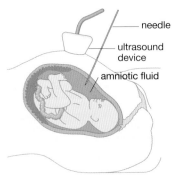

**Left:** Amniocentesis: a sample of fluid is taken from the amniotic sac with a needle.

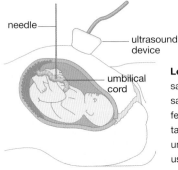

**Left:** Fetal blood sampling: a sample of fetal blood is taken from the umbilical cord using a needle.

fetus are made up of the same cells, an analysis of the cells of the placental tissue provides information about the fetus itself. Analysis of the chromosomes in these cells will detect any abnormalities, while analysis of the individual genes will reveal any genetic defects. Most women describe the procedure as uncomfortable but not too painful. Afterwards, it is normal to experience some abdominal discomfort, which can be relieved by mild painkillers. If the symptoms worsen or any bleeding occurs after this test, you should contact your midwife or doctor urgently.

## Amniocentesis

Amniocentesis is the removal of a small amount of the amniotic fluid that surrounds the fetus. Amniotic fluid contains skin cells from the baby that can be tested for chromosomal defects, for example, Down's syndrome. As with CVS, many women find the procedure uncomfortable but not particularly painful. Amniocentesis usually takes only about 10 minutes and is thus well tolerated by most women who have it.

## Fetal blood sampling

Another method of diagnostic testing is sampling the fetal blood, either from the cord (cordocentesis) or from a vein in the fetal liver (intrahepatic vein). The technique is similar to amniocentesis and CVS except that the aim is to obtain a small sample of fetal blood rather than amniotic fluid or placental tissue.

## Diagnostic tests
# Common questions

**Q** Do I have to consent to a diagnostic test?
**A** The decision to undergo diagnostic testing is often difficult and causes a huge amount of anxiety. The midwife or obstetrician is there to ensure that you fully understand the benefits and risks of any test. But remember, no one has to have a diagnostic test. The final decision has to be made by the parents. In the case of CVS, your doctor will discuss it with you fully and will usually obtain your written consent.

**Q** What happens once the test results are through?
**A** If the test result is abnormal, you will be invited to discuss the available options with your obstetrician. Do not forget, however, that a normal result, although reassuring, does not rule out the possibility of there being any other problems.

**Q** Why are certain tests carried out after specific weeks of pregnancy?
**A** In some cases, performing the tests too early can be harmful for the baby. For example, evidence suggests that CVS performed before 10 weeks can result in limb deformities, while amniocentesis performed before 14 weeks carries an increased risk of talipes and the chances of causing a miscarriage are raised.

# Tests during pregnancy
## Benefits and risks of diagnostic testing

| What is the test? | When and how is it performed? |
|---|---|
| **Chorionic villus sampling (CVS)** | After 11 weeks. It involves injecting a local anaesthetic and then, under ultrasound guidance, passing a needle through the skin and layers of your abdomen into the placenta. A sample of the placenta is then taken and sent for analysis. Occasionally the procedure is performed through the cervix, for example, if the placenta is very low or the uterus is tilted back (retroverted). If you are Rhesus negative, you will be advised to have an injection of Anti-D (see page 141). |
| **Amniocentesis** | The procedure is only performed after 15 weeks. You may not require an anaesthetic because the needle used for amniocentesis is finer than that used for CVS. The procedure is conducted under ultrasound guidance and involves passing a needle through the skin and layers of your abdominal wall into the uterus, avoiding the fetus and, if possible, avoiding the placenta. A small sample of fluid (for example, 15 ml (1 tbsp) at 15 weeks) is then removed. If you are Rhesus negative, you will be given an injection of Anti-D (see page 141). |
| **Fetal blood sampling** | After 18–20 weeks of pregnancy. For cordocentesis, ultrasound is used to locate the point where the umbilical cord is inserted into the placenta. The procedure then involves inserting a fine needle through the abdomen and uterine walls into the umbilical cord, using ultrasound as a guide. Once the fetal blood sample has been obtained, it is sent to the laboratory for analysis. Blood samples from the intrahepatic vein are taken in a similar way, except that the needle is guided into the fetal liver. |

| What is it used for? | When will I know the results? | What are the risks? |
| --- | --- | --- |
| CVS is used to detect chromosome abnormalities (for example, Down's syndrome) and genetic disorders (for example, muscular dystrophy, Huntington's chorea, sickle-cell anaemia and cystic fibrosis). | An initial result is usually available within 2–3 days. The full culture result takes about two weeks. | The risk of miscarriage is about 1–2 per cent. If miscarriage does occur, it usually takes place within a week of the test. In rare cases (about 1 in 100), an abnormality is seen in the placenta cells that is not found in the fetus. In this case, it may be necessary to perform another amniocentesis in order to confirm that the fetus is not affected. In about 1 in 200 cases, no full culture result is obtained. |
| Amniocentesis is generally used to detect chromosome abnormalities (for example, Down's syndrome, or trisomy 21), genetic disorders (such as cystic fibrosis) and fetal infection. | Some hospitals offer rapid tests in addition to the full culture test. These results are available with 2–3 days of the procedure. The full culture results take longer (usually about two weeks). | The risk of miscarriage after amniocentesis is about 1 per cent and it usually occurs within a week of the procedure. In about 1 in 200 cases, no full culture result is obtained, in which case the rapid test results are usually reliable. |
| Fetal blood sampling is now mainly reserved for conditions such as fetal anaemia (for example, as a result of Rhesus disease), fetal infection (for example, toxoplasmosis or rubella) or fetal blood disorders (such as sickle-cell disease). If fetal anaemia is diagnosed, the fetus can be given a blood transfusion using the same needle. | A full chromosome result is usually available within 72 hours. | The major risk of fetal blood sampling is a 1–2 per cent risk of miscarriage. |

# Twin pregnancies

The number of twin pregnancies has steadily increased over the last decade. In Europe, approximately 1 in 80 pregnancies are twins, and multiple births are also more common nowadays. This is partly due to the increased use of fertility treatment and also because many women are now delaying getting pregnant until they are older, which increases their chances of twin or multiple pregnancy.

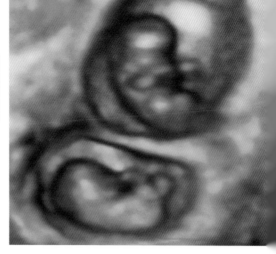

**Above:** If you are bearing twins, it is important that you have regular antenatal check-ups.

## What to expect

Being pregnant with two babies is especially exciting, and even a little awesome, for both you and those around you. The experience can also feel overwhelming at times. If you are carrying twins, you should have regular antenatal checks to identify if there any potential complications. Many obstetricians recommend taking iron and folate supplements to prevent anaemia.

In early pregnancy, an increase in the common symptoms, such as pregnancy sickness or excessive tiredness, or simply an unusually large uterus, may suggest that you are carrying twins. However, the obstetrician needs to know not only how many babies there are but also the number of placentas present. In the majority of twin pregnancies, there are separate placentas (dichorionic twins). In about 20 per cent of these pregnancies, however, the placenta is shared (monochorionic twins). Monochorionic twins have much higher complication rates and therefore will need closer monitoring.

Since early birth is a much more common occurrence in twins and multiple pregnancies, you should visit the hospital to be checked over if you notice any hint of labour occurring. You are more likely to go into premature labour if you have a short cervix, and some hospitals offer a scan at 24 weeks to measure the length of this. Almost all twins are delivered in hospital and both of them are monitored continually throughout labour.

### Twin-twin transfusion syndrome

Identical twins who share a placenta have a small but significant risk of developing twin-twin transfusion syndrome (TTTS). One twin receives more blood than the other because of abnormal blood vessels that connect across the placenta. Treatments include destroying these vessels with a laser and draining excess amniotic fluid.

# Twin pregnancies **Common questions**

**Q** Are there risks involved in carrying twins?

**A** Twin and multiple pregnancies are thought to be high-risk for both mother and baby. For the mother, there is an increased risk of complications, for example, gestational diabetes (see pages 138–139), pre-eclampsia (see pages 142–143) and anaemia (see page 160). For the babies, the risk of growth restriction and pre-term labour are of particular concern. Therefore, you will be offered close antenatal care and regular scans to monitor the growth of your babies.

**Q** Will I have the ultrasound scans just as I would if I were carrying one baby?

**A** Yes, twins can be screened for Down's syndrome at 11–14 weeks by looking at the nuchal translucency (see page 192). A detailed scan is also performed at 18–20 weeks. Twins are more likely to have certain structural abnormalities, for example congenital heart disease and neural tube defects (such as spina bifida). In addition to this, twins are often monitored every four weeks by ultrasound to look for growth restriction (although many women would not want to risk both babies miscarrying through the further investigations that can follow the screening tests). Growth restriction affects about 25 per cent of dichorionic twins and almost 50 per cent of monochorionic twins. The major risk to monochorionic twins, however, is the development of twin-twin transfusion syndrome (TTTS, see opposite).

**Q** I have heard that you are more likely to suffer from morning sickness if you are carrying twins. Is this true?

**A** Pregnancy symptoms are often more pronounced with twins and multiple pregnancies – for example, you may experience more sickness, fatigue, heartburn, haemorrhoids – because your body is working harder and carrying more weight than during a pregnancy with one baby. You are also more likely to develop high blood pressure (hypertension) and you may need to give up work earlier – many women stop work at around 26 weeks of pregnancy.

## Five facts about **twin pregnancies**

1 The average length of a twin pregnancy is 36 weeks, and 34 weeks for triplets.
2 Tall women are more likely to conceive twins.
3 Women over 35 are more likely to have twins.
4 Up to 22 per cent of twins are left-handed while for non-twins the rate is just under 10 per cent.
5 The United States has one of the highest rates for multiple births, while Japan has one of the lowest.

7

# labour and birth

# Getting ready

Preparing for your baby involves more than just packing your bag for the hospital and decorating the nursery. You also need time to adjust emotionally to the prospect of the alterations created in your life by having a baby.

## Preparations to make

It is important to know who to ring and what to do when you go into labour. You should have the phone number of the labour ward in your antenatal notes, as well as any other important phone numbers, for example your community midwife or ambulance control. It is always useful to have a list of phone numbers to hand – not only your partner's mobile number, but also the numbers of local taxi firms and all the people you will want to call with your news after the birth of your baby.

If you have already had a tour around the maternity unit, make sure that you and your partner know how to get there and where to go when you arrive. You could even practise driving the route in the rush hour, just to see how long it takes. Remember that, with a first baby, even if you get stuck in traffic, you will probably still have time to spare! Make sure that you can find the correct entrance, especially at night when the main doors to the hospital or maternity unit may be locked.

**Above:** The weeks spent 'nest-building' just before the birth are a very special time for mums-to-be.

## Getting ready
## Common questions

**Q** When is the best time to stop work?
**A** Choosing the right time to give up work is a common problem, particularly if you intend to return to work and have a limited amount of maternity leave. Many women try to make the most of their maternity leave by working as far into the pregnancy as possible. However, it can be very difficult being at home with a baby only a week or two after giving up work.

# What to pack

Your hospital will provide a list of things to bring in, and here are some additional suggestions. It makes it easier if you pack two bags, one for the labour ward and one for after the birth. If you know you are having a caesarean section, pack a few more of everything in your post-natal bag, or ask your partner to bring things in as the need arises.

## Labour ward bag

- Comfortable clothes to wear during labour, for example an oversized T-shirt or nightdress
- Socks and slippers
- Dressing gown
- Three pairs of large disposable knickers (for when your waters break and also immediately after the birth, when your blood loss will be quite heavy)
- Clean nightdress for afterwards
- A sponge or flannel to keep you cool during labour
- Massage oils and equipment if you are using them
- Toiletries, including mild soap, toothbrush and toothpaste, hairbrush and towel
- Sanitary towels (maternity pads or night-time sanitary towels)

- Cartons of fruit juice and high-energy snacks (for example, dried fruit)
- Birth plan
- Camera
- Hot-water bottle for easing backache
- Hand mirror – so that you can see your baby's head emerging, especially useful when you feel you are not making any progress
- Battery-operated music system or radio (electronic items from home are sometimes not allowed on the ward) and a selection of music that you can use to focus on through your contractions
- Change for the telephone (you are not allowed to use a mobile phone in the hospital), address book and important telephone numbers
- For your baby: two baby-grow suits, two vests, nappies, cotton wool, hat

## Post-natal bag

- Nightdress – front-opening if you intend to breastfeed
- Several pairs of knickers
- Nursing bra
- A few breast pads
- Good-quality nipple cream
- Sanitary towels (heavy-duty)

- Something to read – if you get time!
- For your baby: four baby-grow suits, four vests, a small pack of nappies and a hat, cardigan or outdoor suit for wearing home. If you are not planning to breastfeed you may also need bottles, teats and formula, if the unit does not provide them.

# YOUR BABY'S POSITION

## Preparing for the outside world

**The position of your baby in the uterus can affect labour and birth. By 37 weeks of pregnancy most babies will be head down, ready for labour.**

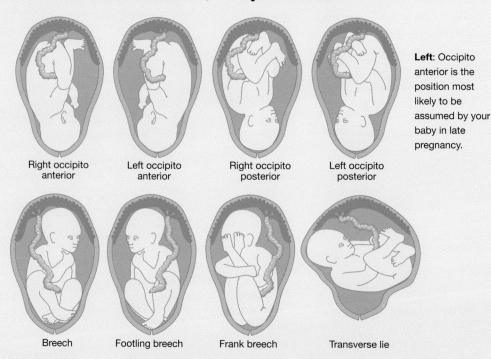

Right occipito anterior

Left occipito anterior

Right occipito posterior

Left occipito posterior

**Left**: Occipito anterior is the position most likely to be assumed by your baby in late pregnancy.

Breech

Footling breech

Frank breech

Transverse lie

The position of your baby is irrelevant until 37 weeks of pregnancy, as she will still be moving. Even after 37 weeks a few babies are mobile, waiting for the softening hormones produced at the start of labour before they engage. Others simply stay bottom down. A baby that is head down and fully engaged rarely changes position.

abdomen. This position is described as occipito anterior or OA (the occipito is the back of the baby's head). This is the ideal position for the baby to pass through the pelvis – she can tuck her chin on her chest, fit through the pelvis neatly and turn slightly to emerge at birth. The majority of babies adopt this position.

## Occipito anterior

Your baby will probably be facing your back, with her back slightly to one side of your

## Occipito posterior

The occipito posterior (OP) position is when your baby is lying with her back against your

## Five steps to the **best position**

You can try to encourage your baby to get into the best position for labour with the following:

1 Sit with your knees lower than your hips.
2 When standing, lean over slightly as much as possible, for example, over a work surface, thus allowing your baby more space to turn.
3 Swim – breaststroke is best – the buoyancy gives your baby more room to move around.
4 Try kneeling on all fours as often as possible so that gravity helps the baby's spine, which is heaviest, to move round.
5 Adopt a knee to chest position for 5–10 minutes four times a day.

back, facing your abdomen. Only about 5 per cent of these babies fail to move into an OA position. If your baby is one of these 5 per cent, it does not mean that you cannot have a vaginal birth. However, in this position your baby cannot tuck her chin in so well and most will have further to rotate to pass under your pubic arch. This is more likely to make labour longer and to give you backache during labour (see below). You are also more likely to need an assisted birth (see pages 230–231).

## Breech

A breech position is when your baby's buttocks are facing down and her head is under your ribs. Her legs may be tucked up (frank breech) or she may have one or both legs pointing down (footling breech). If your baby is breech, you may be offered an external cephalic version (ECV) at about 37 weeks. This is where the obstetrician manipulates your abdomen to try to turn the baby around (see below).

## Transverse lie

A transverse lie is when your baby is lying across your abdomen, with her head towards your left or right side. Unless she turns, you will need a caesarean.

## Unstable lie

A baby that keeps changing position after 37 weeks of pregnancy is known as an unstable lie. Labour may be induced while she has her head down.

## Babies that do not turn

If your baby does not turn head down spontaneously by 36 weeks, you could encourage her to do so (see box). Your doctor might also try, especially if this is not your first baby. This option should be discussed with you first. You will be asked to lie on your back with your knees up and to relax while the doctor massages your tummy. This is called external cephalic version (ECV). No force is used and your doctor will stop if your baby clearly does not want to move. After 36 weeks it is sensible to discuss breech birth with your midwife in case your baby does not turn. Only 3 per cent of babies remain in a breech position at birth.

## Backache labour

If your baby is lying in a back-to-back (occipito posterior) position, you are likely to suffer from considerable backache during and between your contractions. This is because the baby's head is hard pressed against your sacrum and the base of your spine. You can relieve the backache to some extent by getting into an all-fours position during labour. This position makes the baby drop down and away from your spine.

# Overview of labour

A normal gestation is anywhere between 37 and 42 weeks of pregnancy and, in practice, only 5 per cent of babies arrive on their estimated due date. The onset of labour is usually a gradual process and you may have mild, irregular contractions for some days before labour begins in earnest, so do not expect to rush to the hospital at the first sign of something happening, unless you have any obvious complications.

**Above:** The familiar surroundings of home can make labour a much more relaxed experience.

## What happens?

The definition of established labour is the onset of regular contractions with dilation of the cervix. The uterus is made of muscle, which tenses and relaxes during a contraction. At the bottom is the cervix, which also forms the top of the vagina. As part of the birth process, changes must occur in the cervix in order for the baby to pass through and into the birth canal. The cervix will gradually get softer and thinner, and then it will start to dilate (open) in preparation for the birth.

If you are getting contractions but your cervix has not started to dilate, this is still regarded as early labour (latent phase). Early labour is different from established labour, which is the point of no return. (See the box, right, and pages 214–215, 218–219 and 222–223 for more on the three stages of established labour.)

### Established labour

Established labour is divided into three stages:
- **Stage 1** from the start of regular contractions and the opening of the cervix until the cervix has fully dilated (10 cm/4 in). With a first baby this takes an average of 10–12 hours.
- **Stage 2** from full dilation of the cervix to the birth of the baby. When the cervix is fully open you will be able to push the baby down the birth canal. With a first baby, this takes an hour on average. The second stage is often shorter in subsequent pregnancies.
- **Stage 3** from the birth of your baby to the delivery of the placenta and membranes (the bag of fluid that surrounded your baby). This can last between 10 minutes and an hour.

# Labour **Common questions**

**Q** This probably sounds silly, but how will I know when I am in labour?

**A** Many women worry they will not recognize labour – but you will! Most start with mild, period-like cramps that gradually develop a pattern. Some expectant mothers feel it low in their abdomen, others in the back. The latent (very early) phase of labour can last a few days, with 'niggly' aches and pains that start and stop. The general rule is: if you are not sure you are in labour, you probably are not. It might be the start of it, but when you have regular contractions that take your breath away, you will know.

**Q** I am worried that the onset of labour will send me into a panic and that I will not be able to cope. What can I do to prevent this?

**A** Keeping relaxed is the key here. The longer you are able to stay at home the better. A new environment is likely to make you tense, and a labour ward is no exception. It is natural to be excited about going into hospital but being there does not mean that your baby will arrive any quicker. In fact, many women find that the contractions stop once they get to hospital because anxiety inhibits their labour. Therefore, unless your waters break, or the contractions are strong and five minutes apart, it is too early to turn up at the maternity unit. Your community midwife may be able to visit if you are unsure whether or not you have gone into labour. However, as a general rule, if you have any doubts, your labour has probably not started.

**Q** What should I do if I happen to go into labour early?

**A** If you notice signs of labour starting and it is three weeks or more before your due date, contact the labour ward straight away. Many babies come early without problems, but some will need specialist help. If you have several weeks to go, the hospital may try to delay your labour with drugs in order to give your baby more time to mature. Take your notes with you if you stay away from home and contact the nearest hospital if labour does start.

*'When I had a show we just looked at each other, unsure what to do. We had been to antenatal classes, read every pregnancy book and magazine, and there we were, frozen to the spot with a mixture of fear and excitement. It is a good job we did not rush off to the hospital because it was still a week before the contractions started, and then 10 hours after that Jacob was born!'*

*Paula, mother of Jacob*

# Positions for labour
## Stage 1

In the last weeks of pregnancy, practise the positions on these pages a couple of times to see how they feel. You will not know in advance which will be the most effective and comfortable for you in labour so it is a good idea to try them all. Do not stick to just one position but move between them as your body dictates, with your birth partner's help if you need it.

**1** When you feel like resting rather than moving around, it is better to opt for a chair than a bed or an armchair. Pad the seat with a pillow and sit back to front, with your legs either side of the chair back. Relax onto another pillow placed under your chin.

**2** When a contraction comes while you are walking around, stand with your arms on your birth partner's shoulders, lean forwards and let him or her support some of your weight in a reassuring hug until the pain subsides. You can also support yourself by leaning against a wall, worktop or a piece of heavy furniture.

**3** Sit halfway back on a chair, with your knees apart and leaning onto your birth partner for support and reassurance. Alternatively, try adopting the same position on a birthing ball.

# Positions, stage 1 **Common questions**

**Q** Is it true that keeping mobile makes labour and birth easier?

**A** Yes. Although women in the West have traditionally given birth lying on their backs, this is not the most effective position for either labour or birth. Women who remain mobile and adopt a more upright position during labour, and who stand, sit or squat to give birth, generally have an easier time. Mobility affects the speed of the contractions, your ability to cope with them and also the progress of the labour. Labour tends to be shorter, less painful and requires less intervention. However, if your contractions start in the middle of the night, do not leap out of bed: it is also important that you go into labour rested.

**Q** Why do most positions recommended for stage 1 involve leaning forwards?

**A** During this stage of labour, your cervix is dilating and your uterus is rising and tipping forwards, so it makes sense to adopt positions that help these processes and assist in stretching the ligaments that join the bones of your pelvis. Being upright, whether walking around or resting across a chair, means your baby's head is pressing on your cervix, which will encourage contractions, speed dilation of the cervix and move your baby's head down into the pelvis. Changing positions can help her to move further down. By leaning forwards you allow the contractions to work with gravity, pushing your uterus forwards.

**4** Kneel on something soft like a blanket, spreading your knees to make space for your bump and leaning onto your hands. This position is good for stretching your pelvic ligaments. Rocking yourself gently in this position can help to turn your baby if she is facing forwards.

**5** Kneel on something soft and lean into your birth partner's lap with your thighs either side of his or her feet. You could also adopt this position leaning onto an armchair or your bed.

# Positions for labour
## Stage 2

These positions are good for stage 2 of labour. Practise all the positions with your birth partner before you go into labour.

**1** Your birth partner stands behind you, perhaps supported by a wall, with his or her hands under your arms for support. As you bend your knees and push on the floor, your birth partner bends his or her knees as well and takes some of your weight.

**2** Stand or semi-squat, supported by your helpers on either side. As you push and bend your knees, your helpers should bend their knees too, taking your weight so that your feet remain on the floor, giving you something to push against.

**3** Lie on your left side with your knees bent. Your birth partner supports your upper leg as you push into the contractions. This can be a good position for getting rid of the last lip (the anterior lip) of the cervix.

## True story

### A perfect natural birth

'I planned to have my December baby at home. When I was two days overdue, I awoke at 3.50am with period-like pains and knew that this was it. Paul, my husband, and I went into the living room and turned on the Christmas-tree lights. Contractions were coming thick and fast, so I phoned the hospital and shortly afterwards my midwife rang. When the midwife and her colleague arrived, at 5am, they said I was 8 cm (3 in) dilated. At every contraction the midwife massaged my back and I sniffed lavender oil and pushed my tummy out.

'I tried gas and air for the last few minutes, but it interfered with my pushing and I didn't feel any benefit. I pushed just three times and followed the midwife's instructions exactly so I didn't tear. Jamie was born almost under the Christmas tree, just one hour after the midwife arrived. I was standing and Paul caught him as he slipped out! A sweet cup of tea on the sofa finished off my perfect birth and we celebrated with Champagne.'

*Ann-Marie, mother of Johnnie and Jamie*

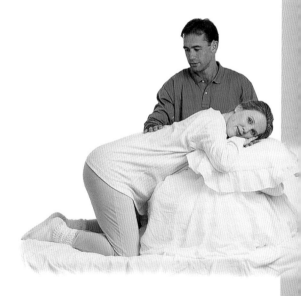

**4** If you are getting too tired to stand, squat between your birth partner's legs and lean into his or her lap with your feet flat on the floor and your arms over his or her knees. This position can be adapted for sitting on a bed, if you are propped up with pillows.

**5** Kneel on the floor or bed, leaning onto pillows or a beanbag. This position will give you something to push against and the midwife can deliver your baby from behind. You could also be on all fours, with your middle supported on pillows or a beanbag.

# RELAXING AND BREATHING DURING LABOUR

## Staying in control

**Knowing how to relax is the key to a labour where you feel in control and increases your chances of giving birth naturally.**

When your uterus contracts strongly, other muscles tend to join in. However, if you can allow your body to relax, the contractions will work more effectively and the natural pain-killing hormones will flow through your body. Relaxation and breathing are closely linked. When you relax, your breathing adjusts to the best level for you and vice versa – by breathing deeply you will achieve a better state of relaxation. You are already used to

unconsciously changing your breathing pattern according to what you are doing, for example, when drifting off to sleep, exercising or sinking into an armchair at the end of a day. Likewise, any kind of stress automatically affects your breathing. It will become faster and shallower, from the upper part of the lungs, and will cause tension in your shoulders.

**Below:** Your birth partner plays an important part in keeping you relaxed during labour.

# Knowing when to relax

During labour, the majority of women find that the stress of being in an unfamiliar environment (if they are giving birth in hospital rather than at home) and coping with the pain of the contractions makes them tense. Learn to recognize approaching tension so that you can keep it in check: before it engulfs you, pull your shoulders down and let them go, part your lips to loosen your jaw, turn your palms upwards. Practising the following breathing techniques can also help.

- Sit or stand comfortably, with loose shoulders, hands and face.
- Breathe in deeply through the nose and out through the mouth.
- Relax your body as you breathe out.
- Find something on which to focus as you breathe – your partner's eyes or an image in your mind.

Do not wait until you are in labour before seeing if this works, but take time to practise the techniques with your birth partner before you go into labour. He or she will then be able to guide you during labour if necessary, as it may well be that you temporarily forget to concentrate on your breathing once the contractions begin to get more painful. Your birth partner should also remind you to keep your face relaxed during labour. If your face is relaxed, you will find it more difficult to tense other parts of your body.

# Breathing through contractions

At the start of a contraction, breathe in slowly and deeply through your nose. Hold for a couple of seconds and then breathe out slowly through your mouth. Try to keep your breaths the same length throughout the contraction.

# Hypnotherapy

Hypnotherapy is based on the belief that removing fear and promoting relaxation can help relieve pain in labour, and it has met with some very positive results. It uses hypnosis, a naturally induced state of relaxed concentration in which suggestions are communicated to the subconscious mind. That part of the mind influences what you think, how you feel and the choices you make, including pain control. Hypnotherapy teaches that when a woman is prepared for birth and free from fear, the birthing muscles can work in the way nature intended. The following guidelines offer an insight as to how it works.

- Think how you relax and practise going into a deeply relaxed state.
- Create a calm place in your mind. Practise going there – feel, see and hear things as if you are there.
- Indulge yourself by fantasizing about your perfect birth in detail. Do it daily in the final weeks before pregnancy.
- Focus on what you want rather than what you do not want.
- Protect yourself from negative images. When someone wants to tell you a birth horror story, stop them and ask about the good bits.

Your breathing will become a little faster towards the end of your labour, when your contractions become intense. This is fine as long as you do not start to panic and take very short breaths. Always concentrate on the 'out' breath to avoid hyperventilation, but if you do start to feel light-headed, cup your hands over your face and breathe into them until the sensation passes.

# Stage 1 of labour

The first stage of labour is the longest, lasting from the start of regular contractions and the opening of the cervix until the cervix is fully dilated at 10 cm (4 in). When the cervix is dilated to this extent, the baby is able to pass through it. Although this stage is long, it is not relentless as, in between contractions, you will have the opportunity to move around or just rest.

## What happens?

Before labour begins, the cervix resembles a small, thick tube with a dimple in it, which nestles at the top and to the back of your vagina. The cervix moves forward, softens and thins and then gradually starts to open. Putting a finger into a cervix that is 1 cm (½ in) dilated feels a bit like putting a finger in a nostril! As the cervix gets thinner and more stretchy, it feels more like a hole in a piece of bubble gum. Because of the amount of stretching and softening that needs to take place, the longest part of labour can often be the dilation of the cervix to 4–5 cm (2 in). Once you are getting strong, regular contractions, your midwife can perform a vaginal examination to establish just how far into labour you are. She can feel how far your cervix is dilated and confirm the exact position of your baby.

There are a number of signs that indicate impending labour, but experiencing any of them does not necessarily mean you will go into labour immediately. They include:

- A 'show'
- Contractions
- Diarrhoea
- Your waters breaking.

## Contractions

A contraction is when the muscles of the uterus tense and relax, passing in waves from the top, travelling inwards and downwards. During the first stage of labour, they begin to 'take up' the neck of the uterus, making it thinner so it is no longer tube-shaped (this is called effacement). As these muscles stretch and relax, the cervix starts to open until it is fully dilated and the baby moves deeper into your pelvis. This completes the first stage of labour.

During the second stage of labour, contractions play a different role, pushing your baby down the birth canal. After he is born, further contractions push out the placenta, which completes the third and final stage of labour. In the short term, the contractions vary in intensity, rather than getting progressively longer and stronger. However, overall, they become more frequent and last for longer as the birth approaches.

# Stage 1 of labour **Common questions**

**Q** What is a show?

**A** This is the jelly-like blood-streaked 'plug' of mucus that has been preventing infection from getting into your uterus. It often comes away from the cervix at the beginning of labour, although it can still be a few weeks before labour begins. There is no need to tell anyone about this. It is your own sign that there is a good chance of labour starting within the next few days – but it is not a guarantee!

**Q** I hate the thought of internal examinations in labour. Do I have to have them?

**A** Women usually want to know about their progress in labour. By doing an internal examination the midwife can evaluate how dilated your cervix is and tell what position your baby is in. If you use breathing exercises or gas and air and if you empty your bladder first, the examination should not feel too uncomfortable. However, an internal examination can only be done with your consent, and if you are sure you really don't want one, your wish should be respected.

**Q** When will my waters break? What should I do when it happens?

**A** The breaking of your waters (amniotic fluid) usually happens during labour with the force of a contraction, but it can also happen before labour begins. If it does, contact your midwife or labour ward, who can confirm whether labour has started if you are unsure. A midwife will also listen to your baby's heartbeat and probably take a swab from your vagina to check for infection in case you do not go into labour soon afterwards. Most women find that once their waters have broken contractions start within 36 hours. If you do not go into labour, the midwife will tell you how to check for signs and symptoms of infection, for example, by looking for changes in the smell of the amniotic fluid or a rise in body temperature.

**Right:** Keeping upright during labour lets gravity help you and encourages contractions.

# Monitoring the baby

A baby's heart rate can change as the uterus contracts, returning to normal when the contraction ends and blood can flow freely again. Sometimes, however, the heart rate can speed up or slow down too much, or can return to normal too slowly after a contraction, indicating that the baby is in distress.

## Different types of monitoring device

A variety of instruments are used to monitor babies, ranging from handheld devices to more complicated electronic equipment used for continuous monitoring. They are suitable for different birth environments, meaning that you can be monitored even if you opt for a home or water birth.

### Dopplers and pinnards

During your pregnancy, the midwife will have listened to your baby's heartbeat using a handheld instrument, such as a Doppler or a pinnard. A pinnard is a type of ear trumpet that is placed on your abdomen and through which your baby's heartbeat can be heard. Many women prefer the Doppler because the sound is amplified so that they can hear the heartbeat as well. If you have had a straightforward pregnancy and no problems are anticipated during the birth, research suggests that a Doppler is the best way of monitoring the baby's heartbeat during labour.

## Cardiotocograph (CTG)

This instrument consists of two transducers that are held in place on your abdomen by elastic belts and connected to a monitor. The monitor provides a print-out of the baby's heartbeat and also the uterine contractions. The monitor can be moved about so, unless you have an epidural, which restricts your movement, you can still stay upright or get out of bed. If everything is going smoothly there is no need for it. However, there are many instances where continuous monitoring is necessary, for example, during premature labour, if oxytocin or an epidural are being used or if the baby shows signs of distress.

## Fetal scalp electrode (FSE)

Sometimes there are problems picking up an accurate and continuous reading of the heartbeat with the abdominal transducers, often because of the baby's position. In this case it may be necessary to use an FSE. The midwife or obstetrician will carry out a vaginal examination to determine the position of your baby and then attach a small metal clip to your baby's scalp. This is linked by a lead to a CTG (see above).

*'I had to be monitored because of the epidural. But the CTG was like having a huge TV on in the middle of the room. We all just stared at it.'*
*Ceri, mother of Sofia*

# Monitoring **Common questions**

**Q** I am keen to have an active birth. How can I do this if the midwife has to monitor my baby's wellbeing the whole time?

**A** As long as your pregnancy and labour are straightforward, you should be encouraged to have an active birth, without the interference of continual monitoring. In a normal labour, the appropriate method of listening to the baby's heartbeat is with a handheld Doppler or pinnard – as would be done during a home birth. If your baby does need continual monitoring throughout labour, two belts will be strapped to your bump and attached to the machine that provides heart-rate readings. You do not have to stay on the bed, as long as you stay close to the monitor.

**Q** Can my baby's heartbeat still be monitored if I opt for a water birth?

**A** If you labour in a birthing pool, your baby's heartbeat can easily be monitored using a handheld Doppler. Some Dopplers are designed to work under the water but, if one of these is not available, all you have to do is lift your bump above the surface of the water so that the midwife can listen in. Even while you are in the water the midwife can lean over and do a vaginal examination, check your blood pressure, or whatever else might be needed to monitor your and your baby's wellbeing.

**Below:** Your midwife can listen to your baby's heartbeat using a handheld pinnard or Doppler.

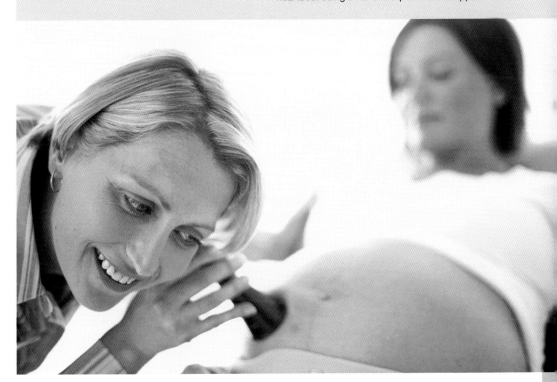

# Stage 2 of labour

The second stage of labour lasts from full dilation until the birth. The contractions associated with this stage are described as expulsive and feel very different to those of the first stage, and many women find it easier to cope with them. Second-stage contractions cause an overwhelming urge to bear down and push out your baby, which is why women become more vocal at this stage.

## What happens?

With each contraction, your baby will move further down the birth canal until a small part of his head becomes visible. If this is your first baby, the head will slip back between contractions, but, eventually, the head will stay in position and more of it will be seen. This process is called crowning and some women experience a burning sensation at this point. When the baby's head crowns, the birth itself is not far off.

## The signs

The onset of stage 2 of labour can be confirmed by a vaginal examination, although many midwives find this unnecessary because there are often other signs that the cervix is fully dilated. These other signs include:

- Involuntary grunting with the effort of the contraction
- A heavy, blood-stained show (different to the show in early labour, see page 215)
- Bulging of the back passage
- A slight dip of the baby's heartbeat with the contraction.

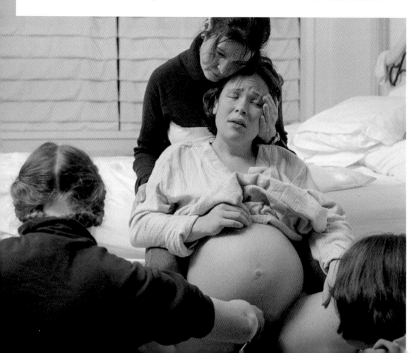

**Left:** Knowing that the baby will soon be born helps many women cope with labour.

# Stage 2 of labour **Common questions**

**Q** How will I know that I have reached stage 2 of labour?

**A** There are always exceptions to the rule, but most women in the second stage of labour will feel an overwhelming, involuntary urge to bear down and push. It builds up like a wave and is impossible to fight, and some women even describe the feeling as sexual. Some women initially find the feeling scary as it is so powerful, not painful, but it becomes far less scary if you stop fighting it and just go with the feeling. Most women find it a relief to do so and push as their body tells them to.

**Q** I am scared of losing control during labour and making grunting noises. Should I have an epidural to prevent this?

**A** Women often worry about whether or not they will make strange noises or behave out of character during labour. It is usually during the second stage of labour that expectant mums become more 'vocal', because they have an overwhelming, involuntary urge 'to bear down'. Although women may make noises, it does not mean they are out of control. In fact, you may feel more out of control with an epidural if you cannot feel what is actually going on. If you do start to make involuntary sounds, it is a positive sign that you are approaching the second stage of labour and, therefore, usually suggests that you are making good progress.

**Q** What should I do once I get the urge to push?

**A** The best thing for you and your baby is simply to listen to your body and push spontaneously. If you do this, you will naturally give three or four short pushes, lasting about five seconds each, with every contraction. If you have an epidural and, because of this, cannot feel the contractions for yourself, the midwife can feel them by placing her hand on your abdomen and will tell you when you are having a contraction.

**Q** Will I open my bowels during this stage of labour?

**A** Many women have diarrhoea as a first sign of labour, and this is nature's way of clearing out the bowel before labour starts. A lot of women still open their bowels during labour and, if this is going to happen, there is nothing that you can do to stop it. 'Holding back' will make you more uncomfortable. If your bowels do not open when you push, it will feel as if they are, so you probably will not know for certain. During stage 2 of labour the baby's head puts pressure on the rectum, which is why you feel the need to open your bowels. This is a sign that the birth is imminent.

# Birth

As the birth approaches and the baby's head crowns, your midwife may ask you to breathe rather than push, in order to control the birth of the head and reduce the risk of tearing. Once a small part of your baby's head appears, try reaching down and touching it.

## Your baby's arrival

Many women find that feeling their baby's head for the first time helps them to focus on where they are pushing, as well as giving them the encouragement of knowing that they are making progress and will soon be meeting their baby. Once the head is actually out, you will probably feel a sense of relief. Your baby will turn her head to come in line with her

## Twin and multiple births

Most twins are born in hospital and you may be advised to have an epidural in case you need an emergency caesarean or an assisted birth for the second twin. Both babies are usually continuously monitored during labour. In some hospitals, it is policy to deliver twins in an operating theatre (even for vaginal deliveries) or in a larger delivery room, for safety and to accommodate a midwife and a paediatrician for each baby, as well as the obstetrician.

Although around 60 per cent of twins are born by caesarean section, it is possible to have a normal birth, particularly if the presenting twin is in a head-down position. If the first twin is in the breech position, your obstetrician might advise a caesarean section. During labour, an emergency caesarean may be required, either because labour is not progressing well or because there is evidence of fetal distress.

After the birth of the first twin, the second twin may be lying across the uterus, in which

case it may be possible to turn her into either a breech or a head-down position so that she can be delivered vaginally. The midwife or doctor will confirm the position of the second twin and break the waters if necessary. Usually, you will be given a hormone drip to make sure that your contractions continue. The second twin is usually born within 20 minutes of the first. Occasionally, she will show signs of distress, in which case you will be given an assisted birth or a caesarean section.

You will be given a hormone drip after the birth. This encourages the uterus to contract to lessen the risk of bleeding because of the large area covered by the placenta.

Triplets or more are usually delivered by caesarean section. Whether you can give birth naturally or not depends upon the position of your babies when you go into labour.

shoulders, which will be turned to one side. The midwife will gently feel around her neck for the umbilical cord, which can be slipped over her head.

The rest of your baby will be born with the next contraction. The first shoulder will emerge from under your pubic bone. Your midwife will gently lift up this shoulder and your baby's head to give the second shoulder (the one nearer the spine) more room. The rest of her body will then slip out easily accompanied by a further rush of amniotic fluid. Your baby can be placed directly onto your abdomen, either naked or, if you prefer, wrapped up. The cord can then be clamped and cut, either by the midwife or by your birth partner.

# Birth **Common questions**

**Q** How will stage 2 of labour be different if my baby is in a breech position?

**A** You will probably be advised to have a caesarean section, particularly for a first baby if your baby is not in a 'frank breech' position (see page 205), or is thought to be quite large. If your baby is found to be in a breech position when you are already in labour you may be advised to have an emergency caesarean, unless it is too late and the birth is imminent. Ultimately the decision is yours, so make sure that you are confident that you have had lots of information from your midwife or doctor.

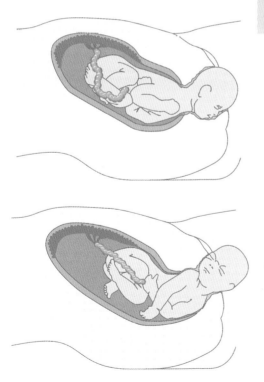

**Above:** The baby's head first crowns and then fully emerges

**Above:** Leaning forwards is a great position for giving birth.

# Stage 3 of labour

The third stage of labour is the expulsion of the placenta by contractions of the uterus. There are two ways of managing this stage: naturally (physiologically) or with an injection (actively). You should be given the opportunity to discuss the options beforehand, or put your preference in your birth plan (see page 186), but what happens on the day will depend partly on the nature of the birth.

## Stitches

After the delivery of the placenta, the midwife will check your vagina and perineum for any tears or grazes. A small tear that is not bleeding will heal naturally if kept clean and dry. A cut or a larger tear will need stitching soon after the birth. You will be given a local anaesthetic in the area before the stitches are put in. If you have had an assisted birth (see pages 230–231), the doctor will stitch the cut as soon as the placenta is out, while your legs are still raised.

Stitching usually takes about 20 minutes and you may be able to use gas and air, although the local anaesthetic should provide enough pain control.

The stitches do not need to be removed because they will dissolve after around two weeks (longer if there are knots close to the skin or an infection).

## Natural delivery

Women who have given birth naturally, with no intervention, often want to complete the process naturally, without drugs. Once the baby has been born, the umbilical cord is left attached until it has stopped pulsating, after which it is clamped and cut. The uterus will contract naturally, but it can take longer to expel the placenta. Blood loss tends to be heavier initially, but this is seldom a problem as long as the mother is healthy and not anaemic.

## Active management

If you had an intervention during labour, for example, an induction, an epidural or an assisted birth and are therefore at higher risk of bleeding, it is advisable for the third stage of labour to be actively managed.

In an actively managed third stage, the midwife will inject an oxytocic drug (ergometrine plus oxytocin) into your thigh immediately after the birth. This drug is a synthetic hormone that causes the uterus to contract and the placenta to detach from the wall of the uterus. You will feel a contraction and the midwife will place one hand on your stomach while she gently pulls on the cord with the other hand. The blood loss tends to be lighter using this method, although the drug can make some women vomit.

If you have high blood pressure, you will be given an alternative drug containing oxytocin alone, intravenously. This is because the drug ergometrine can cause a rise in blood pressure.

# Stage 3 of labour **Common questions**

**Q** With my first child, I remember shaking all over after the delivery of the placenta. Why was this?

**A** It is perfectly normal to get the shakes after the delivery of the placenta. Your legs may feel wobbly as a result of a change in body temperature and loss of fluid, as well as the sheer effort of childbirth. All being well, you will now be given a chance to spend some special time with your baby, so that you can get to know each other, before he is checked over.

**Q** What happens if the placenta fails to come out completely?

**A** If various efforts to expel the placenta, for example, putting the baby to the breast as well as encouraging the mother to empty her bladder, have failed it will have to be removed manually in an operating theatre. This procedure is undertaken under spinal anaesthetic and you would be given a course of antibiotics afterwards in order to reduce the risk of infection.

**Q** My sister suddenly started bleeding heavily about a week after her baby was born and had to go back into hospital. What causes that and how common is it?

**A** Secondary post-partum haemorrhage – heavy bleeding that usually occurs 8–10 days after birth – occurs in approximately 1 per cent of all births. It is usually caused by a piece of placenta retained in the uterus. A secondary PPH would normally be treated with a drug to make the uterus contract, a scan to see if there was any placenta left and, if that is suspected, an operation to remove it followed by a course of intravenous antibiotics.

'During my pregnancy I used to worry about having stitches after the birth. When I tore, I was not even aware it was happening. The midwife put the stitches in as I was cuddling Annabel, and to be honest I did not give it a second thought.'

*Sue, mother of Annabel*

# Overdue babies

It can be really depressing to see your due date come and go with no sign of labour. Although the majority of babies arrive after the due date – most of them within 10 days – waiting for the first sign of labour can seem like the longest part of your pregnancy. If you reach 10–12 days overdue, induction may be advised.

## Being induced

You will probably be offered induction when you are 10–12 days overdue because the placenta – the source of your baby's nutrition – may stop working efficiently after this time. This could mean that your baby is not getting all the nourishment she needs.

In the first instance, your midwife may try giving you a 'stretch and sweep'. This is an internal examination that is sometimes effective in starting labour, in which the midwife runs her finger around the bag of waters, through the cervix.

## True story

**Worth waiting for**

'My baby decided to be fashionably late, and so there I was at 42 weeks in hospital, waiting to be induced. Typically, the contractions started up practically the moment my partner, Neil, left. I spent the night walking around the unit. Sitting or lying down were agony, and although I was having strong contractions, I wasn't dilating.

'The morning dawned and the midwife recommended breaking my waters to move things along. At last I started to dilate, albeit slowly. I managed to sleep for about an hour before my in-laws arrived to see me – just as I was being wheeled out of the ward to the delivery room.

'My contractions were so strong they were going off the scale. They were also close together, but unfortunately I still wasn't dilating very quickly. I asked for an epidural to help ease the discomfort. I wasn't fully dilated until 7am, but by that time the contractions had slowed down, and when I was told to push, I didn't feel I had any contractions to work with. I pushed for two hours, but the baby hardly budged.

'At this point another doctor was called in. He turned out to be the same doctor I had seen during my pregnancy and who'd broken my waters earlier. That put me much more at ease. He decided I needed forceps, and after an episiotomy he delivered my beautiful baby boy. Despite all the problems I had, he's absolutely perfect, and giving birth to him was the most emotional experience of my life.'

*Melissa, mother of Liam*

# Overdue babies **Common questions**

**Q** How long after my due date will the hospital recommend I am induced? Do I have to follow their advice?

**A** Nobody can say exactly when your labour is supposed to start – a 'normal' gestation is anywhere between 37 and 42 weeks of pregnancy. However, women are usually offered an induction of their labour 7–14 days after their due date. If you do not want to be induced, talk to your obstetrician or midwife. They should offer to monitor your baby's heartbeat at least twice a week with an electronic monitor, and to measure the fluid around your baby with ultrasound. You will also be advised to monitor your baby's movements as a guide to her wellbeing.

**Q** I have heard that having sex can trigger labour. Is this true?

**A** Nothing can trigger labour unless your baby is ready. However, during an orgasm, your body releases the hormone oxytocin, which can cause your uterus to contract, leading to labour. Similarly, if you lie down after sex for as long as you can, with your legs raised on a couple of pillows, the semen will bathe the cervix, which can help to soften it and encourage labour to start. (Semen is a natural source of the hormone prostaglandin, which is used in hospitals to induce labour.)

**Below:** The wait for labour to begin can seem endless if the baby is overdue.

If that doesn't work you will probably be asked to go to hospital, where the induction procedure will begin. If your cervix is closed, you will given a prostaglandin pessary, to help soften and open the cervix. This might need to be repeated a few hours later, and the process can take a couple of days.

When the cervix is starting to open, the midwife can then break your waters with an amnihook (a bit like a crochet hook). If contractions still don't become established, an intravenous drip of an oxytocic drug will be recommended to get your uterus contracting. By now even the most reluctant baby should be on her way. In very rare cases where labour cannot be induced, the baby is delivered by caesarean section (see pages 232–233).

# Unusual labours
## Precipitate labour

There are times when a birth does not go quite according to plan. Some babies appear before time and rapidly, while others take a lot longer than average. One thing is certain: everyone's experience of labour and childbirth will inevitably be slightly different and therefore your labour is unlikely to match your expectations in every respect.

## Sudden and fast birth

Many couples worry that labour will progress so quickly that their baby is unexpectedly born at home or on the way to the hospital. This is called precipitate labour. It is unusual for this to happen, particularly with a first baby, and is more common in women who have already had a child. If you feel that your labour is progressing very quickly, you can always call your midwife to attend you at home or telephone for an ambulance rather than risk a car journey to the hospital. Bear in mind that there are rarely any problems if a baby is born quickly. Problems are far more likely to occur if a labour progresses slowly.

### Coping in an emergency

Your partner will probably be reassured if he knows what to do in the event of a sudden birth – even if it never happens:

- If you feel the urge to push, get down on all fours, with your bottom in the air, and 'pant' through the contractions. This can help to delay birth.

- Have some clean towels ready to dry and wrap your baby in, and to put underneath you.
- If there is time, your partner should wash his hands.
- If your baby's head is visible, your partner should encourage you to pant and try to 'breathe' your baby out rather than push.
- Putting his hand on your baby's head will help to 'control' the speed of the birth.
- When your baby's head is out, stay calm and do not try to pull out the rest of his body. The body will be born with the next contraction. Your partner should carefully run a finger around your baby's neck and, if he can feel a cord, try to gently loop it over the baby's head.
- Support your baby's head as his body is born to prevent him falling onto the floor.
- Dry your baby with a towel to stimulate him if he initially appears to be floppy.
- Wrap him up and cuddle him, keeping the cord attached.
- Do not try to cut or pull on the cord.
- Put your baby to the breast to feed as soon as you feel like it. This will help the uterus to contract.
- If you feel the urge to push out the placenta after a contraction, do so, but otherwise leave it alone. If the placenta is expelled, still do not attempt to cut the cord.
- Your partner should keep both of you warm until help arrives.

# True story

### Taken by surprise

'As my first two babies were born safely and easily at home, there was no doubt where I wanted the birth of my third child to take place. There was little for me to worry about – same home-birth midwifery team, same birthing pool, same experienced father – so I put it to the back of my mind and focused on a work deadline in the week of my due date.

'My two previous labours had both been around four hours, so I knew we didn't need to call the midwife until I'd been having contractions for at least two hours. But the labour accelerated very quickly and my husband ended up catching the baby himself! Before he'd had time to wipe his hands he was on the phone to the ambulance men, who told him to leave the cord and keep the baby warm until the midwife arrived. She appeared shortly after – to find a by then calm set of parents. The water in the birthing pool was very calm too, as I hadn't had a chance to even get in!

'While I'd planned on a birth with the minimum of medical assistance, I hadn't quite had this in mind – but the elation and excitement afterwards were incomparable. They even gave me the energy to tackle that unmet deadline just a few days later!'

*Tessa, mother of Lewis, Owen and Carys*

# Precipitate labour **Common questions**

**Q Will I make it to the hospital?**

**A** Many women who have had a short labour the first time around worry that they may not get to hospital in time with their second child. If this is something that worries you, why not plan on a home birth? If you have a home birth the midwives will come to you, rather than you having to go to them. Alternatively, if you have had a previous precipitate labour, and do not wish to have a home birth, you may prefer to go into hospital and be induced in a subsequent pregnancy, rather than risk a journey in labour.

With a first baby, it would be unusual to have a very quick labour. However, if that were to happen, don't panic. Simply keep the baby warm until help arrives (see left for more instructions on what to do).

# Unusual labours
## Prolonged labour

An average first labour lasts about 10–12 hours, but it may be much shorter or longer. If you have had no problems during pregnancy, the best thing you can do is to stay at home for as long as possible. Many women find labour slows down when they get to hospital.

## Extended labour

There are a number of possible reasons for a prolonged labour and it is more common for first-time mothers.

- **Your baby's position** If your baby is in an occipito posterior position (see

**Below:** Prolonged labour can be a very tiring and frustrating experience

## Tension

There is a cycle of tension-causing events that midwives recognize all too readily, which is why they will encourage you during labour to keep moving around for as long as possible.

- Your muscles tense whenever you feel anxious. The uterus is a muscle so tension can affect the contractions and slow them down.
- Rather than staying upright and moving about when you get to hospital, you may lie down on the bed. This can also slow down the progress of labour.
- If you are tense, you might find it difficult to deal with the contractions and ask for pain relief at an early stage of your labour. If you are given an injection of pethidine or an epidural you will become less mobile, in which case the contractions can slow down.

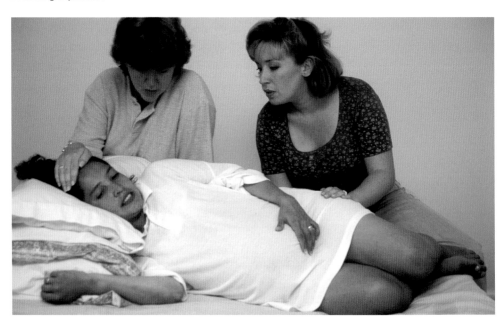

# Prolonged labour **Common questions**

**Q** What will happen if progress continues to be slow?

**A** The doctor may suggest an oxytocin drip to produce stronger and more regular contractions, but it's also important that a normal labour does not become too much of a timed event, as most babies will rotate as long as you can keep upright. You may want to consider an effective form of pain relief, such as an epidural, as you may already be distressed and tired from a long labour. If the cervix still does not dilate, despite the drip, a caesarean section will be necessary to deliver the baby. This may be a relief if you have genuinely had a prolonged labour or failure to dilate, even if this is not how you originally planned to give birth.

**Q** Why is it so uncomfortable if the baby is in an occipito posterior position?

**A** Because of the baby's position, you will probably feel much of the pain in your back, which can be distressing if there is a strong urge to push before the cervix is fully dilated.

This is because the back of the baby's head is pressing on your back passage. A good position to adopt for this type of labour is on all fours, which takes the pressure off your back and allows your birth partner to massage you or put hot towels on the base of your back.

**Q** What is a 'deflexed' head?

**A** For your baby's head to fit through your pelvis, she needs to have her chin tucked onto her chest. In some cases, the baby's chin is higher than this – 'deflexed'. If the contractions are effective, your baby will tuck her chin down but waiting for this can prolong labour.

**Q** How will we know if prolonged labour is the result of the baby's head being too large? Are there any signs?

**A** If this is the case, you may show signs such as a rise in temperature and pulse rate. A vaginal examination may show swelling on your baby's head. If these signs accompany slow progress, it may indicate that the head might not fit through the pelvis.

pages 204–205), this can cause a prolonged labour. It is quite a common occurrence. With regular contractions, most of these babies will eventually turn round, but labour can be long.

- **The size of your baby's head** Labour will be prolonged if your baby's head is large in proportion to your pelvis.

- **Cervical dystocia** This is a very rare condition that affects the structure of the cervix. Some women are born with cervical dystocia, while others develop it as a result of scarring from infection and surgery. If you have the condition, your cervix will remain firm and will not dilate even if you are having strong uterine contractions.

# Assisted birth

Forceps and ventouse are both types of assisted birth, in which instruments are used to assist with the birth of your baby. They can only be used during the second stage of labour, so, if your baby needs to be born quickly before this stage, he would be delivered by emergency caesarean section (see page 232). An obstetrician will perform both types of birth.

## Ventouse

In this type of assisted birth, a ventouse is used to help guide your baby out by means of suction. A metal or plastic cup is placed on your baby's head and the cup is given its suction either by a separate machine via a tube or through a handheld device. While you push with each contraction, the obstetrician will gently pull the cup, guiding your baby out. It is not always necessary to have an episiotomy with this procedure.

## Forceps

Forceps are a pair of metal instruments that look rather like two large salad servers. They link together and are placed inside the vagina. The forceps cradle the baby's head and guide him out, although you still need to push with the contractions. Forceps known as Kielland's are used to help turn your baby if he is facing the wrong way. Neville Barnes' or Wrigley's forceps are used to guide and lift your baby out. Unlike with a ventouse birth, an episiotomy (see page 234) is nearly always necessary in a forceps birth.

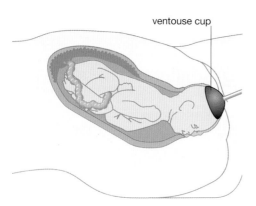

ventouse cup

**Above:** An anaesthetic may not be required with a 'lift-out' ventouse birth.

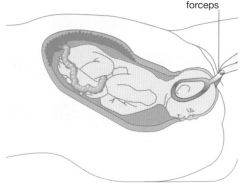

forceps

**Above:** In a forceps birth, the mother will usually have a local anaesthetic or epidural.

# Assisted birth **Common questions**

**Q** Who decides whether to use ventouse or forceps? What is the procedure?

**A** The obstetrician will carry out a vaginal examination in order to decide on the most appropriate instrument to help deliver your baby. This will depend upon the position of your baby and how far down the birth canal he is. If there is a significant chance that the instruments may still fail to deliver your baby then you will be advised to have the procedure attempted in the operating theatre. The obstetrician can then proceed to a caesarean section quite quickly. This is called a trial of ventouse/forceps. Your bladder will be emptied prior to the procedure, using a catheter, and your legs will be placed with your feet higher than your hips. Your midwife will stay with you throughout the process.

*'I never wanted a forceps birth but when the midwife told me that my baby's heartbeat was slowing down because he was becoming distressed, I just wanted him to be born – and I did not care how. My birth plan went out of the window but I was so relieved that David was all right that nothing else seemed important.'*

*Sandra, mother of David*

**Q** In what circumstances might I need an assisted birth?

**A** This type of approach is commonly used if you have been pushing for a long time and your baby is making slow progress down the birth canal, particularly if he is showing signs of distress. This is more likely if progress has already been slowing during stage 1, perhaps indicating that you have a large baby or that the head is not in an occipito anterior (OA) position (see page 204).

**Q** What are the effects of an assisted birth on my baby?

**A** The birth can cause distress or trauma to your baby, so it is usual to have a paediatrician in the room with a resuscitaire. Babies who have had a ventouse birth commonly have a bump on the back of their heads. This is usually reddish purple in colour and can be quite prominent. Forceps can sometimes leave two red marks on the side of your baby's head, but any bruises or bumps should go down within the first week. Because of the bruising, these babies are more likely to develop jaundice. Occasionally, a baby appears irritable after an instrumental birth, so it may be best not to let too many different people handle him for the time being.

**Q** What will be the effects on me?

**A** Some assisted births are easy – the baby is simply lifted out and the mother feels much the same as she would after a natural birth. Others are hard work for all concerned and you may feel bruised and sore afterwards.

## Caesarean section

A caesarean section is a major operation involving an incision through various layers of tissue, and into the uterus, in order to deliver your baby. Unless there are medical grounds that make it the safest form of birth for your baby, electing to have a caesarian section is not a decision you should take lightly.

### The three types of caesarean

- **Elective** This is where the decision has been made before labour to deliver the baby this way. Reasons could include breech position, placenta praevia or if the mother is HIV positive. It is normally done at around 39 weeks.

- **Emergency** This is an unplanned caesarean. It may happen because the baby has started to show signs of distress in early labour or because there has been little progress during labour. Another cause may be the discovery that the mother's pelvis is too small for the baby's head to pass through.

- **Crash** This is a true emergency situation, in which the baby has to be delivered at once. Reasons include placental abruption (see page 131), a prolapsed cord or severe signs of distress with the baby's heartbeat. If you have a crash caesarean,

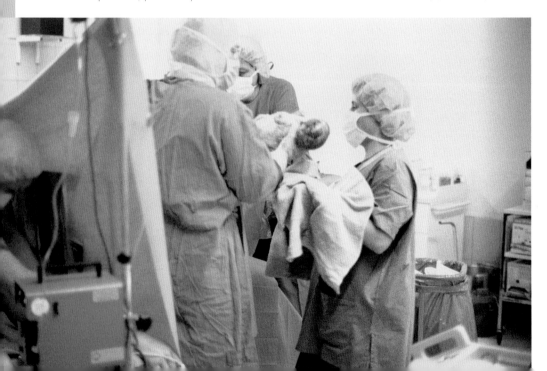

**Below:** Caesarean birth takes place in a surgical environment, but can be a very positive experience.

you would need to be given a general anaesthetic if you did not already have an epidural in place.

## What happens?

A caesaraean is no different from any other operation. The top of your pubic hair will be shaved and the midwife will insert a catheter into your bladder just prior to the procedure. A needle will be put into the back of your hand through which fluid will drip in case your blood pressure falls. You will usually be given a spinal block or epidural rather than a general anaesthetic, in order to enable you to stay awake during the operation and hold your baby soon afterwards.

The procedure will not hurt but you will be aware of the pushing and pulling inside of you. Some women describe it as 'someone washing the dishes inside of their stomach'. The operation takes about 10 minutes from the first incision until the birth of your baby, and about another 40 minutes for the stitches to be put in the layers of muscle, fat and skin. The scar will be just below the bikini line and will fade in time.

## Caesarean section
# Common questions

**Q** My friend was very disappointed to have a caesarean. Is there any way to make it a positive experience, if it happens to me?

**A** Many women make a caesarean birth a positive experience. It is worth thinking about what you would like in the event of it happening and putting it in your birth plan. Consider how you and your partner might respond. Would you like to have your choice of music played in the operating theatre? (If so, take some CDs with you and ask for them to be played). Would you like your baby to be placed straight onto you, skin to skin, providing there are no complications? Do you want to find out the sex of your baby yourself? Would you like to see the baby being lifted out? (If so, you can ask for the screen to be lowered at that point.)

**Q** What should I take to the hospital?

**A** Big knickers are a must, as you will have a wound that runs along the top of your pubic line. You will bleed after the operation so do not forget sanitary towels. You will stay in hospital a bit longer – about four days – so you will need extra clothing for you and your baby.

*'I had to have a caesarean as my baby was large and in the breech position. I was really nervous, but I had a look at the operating theatre a couple of weeks before the date, which helped. My husband and I went to the labour ward at 8am and our baby was born at 9.30am – quite civilized really!'*

*Joanna, mother of Thomas*

# Episiotomy and tearing

An episiotomy is a small cut made at the vagina entrance to give the baby more room. In the 1970s episiotomy was routine procedure, particularly in the case of a first baby. Today it is usually given only when the baby is showing signs of distress and a quick birth is needed or when forceps are required (see page 230).

## What happens?

Although an episiotomy may sound daunting, once you are in labour the procedure becomes much less of an issue. If you are thought to need an episiotomy, the midwife will get your consent first and then inject some local anaesthetic in the area where the cut is to be made. This area is very thin at the height of a contraction, and it is then that the incision is made – with just one quick snip of a pair of sterile scissors.

## True story

### A necessary episiotomy

'My contractions started on the Sunday morning. My midwife, Kate, popped round to check me over, and reassured me that my baby and I were fine and that she would return later. She was back at 2pm, and after a couple of hours I was getting an overwhelming urge to bear down. I just knew the baby was ready to be born. Kate kept listening to the baby's heartbeat with her handheld Doppler, and towards the end of labour it started to get slower. This is normal, apparently, as the baby gets squashed travelling down the birth canal.

'I remember feeling a burning sensation as the head started to crown, and Kate telling me that I needed to push, as the baby was getting tired. I kept pushing and pushing, and still there was no baby! Kate told me that she needed to do an episiotomy and I didn't question it – I trusted her implicitly. A few seconds later our beautiful Gracie was born.

'I never even felt the cut as it was done with a contraction, and Kate had applied some local anaesthetic to the area. She explained that she'd only ever had to do two episiotomies, but my baby was showing signs of distress and needed to be born as quickly as possible. I sat on the edge of the sofa cuddling my gorgeous new baby while Kate stitched the cut. It soon healed, with the help of a few lavender baths, and was a small price to pay for our beautiful daughter!'

*Sarah, mother of Grace*

# Episiotomy and tearing **Common questions**

**Q** Where am I most likely to tear?

**A** The most common tear goes from the entrance of your vagina towards your back passage. This area is called the perineum. A first-degree tear involves only the skin; a second-degree tear involves skin and muscle; while a third-degree tear, which is less common, involves the lining or muscles of the back passage. Sometimes tears are towards the labia or clitoris, and these can be extremely sore, particularly when passing urine.

**Q** Is it possible to prevent tearing?

**A** Nobody can guarantee that you will not tear because it depends to some extent on factors such as your baby's position and whether the birth needs assistance. However, there is some evidence that you can help to avoid damage to your perineum (the tissue between your vagina and anus) with gentle massage. In the last weeks of pregnancy, try massaging the area with sweet almond or wheatgerm oil for about five minutes each day. Practising your pelvic floor exercises (see pages 108–109) will also help you to become more aware of the area and relax it when it comes to pushing out your baby. As the baby's head is delivered, the midwife will ask you to breathe, not push, in order to control the speed at which the head is delivered and to reduce the chance of tearing.

**Q** My midwife told me that I am more likely to need an episiotomy if I have an epidural. Why is this?

**A** Having an epidural tends to affect mobility. Keeping upright and active stimulates your contractions and helps your baby descend lower into the birth canal, which reduces the risk of an assisted birth. This, in turn, lessens the likelihood of an episiotomy. If progress is slow, it is more likely that your baby will show signs of distress and his birth will have to be speeded up with medical intervention.

**Q** My friend was really uncomfortable the first week after she had an episiotomy. Is it always like that?

**A** Usually, yes, but there are exceptions. There are also things you can do to alleviate the pain. Lavender oil in the bath can make the sore area feel more comfortable. Restarting your pelvic floor exercises as soon as possible after the birth will also help with healing, as it increases the blood flow to the area.

**Q** How long does it take for an episiotomy to heal?

**A** A small episiotomy or tear may take up to 10 days to heal; a large episiotomy could take longer. The midwife will ask if your stitches are comfortable and take a look if there is any sign of infection or you have any concerns. Good hygiene is important to avoid infection, which would increase discomfort and delay healing. Wash your hands before and after changing sanitary pads and use medical wipes on toilet seats in hospital.

8

# the first few days

# First moments

Nothing can prepare you for how you will feel when you first see your baby. Don't worry if she doesn't look quite as you expected. She may look a little blue when she is born, but her colour will change as soon as she takes her first breath. If you had an assisted birth, your baby may still have some marks or bumps – and her head may be rather elongated or even lop-sided! All this is normal and will resolve given time.

## Time together

Whether you are breastfeeding or bottle-feeding, try to have some skin-to-skin contact with your baby immediately after the birth, to start the bonding process. Cuddle and stroke your baby, and give her an opportunity to smell and feel the warmth of your skin and listen to your voice talking to her. It is important that you, your partner and your baby spend some time together in order to get to know each other. Your baby does have to be weighed and measured, but there should be no rush to get this done immediately. After all, the measurements are not going to change drastically in a few hours. The midwife will make sure that you are comfortable and that the bedding is changed for you.

## The Apgar score

Parents are often unaware that their baby's first check takes place at one minute of age. This Apgar test (after the doctor who devised it) is repeated again at five minutes. Five categories are assessed, which are each given a score of 0, 1 or 2, the total being out of 10. A healthy baby will have a score of 7 or higher, whereas a baby with a score lower than 7 may need time to recover from the birth. A baby with a very low score may need medical attention. The five Apgar categories are as follows:

- **Appearance (colour)** Many newborn babies are not pink, but tinged with blue. However, they do pink up quickly after the birth. Non-Caucasian babies are assessed by examining the inside of the mouth, the whites of the eyes, the soles of the feet and the palms of the hands.
- **Pulse** The heart rate should be over 100 beats per minute.
- **Grimace (reflexes)** The baby should respond to stimulation, such as being handled.
- **Activity (muscle tone)** The baby should be able to actively move her arms and legs.
- **Respiration** The baby's breathing should be strong and regular.

# First moments **Common questions**

**Q** Will my partner be allowed to cut the cord himself?

**A** Many partners love the thought of being the one to cut their baby's cord, and find it symbolic that they are making that separation between you and your baby. Occasionally the cord is around the baby's neck, in which case the midwife will slip it over the head or clamp and cut it. Otherwise there is no reason why your partner cannot do it. Even if he is not keen at the moment, it is worth asking him again because he may change his mind when the baby is born.

**Q** What happens after the placenta is out?

**A** Soon after you have given birth, the midwife will check over you and your baby. She will make sure that your baby is breathing regularly and that there are no obvious problems. She will put her hand on your tummy to feel that your uterus is well contracted so that the blood loss is not too heavy. If you have torn during the birth, or had an episiotomy, the midwife will stitch it as soon as she can. However, not every tear needs stitching – it depends on how deep it is, and whether or not it is bleeding. Your midwife will look at it and advise you.

**Q** I noticed a mention of vitamin K in an article about birth plans. What is this for and how is it given?

**A** Vitamin K helps blood clotting, and newborns do not have much of this vitamin. In rare cases, babies develop a problem known as haemorrhagic disease of the newborn (HDN), or vitamin K deficiency bleeding, which can be fatal, so most babies are given vitamin K either in the form of an injection after the birth, or as drops into the mouth (twice during the first week and, if breastfed, again at 1 month old).

**Above:** Skin-to-skin contact with your newborn is just the start of the bonding process.

*'I was a bit shocked by how blotchy and spotty she was when she was born, but the midwife told me that nearly all babies have small, white facial spots – called milk spots – in the first few days. They disappeared within a few weeks and her skin is beautiful now.'*
*Caroline, mother of Freya*

# Premature babies

All babies born before 37 weeks of pregnancy are deemed to be premature. However, a baby born at 24 weeks is obviously going to require a lot more assistance than one born at 36 weeks, because, at 24 weeks, he will still be very immature.

## What happens?

Sometimes labour just starts unexpectedly early. In other cases, labour may need to be induced before 37 weeks because there are serious concerns about the wellbeing of the mother and baby, for example, if the mother has severe pre-eclampsia or if the placenta is not functioning properly. Women with a multiple pregnancy, such as twins – or especially triplets – are more likely to go into early spontaneous labour.

Early labours tend to be quicker than full-term labours, as the cervix does not have to dilate to the full 10 cm (4 in) to allow a small baby to pass through. However, an early labour can come as a great shock because you are seldom totally prepared.

## Special care

The special-care baby unit (SCBU) is a separate ward run by specialist nurses and paediatricians. Although it deals mostly with premature babies, there are other babies who also need to spend some time here. With so many screening tests available nowadays, parents assume that any significant problems or disabilities will be picked up during the pregnancy, but this is not always the case and some medical conditions or disabilities, such as cerebral palsy, are not always identified before the birth.

Your initial reaction may be denial, thinking that the professionals have made a mistake. More commonly, the feeling is guilt. What did I do wrong? Did I eat or drink something to affect my baby? You will be reassured that you are not to blame, but you may still blame yourself. It can help to get in touch with an organization where you can talk to other people with similar experiences. These groups can be a great source of comfort, advice and support.

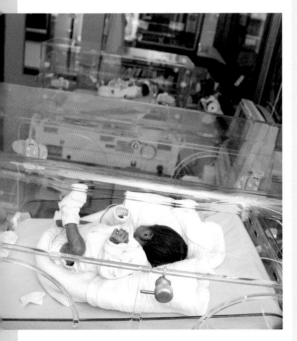

**Above:** It is upsetting to see your baby in a SCBU; be reassured he is receiving the best care possible.

# Premature babies **Common questions**

**Q** What kind of care does a premature baby need?

**A** Many premature babies need help with their breathing because it is not until the final weeks of pregnancy that their lungs are fully mature. A mechanical ventilator may be used to push air in and out of your baby's lungs until he is able to do so himself. Also, small babies do not have much fat laid down and can lose heat very easily. If they get cold, they will not feed and their blood sugar level will fall. Many premature babies are therefore cared for in an incubator, where they can be kept warm.

**Q** My premature baby is doing well in hospital and we have been asked to join a research study on the special-care baby unit. What do you think?

**A** It must be hard when you are facing the stress of your baby still being in hospital, to have to consider the benefits that could be derived from research. Most parents do prove willing to participate in studies, many of them believing that it is good to have their baby treated in a hospital that is involved in a lot of research. If you are not sure, give yourself time to think about it and ask for more information so you know what you are letting yourself in for. Do not be pressurized into a quick decision. The medical team will understand that you must do what is right for your family.

# True
## story

**An early birth**

'I went into labour in the middle of the night, but I didn't believe it was labour, because I was only 32 weeks pregnant. He was huge compared to most other babies in the neonatal unit. Also, because I'd had steroids, he was able to breathe from the start without any help. He went straight into intensive care, but was only there for a few days. We were really lucky and he was home after about three weeks. However, I was shell-shocked. It had never entered my head that I might have a premature baby.

'The worst thing was being on the ward with all the other post-natal mums who had their babies by their beds, while I had nothing. It was even more weird going home after a week and leaving Ned in the hospital. I'd had a baby, but I had no baby. Also, people aren't quite sure how to react to you – they don't know if they should congratulate you or not.'

*Kirsty, mother of Ned*

# Hospital routines

Most hospitals have their own routines and procedures. Being away from home with your new baby can be quite daunting, so be prepared and make sure that you know what to expect. Most hospitals have unrestricted visiting hours for partners but other visitors may only be allowed to visit during certain hours of the day.

## Midwife checks

After the birth, the midwife will check you and your baby to make sure that you are both doing well enough either to go home or, more commonly, to transfer to a post-natal ward. She will want to check that you are recovering well from the birth, that your blood loss is not too heavy and that any potential problems, such as a rise in blood pressure, have been identified. She will also check that your baby is thriving, feeding properly and that her cord is clean and dry.

## Length of stay

If you have had a normal birth, you can usually have a shower or a bath on the labour ward, change your clothes, have something to eat and drink, and then move to a post-natal ward. Some women choose to go home directly from the labour ward if there have been no complications – particularly if they have had midwife-led care and are confident about feeding their baby. However, women usually go to the post-natal ward after an hour or so and stay there overnight, especially if this is their first baby.

If you have had a caesarean section you will probably need to stay in hospital for around four days. You will also need to stay in for a few days if you had pre-eclampsia during your pregnancy, as your blood pressure still needs to be monitored after the birth to make

**Left:** Hospitals will usually allow your partner to visit you and the baby at any time.

# Hospital routines **Common questions**

**Q** I am worried that I will not know what to do with my new baby. Will I get any help?

**A** Nobody expects you to know what to do immediately. Many women have never even held a baby before and need help and support with caring for their baby. Nursery nurses or healthcare assistants often work on the post-natal ward, as well as midwives, and all of them will be pleased to show you and your partner how to top-and-tail your baby, change a nappy, wind your baby and so on.

**Q** If I am tired, will the midwives look after my baby overnight?

**A** This does not tend to happen nowadays because it is much better if your baby stays with you. However, if you have been particularly poorly, a member of staff may offer to look after your baby for a while so that you can get some rest. Staying with your baby at night is part of

the process of getting to know each other – learning each other's sounds and smells, and feeding her when necessary. Even if you feel tired, which is inevitable, you will probably be more relaxed having your baby with you, where you can see her, rather than wondering whether every cry you hear is your baby!

**Q** Are there procedures for visitors?

**A** Once your baby is born, most hospitals prefer you to wait until you get to the post-natal ward before having any visitors. This is to respect the dignity of women still in labour and to ensure that people are not in the way should an emergency arise. Once you are on the post-natal ward, your partner can usually visit at any time and stay as long as he wants. There may be specific visiting hours and children, other than your own, may not be allowed in.

sure that it settles down. Another reason for a longer stay is that your baby was born prematurely and has been taken to a special-care unit. In that case, you will probably want to remain in hospital for a few days so that you can be close to her.

## Pamper yourself

**Take some luxury toiletries with you to pamper yourself and a large fluffy towel for a shower or bath, as well as suitable clothes to change into. There is no need to sit around in your nightdress each day. When your partner visits you, let him spend time with your baby while you soak in a bath and get changed into clean clothes. You are in hospital because you have had a baby, not because you are ill, so there is no reason for you to stay in bed.**

# Your body after the birth

Many women look in the mirror when they get home and compare their body with a half-deflated balloon, so you are not alone! Do not expect to be able to squeeze into your pre-pregnancy jeans yet. Not only have your muscles and skin been stretched, but you may also be retaining quite a lot of fluid (oedema). Your body also needs time to recover after the birth.

## Post-birth changes

- **Breasts** Around the third day after the birth your breasts will become large, hard and engorged with milk. This will happen even if you decide to bottle-feed, but nowadays you will rarely be given medication to prevent it happening. The milk will come in and the discomfort will go after a couple of days; make sure you wear a good support bra in the meantime.

- **Bladder** Your bladder should return to normal after the birth of your baby, but you may feel bruised from the birth. Passing urine may sting, especially if you have had a tear. If this is a problem, try passing urine in a warm bath or pour a jug of lukewarm water between your legs while you are sitting on the toilet. Drink plenty of fluids and resist the temptation to hold the urine for as long as possible because this will make you more likely to get an infection.

- **Bowels** It may be a few days before you can open your bowels again. You may find being in hospital inhibiting and want to take your time in the toilet and you may also be worried about the stitches. Drink plenty of water and eat fresh fruit, vegetables and other fibre-rich foods. Also, remember that any codeine-based painkillers can cause constipation. If you still have not opened your bowels a few days after returning home, your midwife can arrange for a mild laxative.

**Left:** It will be a while after the birth before you can fit into your pre-pregnancy clothes.

# Your body **Common questions**

**Q** I gave birth three days ago and have had quite a lot of bleeding. Is this normal and how long can I expect this to last?
**A** After the birth you will have a blood loss – called lochia – which is similar to a heavy period. This can last for up to six weeks, even after a caesarean. However, the flow should lessen after the first week and will become more of a brownish discharge, gradually becoming lighter. Use sanitary towels, not tampons as these can cause infection. If you notice any large clots on your sanitary towel, show them to your midwife so she can check they are only blood. Very occasionally, the clots contain a piece of placenta, which means that not all of the placenta has been expelled. If the blood loss is heavy, or smells bad, tell your midwife because this could indicate an infection and you may need some antibiotics.

## After pains

Once you have given birth, your uterus shrinks, taking about six weeks to return to pre-pregnancy size. As it contracts in the first few days, you may feel 'after pains', which are similar to period pains. These pains are stronger with a second or subsequent baby and are more noticeable when you are breastfeeding. Any pains should respond to mild painkillers, a soak in a warm bath or a hot-water bottle held against your stomach. Your midwife will check your uterus by gently pressing on your abdomen.

**Q** When will I lose the weight I put on?
**A** Women vary in the amount of weight they gain in pregnancy and in the time it takes to return to their pre-pregnancy shape. You'll lose some weight almost straight away after the birth, and more weight is lost as the uterus contracts to its normal size. It is important not to do too much when you are a new mother, so rather than aiming to return to your pre-pregnancy weight as fast as possible, try to relax, feel good about yourself, and be assured that with all the exercise you get from looking after a new baby, you will soon lose the weight.

**Q** How should I look after my stitches?
**A** Any stitches given after a vaginal birth will dissolve, so they do not have to be removed. However, you need to keep the area clean and dry. A daily soak in the bath can make a big difference to how you feel. Adding four drops of lavender oil to the bathwater may help. If you have had a tear or a cut (an episiotomy), your midwife will check that the area is healing and that there are no signs of infection.

*'Your body may never be the same after the birth, but it is quite surprising how little you care. I had no trouble with weight, but my episiotomy scar gave me trouble for a full four months afterwards, and I won't even get started on my lost cup size!'*
*Victoria, mother of Jonas*

# Your emotions after the birth

In the first few days, you will probably experience a range of different emotions, including relief, exhaustion, fear, anxiety and elation. Some women feel guilty because they assumed that they would immediately fall head over heels in love with their new baby, but now discover that the relationship is something that develops gradually.

## Baby blues

Whether or not you decide to breastfeed, your milk will still 'come in' at about the third day (see page 244). This coincides with a rush of hormones that can give you the 'baby blues'. Don't worry if you start to feel weepy: it is completely normal and your midwife will reassure you that, in the majority of cases, these emotions pass in a short while.

It can be useful to talk through the birth with your midwife so that you can be sure of understanding everything that happened during the birth. However, nothing will prepare you for the changes in these first few days, not only in terms of your body but also the huge, and sometimes overwhelming, feeling of responsibility towards your baby.

## Post-natal depression

The 'baby blues' may continue, or they may not appear until a few weeks after the birth, which may indicate that you are suffering from post-natal depression. This affects about 12 per cent of women and seems to work in different ways, leading to feelings such as detachment, anxiety, inability to cope, weepiness and unhappiness. Some women regard this as a natural reaction to a life-changing event. For others there is a particular reason, for example, their baby being on a special-care unit, a traumatic labour or insufficient support after the birth. Whatever the reason, you should tell you midwife, health visitor or doctor so that you can get help.

Often you can find support from groups of women who have had experience of post-natal depression. Nowadays, there is great social pressure for your life to return to how it was before your baby is born – your body, your home, routines and relationships – but the reality is that things have changed. Feeling low does not mean that you have failed as a mother – just that you need some support and help to get you through it.

*'One day I was sitting in the garden with Gabriel when a huge wasp swooped down on him. Without even thinking about it, I swept him up into my arms and I felt so utterly protective – it was then that I knew I loved him.'*
*Gina, mother of Gabriel*

# Your emotions **Common questions**

**Q** After my baby was born I found life exhausting. How can I avoid it this time round without upsetting people?

**A** It is only natural to want to show off your baby to the world, but some visitors can be hard work. You need to catch up on your sleep during the day, so it is a good idea to put a note on your door saying 'Mother and baby sleeping' or leave a message on your answering machine to say that 'Much as I would love to see people, the best time is between. . .' Most people would hate to intrude but, at the same time, they are genuinely excited about seeing your new baby. The most popular visitors are the ones that bring a cooked meal or take away a bag of ironing. Do not be shy of asking for help from friends and family, or accepting it if they offer. It will not only make them feel good but will also make a real difference, allowing you to spend time with your new baby and not worry about the other things.

**Q** Instead of bonding with my newborn, once I got her home, I found her total dependence on me really suffocating. It was several months before I could say I actually 'bonded' with her. Is this normal?

**A** Bonding is a very individual experience and the process varies from mother to mother. Some women feel a bond the moment they see their new baby while, for others, it takes a number of weeks. In addition to the hormonal changes that are taking place as you recover from the pregnancy and birth, you also have a host of lifestyle and relationship changes to cope with, and all of this can have a significant

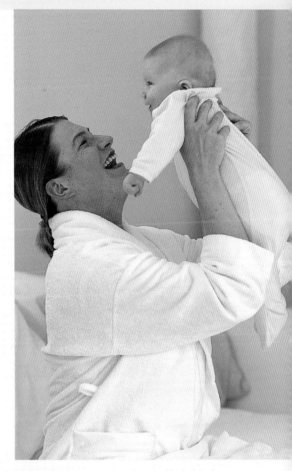

**Above:** Some women can bond with their baby immediately; for others, it takes weeks or months.

effect on the bond with your baby. The main thing is not to feel guilty if you do not feel that surge of love that many mums talk about. As you get to know your baby and learn how to soothe her and enjoy her presence, your feelings will deepen.

# RECOVERING FROM A CAESAREAN

## What to expect

**If you were fit and healthy before the birth you are likely to recover quickly after a caesarean section, although you will feel a bit wobbly to begin with.**

After a caesarean, you will probably find it frustrating to be unable to do such simple tasks as lifting or holding your baby. Your midwife can help by showing you different positions to use while you recover, for example, placing a pillow on your lap, lying down or holding your baby under your arm to feed him. Even though you did not have a vaginal birth, it is still important to continue your pelvic floor exercises (see pages 108–109) because your muscles will have lost tone during the pregnancy. However, you should avoid other forms of exercise (including driving, lifting and housework) for at least the first six weeks. Make the most of any help offered as you will need time to recover from the operation as well as having a new baby to look after.

## Handling pain

Pain varies from person to person and can be severe at first, but adequate pain relief will help speed your recovery. You may be given suppositories to help reduce inflammation, plus an injection or epidural top-up. Some hospitals use patient controlled analgesia (PCA), where you give yourself pain relief through a machine with a device to prevent overdoses. Some women also use a TENS machine or the breathing techniques they learned for labour (see pages 212–213). In a couple of days, paracetamol may be sufficient pain relief. Tell the staff if the pain does not diminish, or gets worse, as this could indicate an infection that needs antibiotics.

**Left:** Breastfeeding on your side in bed may be the most comfortable position after a caesarean.

## Five tips for **conserving energy after a caesarean**

1 Delegate as much as possible. Write down all serious offers of help and suggest specific jobs like vacuuming or taking older children to playgroup.

2 If in doubt, do not do something straight away, put it off until the following day or, better still, week.

3 Have somewhere for your baby to sleep and a set of nappy changing equipment upstairs and downstairs to save journeys. A table at the right height for nappy changing saves any bending.

4 Have a thermos flask of tea and a snack beside you to keep up your strength, especially if you are breastfeeding.

5 Stock up your freezer in the last few weeks of pregnancy, or buy some convenience meals to get you through the first few days. Check that you have the basics, such as washing powder, and list other items, so that someone can shop for you.

# Breastfeeding

Many women worry that they will not be able to breastfeed if they have a caesarean. Be reassured that you will be able to breastfeed, even after a caesarean, just as soon as you feel ready to do so. Anaesthetic drugs cause no problems for breastfeeding and the milk usually comes in around the third or fourth day, although it sometimes takes a bit longer. If your baby is sick or premature you might need extra help, but any difficulties are more likely to be linked to the baby than the type of birth. Experiment to find a comfortable position. You may find it easiest to feed your baby while you are in bed.

# Full recovery

Full recovery after a caesarean birth takes anything between a month and two years, but the average recovery time is about six months. Your scar will be red, then pink; finally it will fade to white or silver, possibly remaining numb for several months. However, physical healing is only part of the process of recovery. An emergency caesarean can test your reserves of courage more than a normal birth. Most women find themselves overwhelmed with fear. This fear does not always disappear once a crisis is over, and the reaction can sometimes be delayed.

# 'Once a Caesar, always a Caesar'

This is an old wives' tale and, just because you had a caesarean with your first baby, it certainly does not mean you will need one with your second. Whether you have a caesarean again or not depends on the circumstances – for example, if fetal distress occurred in the first birth, it is unlikely to happen twice. Regardless of the reason for their first caesarean, more than two-thirds of women go on to have a normal labour with the subsequent child. If you have had an uncomplicated operation with a bikini-line scar, a close eye would be kept on your progress, but hopefully you would go on to have a normal birth – if that's what you choose to do.

# Feeding your baby

Breastfeeding is undoubtedly better for your baby's health and development and 98 per cent of women are able to breastfeed. Nevertheless, it is not always possible, either because of a medical condition or because the mother just does not feel comfortable with it. If you are unable to breastfeed or decide not to, there is no reason why your baby will not thrive on formula milk.

**Above:** Breast milk is the best nutrition for your baby, but breastfeeding is not right for all mothers.

## Five good reasons for breastfeeding

There are many good reasons for breastfeeding if you are able to do so:

1 Breastfeeding helps to protect your baby against serious infections of the ear and chest, as well as gastroenteritis (vomiting and diarrhoea).
2 Breastfeeding helps to reduce the risk of eczema and asthma, particularly if you have a family history of these conditions.
3 Breastfeeding can help you to bond with your baby.
4 Breastfeeding helps you to lose weight because it burns off any extra fat that you have accumulated during pregnancy.
5 Children who were breastfed for eight months or longer show a higher IQ score than those given formula milk.

## Breastfeeding

Breast milk is produced on a supply and demand basis. For the first two or three days, until your milk comes in, your breasts produce colostrum. This is a thick, creamy substance, packed with antibodies to help protect your baby from infections and disease. The more your baby feeds at the breast, the more milk you will produce. The milk is made up of thirst-quenching foremilk, followed by a thicker hind milk.

## Bottle-feeding

If you are bottle-feeding a newborn, you should still feed on demand. Your baby will let you know when she is hungry and, unless she is jaundiced, very small or poorly, you should not wake her for a feed. You may find that she will take more at some feeds than others and that she will feed more frequently at certain times of the day. It takes longer for babies to digest formula milk so they do tend to go longer between feeds. A newborn baby will probably take six or seven feeds in 24 hours and, in the first two or three days, will be taking approximately 60 ml (2 fl oz) at a feed.

## Feeding your baby
# Common questions

## Three tips for
## bottle-feeding

1 If your baby seems hungry but does not take much milk at a feed, try using a larger teat, for example, a medium flow one. Some babies get tired quickly and give up feeding too early.

2 Do not leave your baby to feed on her own, with the bottle propped up. She could easily choke on the milk.

3 Do not increase the amount of powder in the feed just because your baby seems hungry. It can be very dangerous if the feed is not made up correctly.

*Research shows that your partner has a strong influence on the way you choose to feed your baby – so make sure that he is aware of the advantages of breastfeeding!*

**Q** I struggled to breastfeed my first baby and gave up. Will I be able to feed my next?
**A** In fact, you are more likely to succeed now that you have the experience. Do not be disheartened by earlier experiences – even one day's feeding benefits your baby. Talk to your midwife and health visitor and get good information before the birth. Breastfeeding counsellors and clinics can support you after you have given birth. Each breastfeeding experience is different, so you have every chance of success with your next baby.

**Q** How do I know my baby has latched on?
**A** You may need to experiment to see what suits you in terms of position, but essentially you should follow these steps for latching on. Hold your baby so that she is facing you so she does not have to turn her head towards you. Her head should be level with your nipple. Tease your baby with the nipple or let her smell your skin. As soon as she opens her mouth wide, bring her head to your breast. She should not only suck on the nipple but also have as much of the area around it (the areola) in her mouth as possible. If she only has the nipple in her mouth, break the seal with your finger, remove her from the breast and try again.

When she is latched on properly her mouth should be wide open, with the nipple drawn deeply into her mouth. You will see the muscle in front of her ear working as she sucks. When she has finished suckling she will be content. This could take five minutes or 35 minutes. Placing your little finger in your baby's mouth to release the seal will avoid painful pulling on your nipple.

# HOW IS DAD DOING?

## He has to adjust, too!

**It can be hard for a new dad to feel involved in the day-to-day care of a new baby, especially as, on the surface, not that much may have changed for him.**

**Above:** A father has a special place in a child's life, so give him the space to get involved.

Your partner may well still be getting up at his usual time and going out to work, just as he did before your pregnancy, and he may initially lack confidence when it comes to handling the baby. In some cases, a mother can be so focused on her own relationship with the baby that the father hardly gets a look in. For men to be successful as dads, they have to be given the chance to get involved and learn parenting skills. This can be hard for you, especially if you feel that you are the only one who really understands your baby. But you have only

## Five ways for **dads to get involved**

1 Bath your baby. It is the perfect way to end the day and can be great fun.
2 Schedule regular dad time. Take over for a couple of hours in the evening while your partner gets some rest ahead of night feeds.
3 Pop your baby in a sling or his pram and get some fresh air with him.
4 If your partner can express milk, help out with night feeds.
5 Make the early morning nappy change you and baby's special time together.

come to know his ways through trial and error, and your partner needs to be given the same opportunity. Stand back and let him make his own mistakes. If you cannot watch him without trying to correct him, walk away.

## Make some family time

As you both become competent at the day-to-day elements of parenting, it can be easy to turn into serial parents. You may find, as you get on with the chores of child care and running a home, that you slip into a routine in which one of you takes over as the other goes to work, swapping roles later in the day. But do not forget that you are a family. Make time to do things together, whether that involves a day out or simply both being there at bath time occasionally. Enjoying family time is what having a baby is all about – and your child will see that you are a team.

Allowing your partner to be a hands-on dad brings benefits to the whole family. Your baby will have even more love and attention and will thrive from experiencing different parenting styles. At the same time, your partner will relish the opportunity to get to know your baby and to explore his new role as a father. Studies have shown that dads who get more involved in the day-to-day babycare tend to be much closer to their children.

Although research suggests that dads parent babies in a very similar way to mums, men also introduce unique and irreplaceable aspects. Dads often develop a special skill – perhaps bathing the baby, getting him back to sleep or doing a quick nappy change. So try not to see dad as just an assistant mum and instead acknowledge that he will play a special role in your child's life that will grow and develop as your child grows older.

## Your sex life

Some women feel ready to make love again as early as a week or two after giving birth but most take rather longer. If there has been a lull in your sex life, you may find that spontaneity has been lost and it is necessary for you and your partner to make a positive decision together to resume sexual relations. Sex may be painful or remind you of a negative birth experience. Full breasts may be uncomfortable or messy when they leak milk, or you may need reassurance about your appearance. You may be so preoccupied with parenting that you forget about your adult relationship.

Good humour and a willingness to communicate are essential. Your sex life will be different after the birth of your child, but it need not be less good. Remember that penetrative sex is not the only form of lovemaking – there are many different ways of giving and receiving affection. Stroking, kissing and cuddling are all important ways of demonstrating your love. If you continue to show each other warmth and tenderness, and explore other means of providing each other with erotic pleasure, a full sexual relationship can follow in its own time, when you both feel ready for it.

# Index

**Publisher acknowledgements**
**Executive editor** Jane McIntosh
**Project editor** Fiona Robertson
**Executive art editors** Tim Pattinson and Karen Sawyer
**Designer** Colin Goody
**Senior production controller** Martin Croshaw
**Picture research** Aruna Mathur

**Picture acknowledgements**
Alamy/Martin Gardiner 59; /Sally Greenhill 178; /Jennie Hart 206; /Louise Mazzoni 3; /Benno de Wilde 73.
Bananastock Ltd 7, 250, 236, 252.
Corbis UK Ltd 71, 120-121 bottom centre, 218, 232, 248; /Allessandro Bianci 28; /David Raymer 180; /Phillipe Eranian 30; /Brooke Fasani 11; /Owen Franken 200; /Holger Winkler/Zefa 87; /JLP/Jose L.Pelaez 191; /Michael A. Keller/zefa 26; 244; /Layne Kennedy 212; /Floris Leeuwenberg 6, 176; /Mediscan 69; /Sabine Fritsch/Stock4B 86; /H.Schmid 168; /Ariel Skelly 242; /David Stoecklein 174; /Trinette Reed 117; /Turbo 127; /LWA-Stephen Welstead 16; /Jennie Woodcock 138.

Digital Vision 8, 34, 53, 88.
Getty Images/Larry Dale Gordon 43; /Jens Honor.T Photography Ltd 84;/Michael Salas 4.
Octopus Publishing Group Limited/Stephen Conroy 93, 106 bottom centre;/David Jordan 92; /Sandra Lane 19; /Willaim Lingwood 137;/Daniel Pangbourne 210 top right, 210 bottom right, 210 bottom left, 211 left, 211 right; /Peter Pugh-Cook 12, 51,96, 113, 186, 251; /William Reavell 95; /Russell Sadur 23, 247; /Gareth Sambidge 114; /Ian Wallace 110.
Angela Hampton/Family Life Picture Library/Angela Hampton 228.
Photolibrary 124, 166, 239; /Neil Bromhall 1, 27, 54, 83, 89, 116,190, 211, 224, 227, 241, 65.
Photodisc 32, 75, 81, 90, 102, 104, 119, 122, 142, 202, 225.
Science Photo Library/Du Cane Medical Imaging Ltd 82; /Dopamine 64; /Gusto 38;/Ian Hooton 132, 17, 189, 217; /Ruth Jenkinson 215, 172; /Dr Najeeb Layyous 74, 198; /Dr G. Moscoso 57; /AJ.Photo 240.